PRAGMATISM APPLIED

SUNY series in American Philosophy and Cultural Thought
———
Randall E. Auxier and John R. Shook, editors

PRAGMATISM APPLIED

*William James and the
Challenges of Contemporary Life*

Edited by
CLIFFORD S. STAGOLL
and MICHAEL P. LEVINE

Published by State University of New York Press, Albany

© 2019 State University of New York

All rights reserved

No part of this book may be used or reproduced in any manner whatsoever without written permission. No part of this book may be stored in a retrieval system or transmitted in any form or by any means including electronic, electrostatic, magnetic tape, mechanical, photocopying, recording, or otherwise without the prior permission in writing of the publisher.

For information, contact State University of New York Press, Albany, NY
www.sunypress.edu

Library of Congress Cataloging-in-Publication Data

Names: Stagoll, Clifford S., 1965– editor. | Levine, Michael P., 1950– editor.
Title: Pragmatism applied : William James and the challenges of contemporary life / edited by Clifford S. Stagoll and Michael P. Levine.
Description: Albany : State University of New York, [2019] | Series: SUNY series in American philosophy and cultural thought | Includes bibliographical references and index.
Identifiers: LCCN 2018018757 | ISBN 9781438473376 (hardcover) | ISBN 9781438473383 (ebook) | ISBN 9781438473369 (pbk)
Subjects: LCSH: James, William, 1842–1910 | Pragmatism. | Ethics. | Conduct of life.
Classification: LCC B945.J24 P73 2019 | DDC 144/.3—dc23
LC record available at https://lccn.loc.gov/2018018757

10 9 8 7 6 5 4 3 2 1

CONTENTS

ACKNOWLEDGMENTS   vii

INTRODUCTION: Making Pragmatism Pragmatic   ix
   Clifford S. Stagoll and Michael P. Levine

PART 1
ISSUES: PUTTING JAMES TO WORK

CHAPTER 1
Listening to "the Cries of the Wounded": Jamesian Reflections
on the Impasse over Gun Control   3
   James M. Albrecht

CHAPTER 2
Revisiting the Social Value of College Breeding   31
   Loren Goldman

CHAPTER 3
What Makes the Lives of Livestock Significant?   57
   Erin McKenna

CHAPTER 4
Significant Lives and Certain Blindness: William James and the
Disability Paradox   73
   Nate Jackson

CHAPTER 5
Pragmatism and Progress: Has There Been Progress in Race Relations in the United States? 101
Damian Cox and Michael P. Levine

PART 2
THEORY: CLEARING THE WAY

CHAPTER 6
Applying Jamesian Pragmatism to Moral Life: Against "Applied Ethics" 125
Sami Pihlström

CHAPTER 7
Understanding Experience with William James 149
John Ryder

CHAPTER 8
James and the Minimal Self 169
Yumiko Inukai

PART 3
PRACTICE: LIVING WITH JAMES

CHAPTER 9
William James and the Woods 197
Douglas R. Anderson

CHAPTER 10
Taking James to Work: Pragmatism for Managers 211
Clifford S. Stagoll

CHAPTER 11
Habits in a World of Change 237
James Campbell

LIST OF CONTRIBUTORS 257

INDEX 261

ACKNOWLEDGMENTS

The editors gratefully acknowledge the students in their 2015 honors seminar on American pragmatism at the University of Western Australia, and, of course, the contributors to this volume.

Cliff would also like to thank Kelly, Claire, and Davydd for their forbearance, love, and support, and Michael for his ideas and wise words.

Michael would like to thank, in particular, Amy Barrett-Lennard.

INTRODUCTION
Making Pragmatism Pragmatic

CLIFFORD S. STAGOLL AND MICHAEL P. LEVINE

In a letter to his younger brother Henry in 1907, William James (1842–1910) anticipated the triumph of pragmatism, the philosophical movement that he had so effectively helped to define, develop, and publicize, together with the success of his book of the same name. "I shouldn't be surprised if ten years hence it should be rated as 'epoch-making,' for the definitive triumph of that general way of thinking I can entertain no doubt whatever—I believe it to be something quite like the protestant reformation" (James 1926, 2:239). James did not mean to presage pragmatism's ascent just in the universities, public lecture halls, and journals, replacing idealism as the dominant philosophy of his time (although so proud a man as James would appreciate that triumph, too). Rather, he meant quite seriously his comparison with the rise of Protestantism, writing in his book that pragmatism had "generalized itself, become conscious of a universal mission, pretended to a conquering destiny." "I believe in that destiny," he continues, "and I hope I may end by inspiring you with my belief" (1975b, 30).

Not only is James's prophecy extraordinary hubris, but it also evidences an attitude that seems fundamentally at odds with the core tenets of pragmatism itself. In any case, it has proven mistaken. Marian "Clover" Adams (1843–1885) famously said of Henry (1843–1916) (arguably the greatest novelist of his time), "It's not that he 'bites off more than he can chew' but he chews more than he bites off."[1] Leaving aside the merits of Adams's claim (and sibling rivalry), it is clear that William had no trouble in biting off a great deal, and at times not chewing enough. While the pragmatism of Charles Sanders Peirce, James, and John Dewey may no longer be as marginalized as it has been at times during the last century, it has hardly taken the philosophical or nonacademic world by storm, despite the interest generated by Richard Rorty. This of course does not mean that it has not had, or does not now have, its capable proponents, or that pragmatism in various guises has not made substantial advances.

James was convinced that pragmatism would succeed by way of its application: doing away with theoretical complications and confusions so as to leave the way open for human progress, and providing guidance for how people might best lead their lives. He characterized it as "the attitude of looking away from first things, principles, 'categories,' supposed necessities; and of looking towards last things, consequences, facts" (1975b, 32). To this end, James's ideal philosopher "turns away from abstraction and insufficiency, from verbal solutions, from bad a priori reasons, from fixed principles, closed systems, and pretended absolutes and origins" in favor of "completeness and adequacy, towards facts, towards action, and towards power" (1975b, 31).

For James, pragmatism would help to realize a " 'melioristic' " approach to life. Located "midway" between a pessimistic attitude toward "salvation of the world" and an "optimism . . . that thinks the world's salvation inevitable," meliorism is the view that we can contribute to the betterment of the world generally, and our own lives particularly, through deliberate, effortful striving (1975b, 137). This is not to suggest that our lives are characterized by limitless possibilities (far from it), or that constraints can always be surmounted by the exertion of greater effort (far from it)—James was mindful of the unavoidable impacts on his community of the changing technologies, economies, and values of his day, for instance—but only that "some conditions of the world's salvation are actually existent . . . and should the residual conditions come, salvation would become an accomplished reality" (ibid.). Such conditions, James goes on, "are first such a mixture of things as will in the fullness of time give us a chance, a gap that we can spring into, and, finally, *our act*," though just what that act ought to be is as purposefully vague as it is nondescript (1975b, 137–38).

As James reminds his readers, the word *pragmatism* "is derived from the same Greek word, *pragma*, meaning action, from which our words 'practice' and 'practical' come" (1975b, 28). His whole oeuvre can be read productively as so many explorations and enunciations of ideas intended to guide such effort and action; as various perspectives on how we decide the meaning and value of our experiences and proposals for how best to respond to them. In his critical mode, James reveals errors and oversights prevalent in previous philosophies and entrenched patterns of thinking and acting that have tended to disguise or obfuscate prospects for "salvation" (as well as what such a term might mean), and/or prevent their realization. As creatures whose lives are largely products of habitual thought and action, we often proceed mindlessly in one direction or another. In *The Principles of Psychology*, for instance, James alerts us to various aspects of self-conception that play themselves out in, for example, attention-seeking behavior and the attainment of physical possessions (1981, 279–82). In *Pragmatism*, he studies various preconceptions about religion, truth, and "common sense," and proposes alternatives (1975b). For James, uncovering extant "habits of mind" is a crucial step toward conceiving of, and acting on, richer, more productive beliefs.

In more constructive moments, James provides clear and concrete guidance for various challenges of daily life. In his *Talks to Teachers on Psychology; and to Students on Some of Life's Ideals*, for example, he discusses the psychological principles underpinning effective pedagogy, and specifies practical exercises for molding one's habits (1983, 47–53). In his epistemological work, James details the many ways in which we arrive at, deploy, and modify ideas that we take to be true, and how the psychology of these never-ending adjustments influences the ways that we attribute meaning to our experiences (1975a; 1975b). His philosophy of religion (in part) proposes ways of navigating a path between the mystical character of religious experience and scientific understanding of it (1985). Even in his more obtuse moments, as he struggles to enunciate a metaphysics capable of mediating the dynamism and richness of human experience with the facticity of nature's laws, he is at pains to emphasize prospects for altering one's perspectives and locating new ways of assessing and responding to one's circumstances in ways that are beneficial to oneself and others (1977).

But pragmatism's orientation toward action as James conceives of it is not limited to his academic and theoretical investigations. It is evident too in aspects of his biography. For example, as a young man James experienced lengthy periods when the prospect that reality was wholly determined drove him into helpless depression. But by committing to a doctrine of free will suggested by his reading of the French neo-Kantian Charles Renouvier (together with making changes to his personal and professional circumstances), James was able finally to locate a way forward, recording in his diary that he could "see no reason why [Renouvier's] definition of free will—'the sustaining of a thought *because I choose to* when I might have other thoughts'—need be the definition of an illusion," and that he meant to adhere to it in order to "voluntarily cultivate the feeling of moral freedom" (1926, 1:147). In this moment, we have an illustration of the continuity that James so frequently calls attention to between philosophical theorizing, planning, thinking, and acting.

Further examples of James's commitment to the application of his philosophy are evident in his involvement in the public sphere. Following Ralph Waldo Emerson's example, James took seriously an obligation to act on issues of public concern in language and locations accessible to a non-academic audience. From the mid-1890s until the end of his life, James participated in public debates about issues as diverse as American imperialism in the Philippines (he was vice-president of the Anti-Imperialist League), regulation of big business, care of the mentally ill, the awful problem of lynching, homogenization of university teaching qualifications, medical licensing, and the status accorded new and heterodox approaches in science and medicine (especially psychology). He also sometimes engaged with issues facing particular professional groups, as in *Talks to Teachers*, where he also touched upon the "duty, struggle, and success" of farmers in dealing with the challenges of their land (1983, 134). By involving himself in the social, economic, and political changes of his day, and applying insights from his several technical specialties to the realm of public affairs, James was helping, or thought he was helping, to return philosophy to a more practical engagement with the world.[2]

Of course, James was not alone in enunciating and championing links between pragmatist theory and human actions intended to improve our lot. Peirce (1839–1914) was credited by James as the first to introduce pragmatism to philosophy by virtue of his article "How to Make Our Ideas Clear," published in 1878. Peirce discussed the need (and as he proposes in many cases, the unavoidable human tendency) to continually test our conceptions of the world against their practical consequences, and formulated various versions of the "pragmatic maxim" intended to codify it: "Consider what effects, that might conceivably have practical bearings, we conceive the object of our conception to have. Then, our conception of these effects is the whole of our conception of the object" (Peirce 1878, 293). More straightforwardly, in 1905, Peirce expressed pragmatism's main tenet as follows: "that a *conception*, that is, the rational purport of a word or other expression, lies exclusively in its conceivable bearing upon the conduct of life" (1905, 162–63). For Peirce, the "laboratory habit of mind" (to use

John Dewey's phrase), the human tendency to test and adjust one's beliefs on the basis of evident relations between events and their consequences, helps to improve the ways that we respond to our circumstances—albeit that what constitutes such "improvement" is not always specified and, even when it is, often remains unclear.

Peirce's investigations were crucial for James's version of pragmatism. By interpreting Peirce's maxim in terms of a psychology of action, setting aside the experimentally regulative processes of science on which he relied heavily, and referring pragmatism's general tenet to particular consequences and actions for a particular person, James makes of pragmatism a general theory of first-person meaning—specifically, the view that the meaning of one's experiential circumstances is intimately interconnected with their impact upon the way that one thinks and lives. On this wider account, pragmatism becomes less concerned with what is meant by calling a diamond "hard" or a table "flat" (the kinds of examples to which Peirce calls special attention) and more concerned with resolving issues in ethics, the down-to-earth decisions of daily life, religion, and metaphysics. More specifically, it focuses on how one's thinking influences and is influenced by human practices. James writes that "if there were any part of a thought that made no difference in the thought's practical consequences, then that part would be no proper element of the thought's significance" (1975b, 259). Pragmatism becomes, then, a theory of the meaning of *personal experience* in terms of the actions to which it leads.

John Dewey developed and applied aspects of James's work, but deviated from it in several crucial respects. First, he countered James's preoccupation with the lives of individuals by conducting pragmatist investigations of fields as diverse as social theory, democracy in its various forms (politics, education, journalism, and institutions), and social influences on aesthetic judgment. Like James—but to a far greater extent—Dewey pursued the implications of his philosophical analyses as a progressive advocate and activist, particularly on matters of education, women's suffrage, international relations, and preservation of liberal democracy. Second, Dewey championed the advantages of experimental science much more strongly than James—despite James's training in science and medicine, and his significant contributions to the development of modern psychology.

Third, whereas Dewey agrees with James that "it lies in the nature of pragmatism that it should be applied as widely as possible; and to things as diverse as controversies, beliefs, truths, ideas, and objects," he is more careful to delineate "the *distinct* type of consequence and hence of meaning of practical appropriate to each" (Dewey 1908, 87–88). For Dewey, application of pragmatism to real-world problems (or, at least, those with a significant social dimension) demands more deliberate articulation of the context than James thought appropriate. For James, the point is not so much to predefine a problem using philosophical concepts so as to enable a more focused analysis of it, but rather to analyze and propose new ways in which those experiencing the problem might conceive of and respond to it.

All three of these giants of so-called "Golden Age" pragmatism share the view, then, that the meaning and value of ideas, concepts, propositions, and theories ought to be decided by the consequences of their being adopted, and specifically, by how well they help us to adjust to events by guiding our thinking and action. But James is the most approachable and suggestive of them, the one who most encourages bold exploration of ways in which pragmatism might help to realize melioristic intent. This is due in large part to his insight and his willingness to locate and question even those conceptions that seem most basic. ("To believe in the one or the many, that is the classification with the maximum number of consequences," he writes [1975b, 64]). But it is a product, too, of his engaging writing: evocative, rich with literary imagery, suggestive of new paths to pursue, and often bearing the hallmarks of live performance derived from their original incarnation as public lectures. Although there might be merit in claims that James's work is sometimes inconsistent and even downright careless, his desire to tackle so many philosophical and psychological challenges, his employment of myriad theoretical approaches and conceptual resources, and his refusal to systematize links between his projects all contribute to an open-endedness that invites fresh engagements.[3]

This book means to survey and sample some of the ways in which such engagements might extend beyond exegesis and explanation to practical application. In the current climate, in which study of the humanities (indeed, the humanities generally) are increasingly marginalized by a profit-driven tertiary education sector, political misunderstanding, and the preeminence of job-focused training, such an ambition might be interpreted as a proposal for widening the market for Jamesianism. Such a development might be no bad thing, showing to an audience, however small, that, appropriately interpreted and translated, pragmatism has a thing or two of value to say about issues that matter to individuals and their communities. We might even hope that a few more people might come to the realization that John J. Stuhr said was "essential for the public trust and public support of the humanities[:] . . . [that] education in the humanities is essential for the realization of basic professional, personal, and social values" (Stuhr 1997, 10).

But beyond this grand ambition is the desire to do justice to James's own emphases on the action-orientation, consequences, and use-value of philosophy. Despite pragmatism's numerous conceptual links to practices, there is a relative paucity of literature that attempts to apply his philosophy to real-world issues. There are exceptions, of course. John J. McDermott, for instance, apart from being one of the most insightful and provocative commentators on James's philosophy, has drawn deeply and consistently on it for resources to investigate everything from general characteristics of American culture to the phenomenology of private experiences (e.g., McDermott 1986; 2007). Several philosophers (most notably Charlene Haddock Seigfried [1991; 1996] and contributors to a recent collection [Tarver and Sullivan 2015]) have drawn on resources in James to address issues related to feminism, sometimes using them to explain gender-related issues and propose new ways of resolving or dealing with them, and at others using feminism as the basis for fresh perspectives on James and his work. Others have utilized his ideas in discussions of animal welfare (e.g., McKenna 2013) and conceptions of the human body (e.g., Shusterman 2012), and we have seen a resurgence of interest in James's ethics in relation to self-transformation (e.g., Franzese 2008; Marchetti 2015).

But relative to the enormous biographical and interpretative literature on James, such examples are sparse. Further, even in those cases where the relevance of James's work to some field of study or challenging issue is proposed, scholars have tended to describe (usually in technical philosophical language) the *potential* theoretical riches to be had rather than emphasizing how those riches might be *realized*. Their point is usually to show how James might lead us out of some philosophical dispute that bears on the case, rather than to identify means for and consequences of applying pragmatist resources to it. The precise steps to take in order to move from identifying a potentially useful resource to acting upon it are left unspecified, or vague. Such an approach has tended to constrain pragmatism's audience to other philosophers and theorists working in closely related fields—those most capable of interpreting the language and context, and most comfortable with pursuing matters of theoretical import—rather than expanding it to those who might deploy pragmatist ideas in practice, whether professional practitioners or a wider public.

This volume means to encourage an alternative enterprise, emphasizing various ways in which James's theories can be used to conceive of and cope with challenges in contemporary life. The point is not just to locate the inherent usefulness of James's ideas for such matters, but rather, by drawing out some of the ways in which pragmatism might be made "pragmatic" (in the common sense of that word), to promote James's own concern with actions and consequences. On the one hand, this has led the editors to select several chapters that address particular questions directly, such that some idea or theory of James's is shown to be useful in understanding or coping with an issue with which we are confronted. These align more closely with James in a constructive mood. On the other hand, some chapters take a more oblique approach, opening the way for new ways of thinking about our problems and challenges by critiquing assumptions that have tended to constrain our conception of them and make some cases seem intractable. These chapters more closely approximate James's critical moments. Our purpose in what follows is not to produce an abstract of the essays or summary of their arguments, but to give an account of their significance.

Part 1 of the volume includes five chapters that apply James's theory to particular problems or issues. The volume opens with a bang, and what is likely the most contentious and some will say problematic chapter in the volume: James M. Albrecht's "Listening to 'the Cries of the Wounded': Jamesian Reflections on the Impasse of Gun Control." It addresses the issues of gun violence and gun control, and the Jamesian resources, ethics in particular, for understanding and possibly even adjudicating the seemingly implacable impasse. It is an impasse that is one of the most emblematic of the deep and bitter divisions in American society today. Along with Albrecht's specific arguments, the chapter (stirring a hornet's nest) presents an opportunity for appraising fundamentals of James's pragmatic ethics, alongside Albrecht's interpretation of them. Some readers will endorse Albrecht's application of James's views; others may find it misguided or even offensive. In any case, the chapter reveals just how provocative the application of James's ideas can be.

Moving to somewhat safer though no less controversial ground, and taking on issues of great concern to James (as well as the editors), Lauren Goldman in "Revisiting the Social Value of College Breeding" examines James's view that higher education is essential to democracy, and raises broader questions about the purpose and value of higher education and education generally. These issues are especially relevant in this era of the managerialization and corporatization of higher education, now virtually a fait accompli. As Goldman says, "all is not well in higher education." With James, he provides a means to reflect on what has happened to universities and how the changes affect our lives in important practical ways, and an opportunity for querying (another word for challenging) a second enormous and at times bitter division in society (not just in the United States) between the so-called educated elite and so-called working class. The place and value of higher education in society have become particularly pressing matters in what is becoming known as the post-truth (i.e., Trump) world and milieu that we currently live with—a world that would be an anathema to James, Dewey, and Rorty alike. Like the preceding chapter, Goldman's provides ample opportunity for considering first-order interpretive issues related to James. Is it really, as James sees it, intellectuals who are needed to maintain the tried and true ideals of truth and justice?

Moving from universities to fields, farmyards, and slaughtering houses, Erin McKenna in "What Makes the Lives of Livestock Significant?" calls attention to an ambivalence, and possibly a contradiction, in James's writing regarding animal experience and the value of animals. On the one hand, James suggests that just as other humans may experience the world differently than we do and yet deserve respect and tolerance, so too do animals. Their lives are not meaningless or insignificant because they experience things differently from ourselves or other animals. Yet McKenna claims that at other times James seems to see animals as significant only in virtue of their use by humans.

Which is it? Focusing on animals as food, McKenna discusses claims for animal rights and animal welfare in terms of James's central ethical notion of meliorism. To stand the test of time and retain utility, an ethical theory must be applicable and adaptable to new cases, settings, and situations. McKenna's chapter can be also usefully viewed as testing the durability or plasticity of central features of Jamesian ethics to this important and much-debated issue of contemporary ethical concern.

Next, in chapter 4, Nate Jackson turns pragmatism toward "disability" and experiences of the "disabled" in "Significant Lives and Certain Blindness: William James and the Disability Paradox." In particular, Jackson is concerned with examining James's thought as a possible resource for conceiving of disablement in conjunction or as compatible with human flourishing. Jackson claims that scholars have not focused enough on the relation between disability and well-being, and that mistaken intuitions persist regarding disabilities as *necessarily* limiting quality of life.

By way of justifying James's thought as a useful philosophical resource for studying facets of disability, Jackson calls attention to James's own uses of examples of disability (deafness, blindness, and neurodiversity) as well as his own (at times disabling) illnesses. One of the most significant aspects of James (and pragmatism generally) with respect to disability is the view that the testimony of the disabled regarding their experience ought not be dismissed or undermined. An adequate notion of well-being should be indicative of the fact that disabilities (of at least many kinds) are neither contrary to nor incompatible with it. James is a source for an ethics of tolerance and for recognition of limitations to judgments of values. He promotes and recommends a type of "epistemic humility" that counters any tendency to dismiss the testimony of others regarding the value, meaning, and quality of their lives.

Meliorism, as the belief that things can be made better, is an essential part of Jamesian ethics and epistemology. In "Pragmatism and Progress," the last chapter in part 1, Damian Cox and Michael Levine ask what it means to make things better, or in slightly different terms, what it means to say that progress or improvement has been made? They do so by addressing and answering one specific question: "has there been progress in race relations in the United States since legally sanctioned segregation allegedly ended in the 1960s?"

Along with its central role in pragmatism, what constitutes progress is an interesting question in its own right. Apart from some sort of metric, what does it even mean to say that progress has or has not been made (in whatever area)? Indeed, just what is meant by meliorism in James's pragmatism is unclear. This chapter is an attempt to make a first-order contribution to a core doctrine of pragmatism by explaining "progress." It does so in a way that is consistent with and advances an understanding of Jamesian meliorism.

The chapters in part 2 are more concerned with interrogating philosophical notions that influence how we conceive of and respond to real-world issues, and how philosophers have at times encouraged relatively narrow conceptions of relevant terms, including "applied philosophy" and "experience."

In chapter 6, "Applying Jamesian Pragmatism to Moral Life: Against 'Applied Ethics,'" Sami Pihlström argues that although James's pragmatism encourages something like applied ethics ("bringing moral philosophy down to earth from abstract theorization"), the true applications of Jamesian pragmatism to moral life are opposed to the basic idea of applied ethics. Unlike applied ethics, though some applied ethicists might argue against Pihlstrom's characterization, Jamesian pragmatism rejects any sharp distinction between moral theories and their practical application.

From the perspective of a Jamesian pragmatist, "applied ethics" makes little sense. Pragmatists will or should regard ethical theory as, in Pihlstrom's words, "practical all the way down," with "no fundamental distinctions between metaethics, normative ethics, and applied ethics." He argues further that "in this sense, Jamesian moral philosophy is comparable to . . . Wittgensteinian moral philosophy." Ethical theorists may well scratch their heads not so much at the claim that Jamesian moral theory might have significant similarities to Wittgensteinian ethics (though that too might be contested), but rather at the claim that Jamesian pragmatist ethics can do away with the distinctions between metaethics, normative ethics, and applied ethics. What does pragmatist ethics look like from Pihlstrom's perspective, then, and how does it operate, practically speaking?

In chapter 7, "Understanding Experience with William James," John Ryder argues that far from being "superfluous," an account of experience is "central to a clear handle on thought, cognition, emotions, aesthetics, politics, and human action generally." And by central, he means not just to pragmatism, but to any philosophy that deals with these issues. Ryder claims that an adequate conception of experience is to be found "ensconced in the pragmatic naturalist tradition."

In cognitive science, for example, we find "empirical and conceptual support for the idea that mind is embodied, indeed extended into an individual's body and environmental location." These ideas, Ryder argues, "rest to a considerable degree on features of experience and cognition that William James was the first to notice and develop." Ryder points to James's theories regarding the bodily basis of the emotions (emotions as feeling), the qualitative aspect of thought and by implication the bodily basis of reason and logic, and the importance of relations in experience.

Sami Pihlström argues in chapter 6 that Jamesian pragmatism rejects any sharp distinction between moral theories and their practical applications. In a sense, Ryder is doing something similar in trying to show that any application of pragmatism to issues both theoretical and practical regarding cognition, emotions, aesthetics, politics, and other areas should be well grounded in James's account of experience because they are—or should be—intrinsically related to that account.

In chapter 8, "James and the Minimal Self," Yumiko Inukai argues that James, drawing his conclusions from experience, anticipated much of what has developed in contemporary philosophical models of self. This includes, for example, the contemporary focusing on the relationship between phenomenal consciousness and subjectivity—an approach that has yielded "the minimal self" ("the sense of being someone, of a self being present"). The contemporary alternative to the minimal self is the idea of the self as a narrative construction, which includes personalities, beliefs, values, memories, and so on. Inukai sees these characteristics as present in James's account of the stream of consciousness.

Inukai claims that although these two approaches or theories are often seen as conflicting, they are in fact complementary. Both are needed to capture the complexity of self. (Think perhaps of wave and particle theory in quantum physics.) Further, Inukai sees James as offering just such a complementary and necessarily encompassing account.

There is little doubt that Inukai's claim regarding complementarity would be contested by both sides on the basis that the two positions are either incompatible or else delineate two different issues with regard to the self—one metaphysical and the other largely descriptive. In any case it would be useful to see how the competing theorists would respond to the integrative challenge, and to see whether pragmatists take Inukai's approach as distinctively Jamesian.

Part 3 gets personal, and we would like to think not only that parts 1 and 2 point in this direction, but so do James and his pragmatism. Part 3 contains three chapters on how James's ideas might be adopted to help guide one's own philosophical and professional practice.

In 1911, James's former colleague at Harvard, George Santayana, addressing an audience in California, pondered whether, "if the philosophers had lived among your mountains, their systems would have been different from what they are." He concluded that they would indeed be

> very different from what those systems are which the European genteel tradition has handed down since Socrates; for these systems are egotistical; directly or indirectly they are anthropocentric, and inspired by the conceited notion that man, or human reason, or the human distinction between good and evil, is the centre and pivot of the universe. That is what the mountains and the woods should make you at last ashamed to assert. From what, indeed, does the society of nature liberate you, that you find it so sweet? (Santayana 2009, 19)

In chapter 9, "William James and the Woods," Douglas R. Anderson considers the significance for James's work and personality of his time in the country, liberated from "the city and cosmopolitan philosophy," and finds it to have been crucial. Not only did James's excursions to Chocorua and beyond provide "some space for self and world exploration—for contemplative and meditative thought," but they were essential for his maintaining a "life at the borders" between a hectic city existence of professional and social demands and a need for escape from that life to pursue health and simplification. More than that, though, these periods seem to have renewed James's powers of receptivity and perceptual awareness, encouraging his insights into "the poetic and the religious dimensions of human experience."

James's time in the woods shows that, for him, to live productively "at the borders" involved doing away with neat demarcations between private rest and public philosophy, immersion in the natural environment and analyses of the mystical and religious, physical rest (and exercise) and contemplative effort, and rich philosophical themes and the simplest aspects of everyday life. James's experiences in the woods are realizations of the kinds of relationality that are central to his philosophy. Such interactions have been largely ignored or set aside by recent, technically oriented philosophy, Anderson argues, much to its loss and ours, and we would do well to re-engage with natural settings in order to encourage philosophy's re-engagement with diverse human experience.

As Clifford Stagoll writes in chapter 10, "Taking James to Work: Pragmatism for Managers," "the very name 'pragmatism' suggests it as appropriate for use in philosophy of management." But how do we realize this suggestion without pragmatist philosophy being misappropriated in the cause of crass instrumentalism, wholly inconsistent with pragmatism's conception of the world?

Stagoll proposes that the answer lies in using resources from James to engage "directly with the demands of management practice and with practitioners," by which he means using them to improve how managers decipher and draw lessons from their professional experiences. Unlike much traditional management theory, where abstraction is the price paid for general applicability, pragmatism can provide individual managers with tools for coping with disorderly, complicated, and fast-paced work environments. A Jamesian philosophy of management would emphasize and explain the need for managers to draw information from diverse sources, for instance, to take account of qualitative factors in determining the meaning of quantitative measures, and to develop flexible plans for coping with unexpected events.

Stagoll goes on to propose ways to implement a Jamesian philosophy of management, perhaps the most demanding "pragmatic" challenge of all. James provides a range of practical tools capable of helping managers to cope with the personal and professional challenges of their work. Examples include his proposals for adjusting habits, making moral decisions in complicated circumstances (such as those that test the bounds of policy and procedure manuals), and coping with stress. The "'pragmatic" nature of James's pragmatism is likely to appeal to managers, Stagoll contends, in ways that some trite, cliché-addled management theories will not.

The significance of habit in a world of change (the world that we all live in and always have lived in), the importance of relying on habit, and the impossibility of not doing so—these are major themes in James's pragmatism. Habit is a force for the status quo, but by orienting and structuring our lives, it sustains us by both holding us back and enabling us to move forward when we find it necessary to do so. Habit is a necessary, albeit somewhat hidden, condition for meliorism in ethics, epistemology, and daily life generally (socially, politically, and personally). It may sound odd, but without habit there could be no progress.

In the book's final chapter, "Habits in a World of Change," James Campbell "explores the centrality of habit to James's psychology and philosophy, and considers how his largely descriptive emphases can be applied to our current situations." As Campbell says, "habits are means of stabilizing experience, they make us less adaptive to novelty," and yet novelty relies on it. What moves us away from habit to novelty? When and why should we seek difficult paths away from our habitual ways of understanding, interpreting, and relating to the world and others? Questions naturally arise as well as to reasons for, or causes of, resistance to change. How are these to be explained, and to what extent can they be, and when should they be, overcome? Campbell is right in emphasizing the significance of understanding habit for James's pragmatism.

The idea for this volume was motivated by what we took to be the relative dearth of literature applying James's pragmatism to issues of current and practical significance, coupled with our considered view that resources in James's pragmatism can be profitably applied to such issues. We thought this neglect of the practical surprising given that, from its inception, pragmatism's focus has been "applied" in the sense that it was concerned with practices—with outcomes, consequences, and actions in relation to the differences they make in everyday life. We asked for essays that we thought might best address our concern and motivation, essays that considered issues along the lines of "how might James have explained . . . ?" or "how might James's theories guide us in dealing with . . . ?" We requested that authors cover such issues as politics and society, ethics, philosophy (particularly the rise of philosophical professionalism and "the PhD octopus"), religion, and alienation. Insofar as the present chapters reflect our initial motivation and what we perceived as the odd lack of engagement with practical issues, we believe the book achieves our goals.

We acknowledge that important topics are missing from the volume. Ideally, we would have included chapters on James's pragmatism and gender, the built environment, and politically motivated manipulation of "truth." We would have liked to explore the relationship between James's pragmatism and poetry (e.g., Emerson, Robert Frost, Wallace Stevens—to mention only a few—perhaps even Philip Levine and Billy Collins), noting that certain kinds of poetry resonate with life experience to an extent that much philosophy proper does not. Sometimes it takes a book to see what's missing from it.

Edited books tend to assume a final shape that at best approximates their original conception. This is not (necessarily) a bad thing and can in fact be a good thing. Even with relatively detailed abstracts in place, by the time chapters are done and revisions made, an editor's grip on the final product will have loosened. What we think most important about the volume is not so much, or merely, the content, but rather (we hope) the direction it gives to what we have termed "pragmatism applied." The general question that *Pragmatism Applied* raises is whether or not, and to what extent, pragmatism can be a philosophy for our time.

NOTES

1. en.wikiquote.org/wiki/Talk:Literature
2. For a comprehensive account of James's activism and contemporary interpretations of it, see Coon (70–99).
3. The biographical details of William James and his immediate family are well chronicled, but for those unfamiliar with them it's worth investigating for hints at the ways that James's unusual upbringing influenced his philosophy. See Richardson, *William James in the Maelstrom of American Modernism*; Simon, *Genuine Reality: A Life of William James*.

REFERENCES

Coon, Deborah J. "'One Moment in the World's Salvation': Anarchism and the Radicalisation of William James," *Journal of American History* 83, no. 1 (1996): 70–99.
Dewey, John. "What Does Pragmatism Mean by Practical?" *Journal of Philosophy, Psychology and Scientific Methods* 5, no. 4 (1908): 85–99.

Franzese, Sergio. *The Ethics of Energy: William James's Moral Philosophy in Focus.* Frankfurt: Ontos Verlag, 2008.

James, William. *The Letters of William James.* 2 vols, edited by Henry James. London: Longmans, Green, 1926.

———. *The Meaning of Truth.* Vol. 2 of *The Works of William James*, edited by Fredson Bowers and Ignas K. Skrupskelis. Introduction by H. S. Thayer. Cambridge, MA: Harvard University Press, [1909] 1975a.

———. *Pragmatism.* Vol. 1 of *The Works of William James*, edited by Fredson Bowers and Ignas K. Skrupskelis. Introduction by H. S. Thayer. Cambridge, MA: Harvard University Press, [1907] 1975b.

———. *A Pluralistic Universe.* Vol. 4 of *The Works of William James*, edited by Fredson Bowers and Ignas K. Skrupskelis. Introduction by Richard J. Bernstein. Cambridge, MA: Harvard University Press, [1909] 1977.

———. *The Principles of Psychology.* Vols. 8–10 of *The Works of William James*, edited by Frederick H. Burkhardt, Fredson Bowers, and Ignas K. Skrupskelis. Introductions by Rand B. Evans and Gerald E. Myers. Cambridge, MA: Harvard University Press, [1890] 1981.

———. *Talks to Teachers on Psychology; and to Students on Some of Life's Ideals.* Vol. 12 of *The Works of William James*, edited by Frederick H. Burkhardt, Fredson Bowers, and Ignas K. Skrupskelis. Introduction by Gerald E. Myers. Cambridge, MA: Harvard University Press, [1899] 1983.

———. *The Varieties of Religious Experience.* Vol. 15 of *The Works of William James*, edited by Frederick H. Burkhardt, Fredson Bowers, and Ignas K. Skrupskelis. Introduction by John E. Smith. Cambridge, MA: Harvard University Press, [1902] 1985.

Marchetti, Sarin. *Ethics and Philosophical Critique in William James.* London: Palgrave Macmillan, 2015.

McDermott, John J. *Streams of Experience.* Amherst: University of Massachusetts Press, 1986.

———. *The Drama of Possibility: Experience as Philosophy of Culture*, edited by Douglas R. Anderson. New York: Fordham University Press, 2007.

McKenna, Erin. *Pets, People, and Pragmatism.* New York: Fordham University Press, 2013.

Peirce, Charles S. "How to Make our Ideas Clear." *Popular Science Monthly* 12 (1878): 286–302.

———. "What Pragmatism Is." *Monist* 15, no. 2 (1905): 162–63.

Richardson, Robert J., *William James in the Maelstrom of American Modernism.* New York: Houghton Mifflin, 2007.

Santayana, George. *The Genteel Tradition in American Philosophy and Character and Opinion in the United States*, edited by James Seaton. New Haven, CT: Yale University Press, 2009.

Seigfried, Charlene Haddock. "The Missing Perspective: Feminist Pragmatism." *Transactions of the Charles S. Peirce Society* 27, no. 4 (1991): 405–16.
———. *Pragmatism and Feminism: Reweaving the Social Fabric*. Chicago: University of Chicago Press, 1996.
Shusterman, Richard. *Thinking Through the Body: Essays in Somaesthetics*. New York: Cambridge University Press, 2012.
Simon, Linda, *Genuine Reality: A Life of William James*. New York: Harcourt Brace, 1998.
Stuhr, John J. *Genealogical Pragmatism: Philosophy, Experience, and Community*. Albany: State University of New York Press, 1997.
Tarver, Erin C., and Sharon Sullivan, eds. *Feminist Interpretations of William James*. University Park: Pennsylvania State University Press, 2015.

PART 1

ISSUES: PUTTING JAMES TO WORK

CHAPTER 1

LISTENING TO "THE CRIES OF THE WOUNDED"

Jamesian Reflections on the Impasse over Gun Control

JAMES M. ALBRECHT

On December 14, 2012, President Barack Obama addressed a nation shocked by the massacre at Sandy Hook Elementary School in Newtown, Connecticut, where a shooter armed with a semi-automatic rifle and pistol purchased legally by his mother, a gun enthusiast, killed twenty children and six adults, after first murdering his mother and before taking his own life:

> The majority of those who died today were children—beautiful little kids between the ages of five and ten years old. They had their entire lives ahead of them—birthdays, graduations, weddings, kids of their own. Among the fallen were also teachers—men and women who devoted their lives to helping our children fulfill their dreams. So our hearts are broken today—for the parents and grandparents, sisters and brothers of these little children, and for the families of the adults who were lost. (Obama 2012)

Obama spoke eloquently of the victims and their families not only to comfort a grieving nation, but in the hope that focusing on the tragic reality of their suffering might break the political impasse on gun laws. Over the multiple occasions when he had to address the nation after mass shootings,

Obama expressed increasing frustration at Congress's failure to act (Korte 2016). When proposals inspired by Newtown were defeated in the Senate, Obama described the "shameful day for Washington" as a failure to honor the victims' suffering: "I'm assuming our expressions of grief and our commitment to do something different to prevent these things from happening are not empty words. . . . Sooner or later, we are going to get this right. The memories of these children demand it" (Obama 2013). But the multiple mass shootings that occurred during the Obama administration after Newtown did not lead to any federal legislation, and the election of 2016, which gave Republicans control of all three branches of the Federal government, seems to preclude the hope for action in the near future.

This impasse over enacting more effective gun safety laws in the United States provides an intriguing test case for considering the continuing relevance of William James's ethical thought. James's pragmatic theory of truth entails a democratic commitment to confront moral conflicts with an experimental openness, a conscientious respect for the ideals of others, and a genuine willingness to forge consensus around shared values. In some of his central statements on ethics—such as "The Moral Philosopher and the Moral Life" and "On a Certain Blindness in Human Beings"—James insists that moral problems require an approach that is pluralistic, experimental, and democratic: an approach that notably recognizes the tragic choices involved in all moral conflicts (the fact that some ideals are necessarily sacrificed or "butchered," in James's visceral phrase, in order to realize other ideals [1979, 154]), and an approach that thus requires a sympathetic and imaginative effort to understand the ideals and values of others—*including and especially* of our opponents in contentious social conflicts. In considering and implementing any social reform, James argues, we must listen carefully for "the cries of the wounded" to alert us to ideals and consequences to which we would otherwise be blind (158).[1]

In terms of gun violence, James's views provocatively imply that we cannot effectively attend to the sufferings of the victims without also listening to the voices of those who feel threatened by the prospect of gun control. James (1982) himself applies such logic in "The Moral Equivalent of War," where he argues that pacifism cannot hope to succeed unless it works to incorporate and redirect the positive ideals and values that militarists find in war. "Pacifists ought to enter more deeply into the esthetical and ethical point of view of their opponents," he argues: "Do that first in any controversy, . . . *then move the point*, and your opponent will follow" (168). For James, the attempt to imagine sympathetically the ideals of one's political opponents, and as far as possible preserve those ideals in any new consensus on actions to be taken, is both a practical necessity for overcoming the inertia of existing truths and habits, and a fundamental ethical obligation to honor the demands of other beings.

In what follows, I consider how such Jamesian principles might be applied to the partisan impasse on gun control. How might the ideals and values that make gun ownership for some Americans a precious and fiercely protected right be better honored and incorporated in proposed reforms? How would such a Jamesian effort to forge consensus differ from strategies already being deployed by the political Left—whether it be the adoption of a centrist rhetoric on gun control, or a more partisan attempt to influence the minds of voters by promoting an unabashedly progressive rhetorical "frame"? Though my treatment here of so complex a problem can only be suggestive, I hope to show how a Jamesian approach might indicate a practical path forward on the issue of gun control. But my ultimate goal is broader: I hope this exercise in applying James's ethics will point beyond the issue of gun violence, in order to highlight how pragmatism's commitment to an experimental process of inquiry and reform offers a democratic alternative to the partisan dogmatism that besets American politics. In the wake of the most divisively partisan presidential election in recent memory, one that revealed the stark cultural polarizations in U.S. society, a Jamesian ethic of experimental and sympathetic openness to the principles of one's political opponents may seem naïvely idealistic—or more urgently relevant than ever.

THE PROBLEM AND THE POLITICAL IMPASSE

The scope of the gun violence problem in the United States can be captured in statistics all too familiar to anyone who regularly follows the national and local news (Everytown for Gun Safety 2012). More than 30,000 Americans are killed every year by firearms: about two-thirds of these deaths are suicides, the rest homicides. Nonfatal shootings are estimated at an additional 78,000 per year. On average, over fifty women per month are shot to death by their intimate partners in the United States, while seven children and youths die from gunshot wounds every day. The majority of gun suicides are middle-aged white men, while African Americans (especially black men) are disproportionately likely to be the victims of gun homicide. In 2010, the rate of gun homicides in the United States was a whopping twenty-five times higher than the average rate in other high-income countries—five times higher than in Canada (with the next highest rate) and almost one hundred times higher than in such nations as the United Kingdom and Norway. While mass shootings account for a small fraction of gun-related deaths, the list of major shootings during the Obama presidency, and to date under the Trump administration alone—Fort Hood, Tucson, Aurora, Sandy Hook, the D.C. Navy Yard, Charleston, Roseburg, San Bernardino, Orlando, Las Vegas, Sutherland Springs, Parkland, and Santa Fe—invokes the terror that gun violence routinely visits upon American communities. The number of guns per capita in the United States has roughly doubled since 1968 (Horsley 2016): the over 300 million guns estimated to be in circulation today equal almost one gun for every person in the nation. Yet, while gun production and sales have boomed in recent years, the percentage of gun-owning households (about 30 percent) has declined significantly since around 1980, revealing a pattern in which an increasing number of guns are owned by fewer Americans.

In the face of this violence, federal efforts to regulate guns have hardened into a political impasse. The past fifty years have witnessed a pattern of increasing partisan division in which periodic federal reforms—the Gun Control Act of 1968, the Brady Handgun Violence Protection Act (1993), and the Federal Assault Weapons Ban (1994)—have been countered by measures designed to roll back their provisions or preclude future measures. The Firearm Owners Protection Act of 1986 reversed certain Gun Control Act restrictions on the interstate sale of guns and ammunition, and prohibited the federal government from maintaining a registry of firearms owners and sales; and when the Assault Weapons Ban was due for renewal in 2004, Congress allowed it to lapse. Supreme Court decisions in the *District of Columbia v. Heller* (2008) and *McDonald v. the City of Chicago* (2010) struck down municipal bans on handguns, reversing decades of precedent in ruling that the Second Amendment guarantees an individual right to bear arms. Below this struggle at the federal level, state laws have moved in opposite directions (Law Center to Prevent Gun Violence n.d.). Some states, most notably California, have instituted tougher regulations, including universal background checks, permanent records of firearm sales, and bans on assault weapons and high-capacity magazines, while other states have significantly loosened gun laws—Missouri offering the most radical example (*New York Times* Editorial Board 2016). Many states have passed preemption laws that limit the ability of local governments to enact gun regulations, passed "stand your ground" laws that make it easier to claim self-defense in a shooting, and significantly loosened regulations governing the carrying of concealed weapons. These divergent state laws largely follow the Blue State/Red State cultural divide in our nation—with California, Illinois, Hawaii, and Northeastern states having the strictest regulations, and Southern, Midwestern, and interior Western states having the loosest.

Taken as a whole, these developments constitute a weakening of gun laws over the past twenty years (since the 1994 Assault Weapons Ban). The gun rights movement's success at weakening regulations has been undergirded by two larger political trends. Perhaps most significant is the evolution of the National Rifle Association (NRA), since the Goldwater-Reagan transformation of the Republican Party, into a powerful lobby that opposes almost all gun regulations and has turned guns into an enormously effective wedge issue for recruiting blue-collar voters to the anti-government ideology of the GOP (Burbick 2006, 75–99). Concurrently, Democrats have shown a reluctance to advocate gun control measures for fear of electoral backlash at the hands of the NRA and its members (Henigan 2016, 3, 11–12). There have been signs of a shift in this political calculus. After the shooting in Roseburg, Oregon, President Obama (2015) rejected the notion that it is inappropriate to "politicize" gun violence, proclaiming his determination to respond to such tragedies by pushing for more effective gun laws. Congressional Democrats have at times shown uncharacteristic boldness: in response to the June 2016 Orlando shooting, Democrats used a Senate filibuster to force votes on two gun safety measures, and then staged a sit-in takeover of the House floor to protest that body's inaction on gun violence. Despite such efforts, Orlando, like Newtown before it, failed to result in any Congressional action (Steinhauer 2016; Herszenhorn and Huetteman 2016).

This partisan impasse was also on full exhibit during the 2016 presidential campaign. Hillary Clinton (HillaryClinton.com 2016) advocated for new gun safety measures—such as closing the background check loopholes for online and gun show sales and prohibiting persons on the FBI's Terrorist Watch List from purchasing firearms. Donald Trump responded by accusing Clinton of wanting to abolish the Second Amendment—an accusation that was tinged with a threat of violence when Trump remarked that perhaps "the Second Amendment People" would have their own means for stopping a President Clinton (Corasaniti and Haberman 2016). This prospect that the debate over guns might result in political violence felt all too real when right-wing militia groups were reportedly arming themselves in preparation for a possible Clinton victory (Zucchino 2016). With Trump in the White House and Republican majorities in both the House and Senate, the federal government seems predictably unwilling to take any meaningful action on guns. In the wake of the worst mass shooting in U.S. history, the October 2017 massacre in Las Vegas, Congress declined to take up proposed legislation outlawing "bump fire" stocks (that convert semi-automatic weapons into fully automatic ones), which the shooter used to murder 58 people and injure more than 700. Indeed, the only significant action on guns Republicans took during the first year of the Trump administration was to pass legislation reversing an Obama executive order designed to prevent mentally ill persons from obtaining a firearm (Korte 2017).

As this chapter goes to press, the Parkland, Florida, school massacre has unleashed a remarkable wave of student-led activism that seems to be shifting the political landscape in ways other mass shootings have not. Florida's Republican governor, Rick Scott, has supported raising his state's legal age for purchasing firearms and strengthening rules that prevent people with mental health issues or histories of stalking or domestic abuse from obtaining guns (Mazzei and Bidgwood 2018). On the federal level, President Trump has ordered the Justice Department to issue regulations banning bump stocks (Shear 2018)—but at the same time has endorsed the NRA's preferred solution of arming public school teachers and employees with concealed weapons (Davis 2018), and Republicans have so far resisted reinstating a ban on assault weapons. Only time will tell whether the momentum created by the student response to Parkland signals a lasting shift in the nation's response to gun violence.

The current positions in the gun debate have been forged in the crucible of this political impasse. The Brady Center to Prevent Gun Violence (n.d.) describes gun violence as a public health crisis that can be tackled on two fronts: making it harder for those with criminal intent to obtain guns, and limiting the violence—mostly suicides and accidental deaths—involving guns purchased without criminal intent. To address the first challenge, Brady advocates extending background checks to the secondary market of private gun sales—not just at gun shows, but over the Internet and through gun-trafficking sales facilitated by "straw purchasers"—sales that, comprising up to 40 percent of the gun sales in America, constitute a "massive loophole" in the current system. This central policy initiative should be supplemented, Brady argues, by heightened anti-trafficking efforts aimed at "bad apple" gun dealers (whose sales "account for 60% of crime guns"), by requiring gun owners to report stolen guns, and through "smart-gun" technologies that would render stolen guns unusable. Deploying a rhetoric clearly intended to distinguish law-abiding gun owners from criminals, Brady argues that the second challenge, of unsafely stored guns in the home, "isn't a gun problem" at all, but "a responsibility problem" analogous to drunk driving and second-hand smoke—public health threats caused by adults using legal products irresponsibly—and proposes it should be addressed through "major public awareness and education campaigns" about "responsible attitudes and behaviors based on the real risks around guns in the home." Such efforts can be supplemented through legal measures such as child access prevention laws, already adopted in some states, which make an adult criminally liable when a child accesses an inadequately secured gun. While Brady's central initiatives do not stress bans on assault weapons or high-capacity magazines, their approach is representative of mainstream gun safety organizations.

The gun rights position—as articulated by the NRA (2014a–b; 2016a–d), its most vocal and powerful advocate—is diametrically opposed to the Brady approach. On this view, describing gun violence as a public health issue is a liberal ploy to "portray guns . . . as a menace" (2015): guns are not a disease; in fact, more guns wielded by law-abiding citizens provide the only means to a safer America. Violence is not a gun problem, the NRA argues, but a crime problem, and solutions must focus on stronger efforts to enforce existing laws and punish criminals. Measures such as background checks are ineffective at preventing criminals from illegally obtaining guns: instead, they threaten law-abiding citizens' Second Amendment rights (which include even the right to own and use semi-automatic assault weapons and high-capacity magazines), and are dangerous steps down a slippery slope toward the government's ultimate goal of abolishing the Second Amendment and confiscating Americans' guns. Such views shape the NRA's increasingly dogmatic opposition to virtually any new gun safety regulations. After Newtown, the only proposal the NRA put forward was to place armed security guards in schools across the nation—which NRA Vice-President Wayne LaPierre promoted via the gun rights mantra that, "The only thing that stops a bad guy with a gun is a good guy with a gun" (Lichtblau and Rich 2012).

The significance of a Jamesian approach to this political divide can be understood in relation to two developments in progressive thinking and strategy. First, as Molly Ball chronicles, gun control organizations have since the late 1990s strategically adopted more moderate policy goals and rhetoric:

> Gun-control groups don't even use the term "gun control," with its big-government implications, favoring "preventing gun violence" instead. Democratic politicians preface every appeal for reform with a paean to the rights enshrined in the Second

Amendment and bend over backwards to assure "law-abiding gun owners" they mean them no ill will. (Ball 2013)

Such a strategy accords with polls indicating that, although Americans tend in the abstract to favor "gun rights" over "gun control" (Frankel 2015), a majority of gun owners—including NRA members—support various specific gun safety regulations (Everytown for Gun Safety 2012). This approach, pioneered in the wake of the Columbine school massacre by the group Americans for Gun Safety (AGS), has enjoyed success—most notably in state ballot initiatives in 2000 that closed the gun show background check loophole in Colorado and Oregon. These campaigns used "imagery and language that reappropriated the other side's emphasis on sportsmen and the Constitution," and enlisted GOP Senator John McCain to spread the message that "law-abiding citizens have the right to own guns, but with rights come responsibilities" (Ball 2013). The broader success of this strategy, however, has been limited. While the victories of 2000 have been replicated in the passage of other state initiatives, such advances have been limited to Blue States. Moreover, "if the gun-control movement is more strategic than it once was, it's also less ambitious," Ball notes, so that, "the whole debate has shifted to the right." The NRA responded to the success of the AGS strategy by moving further to the right and opposing even moderate gun regulations. The NRA's ability to enforce this hard line is evident both in 2013 recall elections in Colorado (that removed two state legislators who had helped pass a universal background check), and in the fact that five Democratic senators—including Minority Leader Harry Reid—joined Republicans in defeating the universal background check proposal after Newtown. To date, progressive attempts to adopt policies and rhetoric that appeal to the ideals of moderates and gun owners have failed to break our political impasse over guns.

Indeed, a second trend in progressive thought, popularized by cognitive scientist and linguist George Lakoff, questions the very notion of forging consensus around moderate values. Arguing that linguistic and cognitive "frames" play a profound role in unconsciously shaping political behavior, Lakoff explains the partisan divide in American politics as the competition between two moral visions—the "strict father" frame of conservatives and the "nurturant parent" frame of progressives—which, as "long-term concepts that structure how we think," are "instantiated in the synapses of our brains" (Lakoff 2014, 3, 15). Although people "have both models, either actively or passively" in their brains, Lakoff argues that these synaptic circuits are mutually inhibitive (53), so that only one shapes a person's thoughts and actions at any given time. Hence, he divides the American populace into three groups: conservatives and progressives, who think and act consistently through their respective frames, and "biconceptuals" who toggle back and forth between the competing frames, "conservative on some issues and progressive on others" (18). Lakoff seeks to disabuse liberals of the Enlightenment faith that, "if we just tell people the facts, since people are basically rational beings, they'll all reach the right conclusions;" most people, he argues, are incapable of seriously entertaining ideas outside their dominant frame: "If the facts do not fit a frame, the frame stays and the facts bounce off" (15). Accordingly, political discourse is not about rational persuasion and deliberation, but about "reframing" social issues in terms of the core ideals of one's moral vision: the goal is to promote assertively the language of your moral frame to make it more strongly habituated within the minds of the populace—specifically with those "biconceptuals," who are, in Lakoff's scheme, the only segment of the population capable of significant shifts in their political stances (xiii, 45–46, 19). Lakoff attributes the conservative movement's success over the past fifty years, on issues such as guns, to such concerted, long-term efforts to habituate the conservative frame within the minds of American voters: Republicans "say what they idealistically believe, [. . . and] talk to their base using the frames of their base," while "progressive candidates tend to follow their polls and decide that they have to become more 'centrist' by moving to the right. The conservatives do not move at all to the left, and yet they win!" (18).

Lakoff's analysis is a revealing symptom of our times. As a strategic response to the partisanship of the Right, his gospel of "framing"—his view that liberals must more proudly and effectively communicate the moral vision behind their policies—understandably resonates with progressives tired of electoral and legislative defeats. Yet Lakoff's model is troubling in the way it elevates partisanship to a conceptual and cognitive binarism that seems to preclude, or at least seriously circumscribe, the ability to think and act more experimentally—beyond a rigid dualism of "conservative" versus "liberal" approaches. In Lakoff's model, any attempt to appeal to your opponents' ideals in hopes of forging a new consensus is naïve and misguided: indeed, his title *Don't Think of an Elephant* is an injunction to avoid so much as using your opponents' language, even to refute it. A Jamesian ethics demands more, insisting that a charitable and experimental effort to include your opponents' ideals in an inclusive consensus is both a practical necessity and a moral obligation.

JAMESIAN ETHICS IN SOCIAL INQUIRY AND REFORM

The aspects of James's ethics I want to highlight emerge from his pragmatic account of the resistant-yet-malleable role that existing truths and habits play in our efforts to reshape experience. James notes that when a "new experience" reveals the inadequacy of our "stock of old opinions," we seek a "new idea" that "preserves the older stock of truths with a minimum of modification, stretching them just enough to make them admit the novelty." "New truth" is thus "always a go-between" that "marries old opinion to new fact" with "a minimum of jolt, a maximum of continuity" (James 1975, 34–35). James calls special attention to "the part played by the older truths" (35). While he marvels at "how plastic even the oldest truths . . . really are" (37), he stresses that existing truths—because they so profoundly shape our perceptions, actions, and purposes—exert an enormous conservative force: "Their influence is absolutely controlling. Loyalty to them is the first principle—in most cases it is the only principle; for by far the most usual way of handling phenomena so novel that they would make for a serious rearrangement of our preconceptions is to ignore them altogether, or to abuse those who bear witness for them" (35). Accordingly, James encourages a dual attitude toward existing truths: while they must be reformed in order to meet new challenges and realize new possibilities, the most expedient way to facilitate such reform is to preserve, as far as possible, those elements of existing ideals that can be retained and redirected in a reconstructed situation.[2]

The ethical stakes involved in this attempt to honor yet reform existing truths become apparent when we remember that truths are tools for satisfying human demands: that current truths exist because they have proven valuable, that there are flesh-and-blood creatures who find satisfaction in experiences ordered and shaped by these ideals. Hence, James (1979, 141–62) asserts, "the philosopher must be a conservative," and the "presumption in cases of conflict must always be in favor of the conventionally recognized good." Conversely, however, he notes that, "pent in under every system of moral rules are innumerable persons whom it weighs upon, and goods which it represses" (156), and if we merely "follow the ideal which is conventionally highest, the others which we butcher either die and do not return to haunt us; or if they come back and accuse us of murder, everyone applauds us for turning them a deaf ear. In other words, our environment encourages us not to be philosophers, but partisans" (154). Thus, if the moral philosopher must to a large extent be conservative, James counters that, "the *highest* ethical life . . . consists at all times in the breaking of rules which have grown too narrow for the actual case" (158). Preserving existing values in any proposed reform is more than a practical expedient for overcoming political resistance; it expresses a fundamental obligation to honor the demands of other beings, by working to minimize the tragic conflict between those who find value in elements of the status quo and those who feel oppressed by them.

James's ethics are animated by this acute sense that the choice between opposing ideals and courses of action involves a tragic conflict between goods cherished by sentient beings:

> The actually possible in this world is vastly narrower than all that is demanded; and there is always a *pinch* between the ideal and the actual which can only be got through by leaving part of the ideal behind. There is hardly a good which we can imagine except as competing for the possession of the same bit of space and time with some other imagined good. . . . So that the ethical philosopher's demand for the right scale of subordination in ideals is the fruit of an altogether practical need. Some part of the ideal must be butchered, and he needs to know which part. (James 1979, 153–54)

James's visceral metaphor of "butchering" the ideal expresses his claim that "the good" is not some abstract antecedent entity, but merely a summarizing name for the goods that are realized in the embodied experiences of beings with desires and feelings: "Take any demand, however slight, which any creature, however weak, may make. Ought it not, for its own sole sake, to be satisfied? If not, prove why not. The only possible kind of proof you could adduce would be the exhibition of another creature who should make a demand that ran the other way" (149). James accordingly takes the pluralistic stance that there is "no single abstract principle" or "universal underlying kind of motive" that defines the truest or highest good, beyond the definitional claim "that *the essence of good is simply to satisfy demand*" (153).

Moral conflicts, on this pragmatic view, are not theoretical problems but inherently and tragically practical ones, in which our "guiding principle" must be "simply to satisfy at all times *as many demands as we can*" (James 1979, 155):

> That act must be the best act, accordingly, which makes for the *best whole*, in the sense of awakening the least sum of dissatisfactions. . . . Since victory and defeat there must be, the victory to be philosophically prayed for is that of the more inclusive side—of the side which even in the hour of triumph will to some degree do justice to the ideals in which the vanquished party's interests lay. . . . *Invent some manner* of realizing your own ideals which will also satisfy the alien demands—that and that only is the path of peace! (155)

James's injunction here to "do justice to the ideals" of the "vanquished party" by seeking a "manner of realizing your own ideals" that "will also satisfy the alien demands" is a moral mandate for forging political consensus: not only as a practical means to minimize potentially bitter conflict, as "the only path of peace," but because the perceptions, desires, and judgments of all sentient beings deserve respect as indicators of existing and potential goods. A universe in which more demands—including those of one's political opponents—are satisfied is a morally richer universe, and a democratic society, in particular, should strive for such inclusivity.

For James, pursuing the most inclusive synthesis of competing goods requires an experimental process of inquiry and reform. "The Moral Philosopher and the Moral Life" (1979, 141–62) offers a description of the process of moral judgment that encapsulates—as well as any passage in James's writings—how the experimentalism implied in a pragmatic theory of truth also entails a democratic openness and respect for others' views:

> Everywhere the ethical philosopher must wait on facts. The thinkers who create the ideals come he knows not whence, their sensibilities are evolved he knows not how; and the question as to which of two conflicting ideals will give the best universe then and there, can be answered by him only through the aid of the experience of other men. . . . There is but one unconditional commandment, which is that we should seek incessantly, with fear and trembling, so to vote and to act as to bring about the very largest total universe of good which we can see. Abstract rules indeed can help; but they help the less in proportion as our intuitions are more piercing, and our vocation is the stronger for the moral life. For every real dilemma is in literal strictness a unique situation; and the exact combination of ideals realized

and ideals disappointed which each decision creates is always a universe without a precedent, and for which no adequate previous rule exists. . . . He knows that he must vote always for the richer universe, [. . . but] which particular universe this is he cannot know for certain in advance; he only knows that if he makes a bad mistake the cries of the wounded will soon inform him of the fact. In all this the philosopher is just like the rest of us non-philosophers, so far as we are just and sympathetic instinctively, and so far as we are open to the voice of complaint. (1979, 158–59)

This passage is remarkable for the thoroughgoing experimentalism that James—writing in 1891—advocates in social and moral thought. Every problem, he insists, is literally a unique situation; so, while existing principles and rules are of course invaluable, no principle can dogmatically be assumed to provide a solution. We must deploy principles and proposed actions provisionally: actual results in a given situation can never be fully predicted, so we must remain open to changing both our strategies and goals. James also asserts that a genuine experimentalism must be communal and democratic: the results of any course of action can be adequately judged "only through the aid of the experience of other men [*sic*]." In deliberating on possible measures, and in judging their outcomes, we must remain justly and sympathetically "open to the voice of complaint" alerting us to perceptions and values beyond our own.

Consider, in contrast to our current partisan battles over public policy, what such a pragmatic experimentalism might require in relation to the issue of guns. Faced with two conflicting ideals—the belief that democratic citizens have a God-given right to bear arms, and the opposing belief that the right to life, liberty, and the pursuit of happiness includes the freedom from unreasonable fear of gun violence—a pragmatic approach might encourage states and municipalities to experiment with various measures for reducing gun violence, in search of social arrangements that more successfully satisfy both ideals. Pragmatism would also reject any rigid dualism of conservative versus liberal approaches: as John Dewey argued, the critical alternative is not between individualist and collectivist approaches *per se*, but rather between an experimentalism that chooses an approach based on specific conditions and consequences, and an absolutism that precludes such flexible inquiry (Dewey 1988b, 356, 361, 281).[3] Gun rights advocates would have to relinquish a dogmatic opposition to legal regulations, and gun control advocates remain open to measures utilizing nongovernmental channels. Lastly, the processes of proposing, implementing, and judging the results of specific measures would require, at each step, an active effort to understand sympathetically the perspectives of persons whose values and experiences differ from one's own.

This last point is crucial. For if remaining sympathetically "open to the voice of complaint" is essential to guiding an experimental process toward a more inclusive consensus, James warns that such openness does not come easily to humans. A central concern in James's ethics is that the insistently practical nature of our intelligence—focused through our purposes, attention, habits, concepts, and language—threatens to blind us to possibilities in experience beyond our own purposes, and crucially, to possibilities and purposes that other beings hold dear. James famously addresses this topic in his essay "On a Certain Blindness in Human Beings," where he notes that as "practical beings, . . . with limited functions and duties to perform," we are each "bound to feel intensely the importance of his own duties and the significance of the situations that call these forth," but are consequently afflicted with a "stupidity and injustice" about the "significance of alien lives" and the "value of other persons' conditions or ideals" (James 1983, 132). An awareness of this "certain"—that is, inevitable—blindness, imposes a moral obligation:

> It absolutely forbids us to be forward in pronouncing on the meaninglessness of forms of existence other than our own; and it commands us to tolerate, respect, and indulge those whom we see harmlessly interested and happy in their own ways, however unintelligible these may be to us. Hands off: neither the whole of truth, nor the whole of good, is revealed to any single observer. (149)

While we must "at least use our sense of our own blindness to make us more cautious in going over the dark places" (151), a truly democratic and experimental process of inquiry requires more than tolerance, requires a more positive effort to appreciate sympathetically the ideals and purposes of those who differ from us. James offers as a model the profound interest we are capable of taking in the lives of those we love most intimately. Noting that there are persons who extend such sympathy more extensively, who exhibit "an enormous capacity for friendship and for taking delight in other people's lives," he urges us to strive for this challenging standard:

"We ought, all of us, to realize each other in this intense, pathetic and important way" (ibid.).

These various aspects of James's ethical commitment to an experimental and democratic process of reform provide the necessary context for applying his argument in "The Moral Equivalent of War" to the issue of gun violence. It is not particularly useful to focus on James's central, admittedly "utopian" proposal: to create a new social institution (a compulsory civil service in an "army enlisted against *nature*") that will provide a healthier outlet and source for the positive ideals associated with the institution one wants to abolish (war) (James 1982, 165, 171). Dewey, commenting on the "Moral Equivalent" essay, argued that James's proposal understated just how broadly social conditions would need to be reformed in order to replace "the war-pattern" with peaceful dynamics of interaction (1988a). "The problem of war is difficult because it is serious," Dewey concludes: "It is none other than the wider problem of the effective moralizing or humanizing of native impulses in times of peace" (1988a, 82). A similar case must be made about gun violence. Pragmatism—whether James's or Dewey's variety—warns us that ameliorating a serious social problem like gun violence will require ongoing efforts to reform *all* social conditions that perpetuate habits which contribute to it: the various institutions that promote violent forms of masculinity; the glorification of gun violence in our media; our systemic failures in dealing with mental illness; the economic inequality that fuels gang-related crime—to name only some of the obvious culprits.

But if a long-term systemic solution is required, the need for effective gun safety laws remains immediate and urgent. It is here—in relation to the more focused problem of creating consensus for reform in the face of our current partisan impasse—that the core idea behind James's concept of a moral equivalent is most relevant. In asserting that pacifists must "enter more deeply into the esthetical and ethical point of view of their opponents," that militarist's "insistent unwillingnesses" at the prospect of eliminating war, "no less than other esthetic and ethical insistencies have . . . to be listened to and respected" (James 1982, 168), James is applying the more general view outlined above: that a democratic process of inquiry and reform requires a sympathetic effort to understand and, as far as possible, include the values of one's political opponents. Could a more sympathetic understanding of the ideals cherished by gun owners—values that currently fuel their resistance to gun regulations—be used to craft laws they would find consonant with their experiences and values? Might such an effort constitute something more than a strategic adoption of centrist rhetoric, and might it support a renewed democratic commitment to seeking consensus in our hyper-partisan age?

LISTENING TO "GUN GUYS": TOWARD A PRAGMATIC AND DEMOCRATIC IDEAL OF CONSENSUS

Dan Baum's (2013) study *Gun Guys* is a valuable resource for exploring such questions. A freelance journalist and self-professed "gun guy" with otherwise liberal political leanings, Baum describes his project as an attempt to get beyond reductive assumptions about gun owners and, he hopes, to shed light on our cultural divide over guns: "What nobody seemed to be doing," he writes, "was *listening* to gun people;" yet as "almost half our population" they are "worth knowing," since their "enthusiasm for firearms said something about us as a people," and "nothing lasting or decent could happen in gun policy without them" (10). Though Baum encountered, in the wide range of gun owners he interviewed, plenty of off-putting "gun guy anger" that reflects the paranoid extremes of gun rights ideology, he "for the most part" found gun guys "passionate, responsible, and fully aware of the tremendous power they wield every time they pick up a firearm" (274). One can cull from Baum's interviews some of the main reasons many Americans view guns as positive, fulfilling parts of their lives. These include largely amoral satisfactions: the "sensual pleasure" of handling powerful, well-designed machines—"Guys like machines, and guns are machines elevated to high, lethal art" (29); and the heady adrenaline rush of unleashing such destructive force—Baum challenges readers to have any "peacenik" fire a machine gun on a target range, then "strap him to a polygraph and ask him if it was fun" (78). But learning to control such lethal power responsibly also takes on ethical significance: "handling guns can, if done right, . . . impose a welcome discipline on one's life, and, properly supervised, can be particularly healthy for young people" (274). The discipline of carrying a firearm in public entails what Baum describes as an existential sense of confronting and managing the possibility of death, "a little contact high from the grim reaper": "*I am master of this death-dealing device, and you are not. I am prepared for and capable of surviving the kind of situation you can't even bring yourself to think about*" (261; italics in original). This preparedness to wield deadly force can, according to Baum, instill a form of personal and civic virtue, a "sheep dog" mentality characterized by a sense of responsibility for one's own security and a hyper-vigilant awareness of one's surroundings (41, 49). Ultimately, these ethical dimensions take on political meaning. Aside from the Lockean idea that an armed citizenry is a necessary check on government tyranny (a view with many adherents in the American Right), handling guns can be seen to embody virtues of liberty and responsibility that are central to democratic citizenship. America is unique, Baum stresses, in the "amazing amount of trust" it places in its citizens—whether trusting them with a remarkable right to "freedom of information" or supporting their right to own "incredibly powerful weapons" (79). On this view, to own and carry firearms is a patriotic exercise of our democratic liberty.

It is all too easy, from a liberal perspective, to point out ways in which these values are problematic. They are closely tied to traditionally masculine values of power, strength, and control that too often feed violence and inequality in our culture. (Though there are plenty of women who celebrate the values of gun culture, there's a reason Baum's focus is on gun *guys*.) The notion of a "sheep-dog" ethos contains an inherent "us versus them" elitism, directed both at the unarmed "sheep" and at the criminals potentially lurking in any situation. Baum documents how American gun culture trumpets an alleged crisis of crime that is belied by actual trends in our society (35–40, 98–101), and this specter of crime has been used, from Nixon to Trump, as a racially coded wedge issue in American politics. This us-versus-them dichotomy also highlights a familiar contradiction within the stance that carrying firearms is a fundamental democratic right: the claim that "good" citizens can be trusted to wield enormously powerful weapons depends, in part, on the view that they must defend themselves in a dangerous world full of "bad guys" who *can't* be trusted—which explains why the gun rights movement so vehemently insists that criminals, not guns, are the problem.

Without minimizing such critiques, a Jamesian ethics would remind liberals that a failure to appreciate the positive aspects of others' ideals entails a risk of blindness and ignorance, and threatens to perpetuate the misunderstanding and antagonism that impede reform. A recurrent theme in Baum's book is that gun owners feel liberals have failed in precisely this regard: "what was . . . coming through again and again was that gun guys felt *insulted*. They had something they liked to do—own and shoot guns—and because of it they suffered, they believed, a continuous assault on their hobby, their lifestyle, and their dignity" (162). Measures that liberals see as moderate and reasonable—such as banning assault rifles—are perceived by gun owners as revealing an elitist ignorance about and disdain for guns, and by extension gun owners:

> We made gun owners . . . the enemy by threatening to ban their guns. We demonized them by implying—when we inveighed against "gun culture" and "America's love affair with guns"—that they were somehow to blame for Sandy Hook. We alienated them by asking why any "sane" or "decent" person needed an AR-15—the most popular gun in America, enjoyed harmlessly by millions of law-abiding citizens. (280–81)

Baum argues that such dismissiveness carries a high political cost: if liberals "did the instinctive thing and made gun owners the enemy," they "couldn't do the smart thing and make them allies in the struggle against gun violence" (280).

What type of gun safety laws would be more consonant with the experiences and ideals of gun owners? Though Baum is skeptical of the efficacy of most gun control measures, and wary of the damage they do to the larger progressive agenda, his "Postscript," written in the wake of the Sandy Hook and Aurora shootings, offers three proposals that are instructive in terms of both substance and rhetoric:

1. Requiring gun owners to keep their firearms securely stowed—in quick access safes, for example—and making gun owners "criminally liable for crimes committed with guns stolen from their houses."

2. Mandating "stiffer training requirements for concealed carry" permits.

3. Extending background checks to all private sales by placing "the FBI's National Instant Criminal Background Check online, where everybody can access it. . . . As with the current background-check system, the FBI computer would keep no record of the check, preventing the creation of a de facto gun-registration database." (281–83)

These proposals overlap with the types of measures that gun safety organizations have promoted as a centrist approach—and measures already enacted in some Blue States. So why might Baum's proposals offer more hope for enlisting the support of gun owners? Most importantly, because they focus not on banning types of weapons or ammunition, but on promoting responsible handling of guns and keeping them out of the wrong hands, they could be presented, far more intentionally and effectively than groups such as Brady do, in rhetorical terms that gun owners themselves use to defend the right to bear arms: that law-abiding democratic citizens can be trusted to handle firearms responsibly—and that their responsibility sets them apart from criminals and others (the mentally ill, troubled or depressed teens, children) who should not be so trusted. Baum frames his proposal around catchwords like "responsibility" and "training," using NRA-approved rhetoric: "Quick-access safes make guns available to their owners in emergencies, so there's no excuse for not requiring gun owners . . . to obey Rule Five [of firearm safety]: Maintain control of your firearm;" and "Every gun guy urges every other gun guy to get properly trained before carrying, so why not mandate it? Training is not an infringement of Second Amendment rights; it's an *enhancement* . . .—a well-trained armed citizen is more effective in a crisis" (282). Similarly, Baum is careful to stipulate that taking responsibility for making private gun sales safer need not mean subjecting oneself to government control—that law-abiding citizens could perform background checks without winding up in a federal database.

Baum's proposals provide one model of what the initial steps might be in a Jamesian approach to the impasse over gun control. As James notes, the most that ethical theory can do is to provide us with principles, standards, or rules for assessing and acting in particular situations; it cannot prescribe specific measures nor guarantee their success. Whether measures such as Baum proposes would in fact succeed in creating the basis for bipartisan action would be a matter of political art—the art of legislating, coalition building, and public campaigning. Such efforts would require plenty of Jamesian listening in order to build trust and recruit allies who, in turn, would have credibility with gun owners. Such efforts have led to success: in the aforementioned Americans for Gun Safety initiative campaigns of 2000, which featured John McCain appealing to gun owners with a rhetoric of "rights" and "responsibilities" (Ball 2013), and in the 2016 election in Washington State, where the Alliance for Gun Safety used a similar rhetoric to promote Initiative 1491 (creating Extreme Risk Protection Orders, which allow police and families to request a judge to restrict gun access for someone deemed a risk to self or others), which won approval with nearly 70 percent of the vote statewide (Liu 2017, 109–10). And if the polls are correct that a majority of gun owners do not share the NRA's hardline opposition to all gun safety measures, then a Jamesian effort to forge consensus seems well worth trying.

Yet persuading progressives to invest in such a strategy admittedly seems like a tough sell. Since the election of Donald Trump, the emergence of a grassroots movement whose slogan is "Resist!" shows that progressives are in no mood to compromise, and would likely view attempts to forge consensus as a capitulation to the Right. The Jamesian rejoinder—as outlined above—is that, far from being an acquiescence or capitulation, the effort to understand and incorporate the ideals of one's political opponents is both a practical strategy (and perhaps necessity) for effecting reform, and, in broader terms, a requirement for promoting democratic community and experimental inquiry. On the more immediate question of enacting reform, a strong case can be made that meaningful progress on gun safety laws—at least on the federal level—will be achieved only by forging a new coalition that reaches across the current partisan divide. At present (2018), the Republican party controls the Presidency, the Senate, and the House of Representatives, but even if the Democrats had control over all three (which they did as recently as 2010), it is unlikely they could enact meaningful gun violence reforms without some bipartisan support. The Senate's sixty-vote threshold for cloture on legislation ensures that (barring a filibuster-proof majority) no legislation would pass without at least some Republican votes; moreover, without a bipartisan coalition, moderate Democrats from more conservative or swing districts would almost certainly be scared off from tough votes on gun bills. One can also predict that conservatives would be more resistant to compromise than progressives: the current impasse maintains the gun-friendly status quo, serves the conservative agenda of preventing new government regulations, and allows the GOP to retain a powerful culture-war wedge issue.

Given each side's motives for maintaining a partisan line, the prospects for forging consensus seem dim, but the sad truth is that the near inevitability of recurring gun-related tragedies in America will provide repeated occasions for the public to demand that our elected officials take meaningful action—repeated opportunities for politicians on both the Left and Right to consider whether to cling to the security of their party lines or pursue the riskier attempt to forge a bipartisan coalition. From a liberal perspective, if James's advice—"to enter more deeply into the esthetical and ethical point of view of [your] opponents," and "*then move the point*" (James 1982, 168)—resulted in the passage of the laws that Baum suggests, it would represent not capitulation, but concrete progress. On average, seven children in the United States die each day from gunshot wounds, mostly accidental deaths or suicides resulting from their access to improperly secured firearms, and we should remember that the Newtown tragedy resulted from a deeply troubled young man having easy access to guns purchased by his mother. Progressives should not scoff at gun safety laws that might prevent any such tragedies.

A Jamesian strategy, however, would not rest content with such modest measures of success. Steps such as those Baum proposes would be merely initial: focusing on measures consonant with the ideals of gun owners—beginning, in effect, with low-hanging fruit—would be a strategic choice, an attempt, in a situation of partisan gridlock, to forge a sense of shared values and consensus. Passing such laws, if they succeeded in saving lives, would be worthwhile in itself, but the larger goal would be to create, for advocates on both sides, the experience of successful bipartisan action that might create momentum and good faith for tackling tougher issues (such as restrictions on high-capacity magazines) with a more experimental and cooperative spirit. The ultimate goal would be to promote a more genuinely experimental approach to inquiry and reform. Forging consensus need not be a matter of calculated expediency in a partisan standoff—of coopting your opponents' rhetoric in an attempt to push through your own standard partisan proposals, or a static zero-sum compromise in which neither side gets what they want or changes their thinking. A Jamesian model of consensus would require a more genuine experimental willingness to put into practice measures that are consonant with your opponents' ideals.

It is worth repeating that such an experimental openness does not imply an acquiescence or capitulation to the stance of one's political opponents—especially not to a rigid absolutism that would preclude dialogue and compromise.[4] Forging consensus requires flexibility and movement on both sides, and if a Jamesian ethics enjoins us to guard against our blindness or intolerance toward the ideals of others, it entitles us to expect reciprocation. Particularly helpful here is Kenneth Burke's claim that an awareness of the inevitable blindness of human beings requires a "comic" attitude that is "charitable" without being "gullible"—that can view conflict as an inevitable result of our differing experiences and values without excusing malicious intent, intolerance, or cynical political obstructionism (Burke 1984, 41–42, 106–07).[5] Nor does seeking consensus mean suppressing or ignoring conflict. As Martin Luther King Jr. famously argued, a commitment to justice requires a willingness to confront conflict—to promote the "constructive, nonviolent tension which is necessary for growth" (King 2011, 89). While King focuses on the tension experienced by those who are most powerless and marginalized in society, James would remind us that situations of moral conflict require us to attend to the tension experienced by all parties—to listen alertly for the "cries of the wounded" on all sides who feel their ideals or rights are threatened. One can strive to understand the grievances of gun owners without ignoring or minimizing the sufferings of the victims of gun violence; indeed, if the Jamesian logic I have traced here is valid, if the passage of meaningful gun safety laws will require efforts to forge a new consensus, then listening to "gun guys" may be the only way to respond effectively to the sufferings of those victims.

As this chapter goes to press, in the heat of partisanship exacerbated by the Trump presidency, to call for an experimental and charitable search for consensus may seem woefully naïve. But if we understand this Jamesian ethic as a democratic ideal—in pragmatism's melioristic sense of how ideals function—it may seem more relevant than ever. It is instructive here to recall Lakoff's theory that the entrenched partisanship of our politics reflects the extent to which our political thinking is unconsciously governed by mutually inhibitive ideological frames deeply engrained in our brain circuitry—a view that calls into question our capacity to forge coalitions, or even deliberate reflectively, beyond a rigid binarism of conservative versus liberal approaches. In marked contrast, though pragmatism acknowledges the tremendous inertia habit exerts in our individual and collective lives, it also views habit as embodying the fact that our minds and characters, shaped by social conditions, are plastic—educable and reformable. Pragmatism thus encourages us to view the current hyper-partisanship of our politics less as physiologically determined by our cognitive circuitry, and more as a symptom of the ways in which dogmatic, absolutist habits have been instilled by our social institutions. Pragmatism does not minimize the daunting scope of social reconstruction involved in a task such as overcoming the entrenched partisanship of our political culture; nonetheless, it does express faith in our ability to cultivate selves with habits of more flexible and conscientious deliberation, to reshape our institutions (from schools, to media outlets, to political structures) so that they would instill and strengthen such habits, and to create communities that more fully embody an experimental and democratic process of inquiry and action (Albrecht 2012, 156–65, 232–37).

"Faith" is an appropriate term here. For pragmatism, democracy is an ideal whose truth—following the logic of James's "Will to Believe" (1979)—in part depends on our belief in its possibility and our efforts to realize it. The idea of democracy can "become" true, or be shown to be true, only through the process by which any such ideal could *ever* be verified: in its success at guiding us to more satisfactory relations in experience (James 1975, 97, 34). Pragmatism thus encourages the melioristic view that an idea can remain "true" even in the face of daunting challenges and failures—so long as it yields sufficient experiences of and hope for success. Dewey (1988b, 328) described democracy in just such pragmatic terms: as an ideal that can never be fully realized, but provides a necessary standard in our efforts to shape communities that *better* approximate the ideal (Albrecht 2012, 241–43). We will never succeed in creating fully democratic processes of inquiry and reform, or in cultivating selves with perfectly democratic habits of conscientious and flexible openness. A Jamesian effort to consider others' ideals more charitably and openly will never fully overcome our ancestral "blindness" or eliminate dogmatic partisanship from our politics, but it may be a necessary ethos if we hope to make our politics more genuinely experimental, inclusive, and democratic. Striving for such ideals, pragmatism would remind us, is not naively idealistic, but a humane necessity.

NOTES

1. See Albrecht (165–83) for a discussion of how the strand of James's ethics focused on in this article fits within the broader context of his pluralistic meliorism, which envisions a moral self that energetically pursues its own dearest insights, ideals, and purposes while remaining imaginatively and sympathetically open to the ideals and aims of others. Other studies have similarly stressed the importance within James's ethics of a sympathetic openness to others. Seigfried argues that, for James, "concern for the point of view of others . . . is as central to knowledge claims as it is to ethical claims" (93). Edmonds locates in James an "ethics of the encounter," which goes beyond a "passive tolerance" based on an intellectual sense of obligation, and seeks a more profound understanding through the "immediacy of shared feeling" (134). Smith stresses James's "inclusivist" commitment to avoid the potentially damaging consequences of political conflict and to foster instead a healthy dynamic of debate (143–44). Throntveit stresses that empathy is one of the cardinal virtues in James's democratic, communal, and experimental vision of ethics (273). Koopman, citing the "Moral Equivalent of War," views James's "moral inclusivism" as integral to a "transitionalist" meliorism that insists political change must be forged out of the problems and resources of an existing historical situation (167–72). Marchetti stresses that pragmatism's view of "truth as invention" requires efforts to overcome our blindness toward others' ideals and perspectives (198–213), which renders us "not only unable to make sense of their visions and struggles," but "blind toward aspects of the world itself" (201).

2. For a related reading of "The Moral Equivalent of War" as exemplifying James's melioristic and "inclusivist" approach to the conflict between seemingly incompatible ideals, see Koopman (167–70).

3. See Albrecht (252–53).

4. Throntveit (273–74) and Smith (145–46) similarly stress that there are reasonable limits to a Jamesian ethos of charity and inclusivity toward others' political views.

5. See Albrecht (289–94).

REFERENCES

Albrecht, James. *Reconstructing Individualism: A Pragmatic Tradition from Emerson to Ellison*. New York: Fordham University Press, 2012.

Ball, Molly. "How the Gun-Control Movement Got Smart." *The Atlantic*, February 2013. www.theatlantic.com/politics/archive/2013/02/how-the-gun-control-movement-got-smart/272934

Baum, Dan. *Gun Guys: A Road Trip*. New York: Vintage, 2013.

Burke, Kenneth. *Attitudes toward History*. 3rd ed. Berkeley: University of California Press, 1984.

Brady Center to Prevent Gun Violence. "The Pathology of Gun Violence" Video PowerPoint. September 2, 2014. www.bradycampaign.org/about-brady

Burbick, Joan. *Gun Show Nation: Gun Culture and American Democracy*. New York: New Press, 2006.

Corasaniti, Nick, and Maggie Haberman. "Donald Trump Suggests 'Second Amendment People' Could Act Against Hillary Clinton." *New York Times*, August 2016. www.nytimes.com/2016/08/10/us/politics/donald-trump-hillary-clinton.html

Davis, Julie Hirschfeld. "Trump Suggests Teachers Get a 'Bit of a Bonus' to Carry Guns." *New York Times*. February 2018.

Dewey, John. *Human Nature and Conduct*. Vol. 14 of *John Dewey: The Middle Works: 1899–1924*, edited by Jo Ann Boydston. Carbondale: Southern Illinois University Press, 1988a.

———. *The Public and Its Problems*. Vol. 2 of *John Dewey: The Later Works, 1925–1953*, edited by Jo Ann Boydston. Carbondale: Southern Illinois University Press, 1988b.

Edmonds, Jeff. "Toward an Ethics of the Encounter: William James's Push Beyond Tolerance." *Journal of Speculative Philosophy* 25, no. 2 (2011): 133–47.

Everytown for Gun Safety Support Fund. "Gun Owners Poll." Conducted for Mayors against Illegal Guns by Luntz Global. July 24, 2012. everytownresearch.org/wp-content/uploads/2014/10/Luntz-poll-07-24-2012.pdf

———. "Gun Violence by the Numbers." everytownresearch.org/gun-violence-by-the-numbers

Frankel, Todd C. "Support for gun control isn't dead, new poll shows. It just matters how you frame the question." *Washington Post*, June 2015. www.washingtonpost.com/news/wonk/wp/2015/06/03/support-for-gun-control-isnt-dead-new-poll-shows-it-just-matters-how-you-frame-the-question

Henigan, Dennis. *"Guns Don't Kill People, People Kill People": And Other Myths About Guns and Gun Control.* Boston: Beacon Press, 2016.

Herszenhorn, David M., and Emmarie Huetteman. "Democrats End Sit-In after 25 Hours, Drawing Attention to Gun Control." *New York Times*, June 2016. www.nytimes.com/2016/06/24/us/politics/senate-gun-control.html

HillaryClinton.com. "Gun Violence Protection." 2016. www.hillaryclinton.com/issues/gun-violence-prevention

Horsley, Scott. "Guns in America, By the Numbers." National Public Radio, January 2016. www.npr.org/2016/01/05/462017461/guns-in-america-by-the-numbers

James, William. *Pragmatism.* Vol. 1 of *The Works of William James*, edited by Fredson Bowers and Ignas K. Skrupskelis. Cambridge, MA: Harvard University Press, [1907] 1975.

———. *The Will to Believe and Other Essays in Popular Philosophy.* Vol. 6 of *The Works of William James*, edited by Frederick H. Burkhardt, Fredson Bowers, and Ignas K. Skrupskelis. Cambridge, MA: Harvard University Press, [1897] 1979.

———. *Essays in Religion and Morality.* Vol. 11 of *The Works of William James*, edited by Frederick H. Burkhardt, Fredson Bowers, and Ignas K. Skrupskelis. Cambridge, MA: Harvard University Press, [1884–1910] 1982.

———. *Talks to Teachers on Psychology: And to Students on Some of Life's Ideals.* Vol. 12 of *The Works of William James*, edited by Frederick H. Burkhardt, Fredson Bowers, and Ignas K. Skrupskelis. Cambridge, MA: Harvard University Press, [1899] 1983.

King, Martin Luther, Jr. "Letter from Birmingham Jail." In *Why We Can't Wait*. Boston: Beacon, 2011.

Koopman, Colin. *Pragmatism as Transition: Historicity and Hope in James, Dewey, and Rorty.* New York: Columbia University Press, 2009.

Korte, Gregory. "14 mass shootings, 14 speeches: How Obama has responded." *USA Today*, June 2016. www.usatoday.com/story/news/politics/2016/06/12/14-mass-shootings-14-speeches-how-obama-has-responded/85798652

———. "Trump Signs Bill Reversing Obama Rule to Ban Gun Purchases by Mentally Ill." *USA Today*, February 2017. www.usatoday.com/story/news/politics/2017/02/28/trump-sign-bill-blocking-obama-gun-rule/98484106

Lakoff, George. *Don't Think of an Elephant: Know Your Values and Frame the Debate.* 2nd ed. New York: Chelsea Green, 2014.

Law Center to Prevent Gun Violence. "Browse Gun Laws by State." smartgunlaws.org/search-gun-law-by-state

Lichtblau, Eric, and Motoko Rich. "NRA Envisions 'a Good Guy With a Gun' in Every School." *New York Times*, December 2012. www.nytimes.com/2012/12/22/us/nra-calls-for-armed-guards-at-schools.html

Liu, Eric, *You're More Powerful Than You Think: A Citizen's Guide to Making Change Happen.* New York: Public Affairs, 2017.

Marchetti, Sarin. *Ethics and Philosophical Critique in William James*. New York: Palgrave Macmillan, 2015.
Mazzei, Patricia, and Jess Bidgwood. "Defying NRA, Florida Lawmakers Back Raising Age Limits on Assault Rifles." *New York Times*, February 2018.
National Rifle Association. "Ammunition." 2014a. www.nraila.org/issues/ammunition/
———. "Concealed Carry/Right to Carry." 2014b. www.nraila.org/issues/right-to-carry-and-concealed-carry
———. "'Gun Violence' Research." 2015. www.nraila.org/issues/gun-violence-research
———. "'Assault Weapons'/'Large' Magazines." 2016a www.nraila.org/issues/assault-weapons-large-magazines
———. "Background Checks/NICS." 2016b. www.nraila.org/issues/background-checks-nics
———. "Gun Registration and Gun Licensing. 2016c. www.nraila.org/issues/registration-licensing
———. "More Guns, Less Crime." 2016d. www.nraila.org/issues/crime-criminal-justice
New York Times Editorial Board. "Missouri: The Shoot-Me State." *New York Times*, September 2016. www.nytimes.com/2016/09/16/opinion/missouri-the-shoot-me-state.html
Obama, Barack. "Statement of the President on the School Shooting in Newtown, CT." The White House, Office of the Press Secretary, December 2012. www.whitehouse.gov/the-press-office/2012/12/14/statement-president-school-shooting-newtown-ct
———. "President Obama Speaks on Common-Sense Measures to Reduce Gun Violence." The White House, Office of the Press Secretary, April 2013. www.whitehouse.gov/photos-and-video/video/2013/04/17/president-obama-speaks-common-sense-measures-reduce-gun-violence#transcript
———. "Statement by the President on the Shootings at Umpqua Community College, Roseburg, Oregon." The White House, Office of the Press Secretary, October 2015. www.whitehouse.gov/the-press-office/2015/10/01/statement-president-shootings-umpqua-community-college-roseburg-oregon
Seigfried, Charlene Haddock. "James: Sympathetic Appreciation of the Point of View of the Other." In *Classical American Pragmatism: Its Contemporary Vitality*, edited by Sandra B. Rosenthal and Douglas R. Anderson. Urbana: University of Illinois Press, 1999.
Shear, Michael D. "Trump Moves to Regulate 'Bump Stock' Devices." *New York Times*, February 2018.
Smith, Andrew F. "William James and the Politics of Moral Conflict." *Transactions of the Charles S. Peirce Society* 40, no. 1 (2004): 135–51.
Steinhauer, Jennifer. "Senate Rejects 4 Measures to Control Gun Sales." *New York Times*, June 2016. www.nytimes.com/2016/06/21/us/politics/gun-vote-senate.html

Throntveit, Trygve. "William James's Ethical Republic." *Journal of the History of Ideas* 72, no. 2 (2011): 255–77.

Zucchino, David. "A Militia Gets Battle Ready for a 'Gun-Grabbing' Clinton Presidency." *New York Times*, November 2016. www.nytimes.com/2016/11/05/us/a-militia-gets-battle-ready-for-a-gun-grabbing-clinton-presidency.html

CHAPTER 2

REVISITING THE SOCIAL VALUE OF COLLEGE BREEDING

LOREN GOLDMAN

In our democracy, where everything else is so shifting, we alumni and alumnae of the colleges are the only permanent presence that corresponds to the aristocracy in older countries.

—William James, 1907 (1987, 110)

Aristocracy by its very nature degenerates into oligarchy . . .

—Polybius, 2nd century BCE (Polybius 1972, 275)

INTRODUCTION

The purpose of this essay is rather simple: to interrogate the social value of college breeding. This question is admittedly not my own, for it comes directly from William James, who provided his own answer to a slightly different query in a 1907 essay entitled "The Social Value of the College-Bred" (James 1987). James's response shall be discussed shortly, and I will argue that it is no longer plausible (if it ever was). While James approached his essay with characteristic geniality, I fear, furthermore, that any answer today must sound a more despairing tone. The reason is that the college breeding James idealized has been corrupted—and even in 1907 was on the verge of becoming corrupted—by what James memorably called "the bitch-goddess SUCCESS," both in the sense of a fixation on quantifiable yet ultimately meaningless measures of achievement and on what James called "the squalid cash interpretation put on the word success" that he claimed was "our national disease" (James 2003, 267). The ways in which higher education has transformed in the century since James wrote has allowed the "moral flabbiness" James abhorred in the American obsession with lucre to become all the more entrenched and difficult to exercise away (or exorcise). These reflections necessitate, further, a reconsideration of the underlying assumptions of James's own political thought. I suggest that despite James's best intentions, his reflections on higher education are limited by his blindness to what political theorist Jeffrey Green has called "the shadow of unfairness" in modern democracies, namely, that "even the most progressive, well-ordered liberal-democratic regime will not be able to satisfactorily realize a civic life that might be said to be truly free and equal in the fullest sense" (Green 2016, 2).

I begin by discussing James's original essay and several others he wrote concerning higher education. I then offer an overview of the transformations of higher education since James wrote, emphasizing the growth of what Clark Kerr, the influential chancellor of the University of California system, termed the "multiversity" (Kerr 1982), as well as the concomitant shift in expectations of faculty and students alike, not to mention the explosion of student debt, which James was neither historically nor socioeconomically positioned to fathom, and I argue that these transformations have erected significant barriers to James's ideal of higher education. Finally, I suggest that while James's ideals remain inspiring, they are only practicable with a significant transformation in the economic structure of modern education that would require the very sort of "bigness" James rejected (James 2000, 546). As with much else in James, then, the continuing relevance of his thought thus lies in his incisive and ebullient questioning rather than in any particular answer that he provides.

JAMES'S IDEAL OF HIGHER EDUCATION

James set out his conception of higher education's purpose in several essays. The best known of these is "The Social Value of the College-Bred," an address to the Association of Alumnae of Radcliffe College, then the all-female sister institution of the all-male Harvard College.[1] This essay, taken together with "The True Harvard," "Stanford's Ideal Destiny," and "The PhD Octopus" (James 1987), enables a synoptic view of James's thoughts on higher education. In "The Social Value," James gets right to the point, asking in his first sentence, "of what use is college training?" His pithy answer is that it "should *help you to know a good man when you see him*" (1987, 106; italics in original),² a character description James admitted to be "vague" and which must remain "diffuse and indefinite" (112), yet which covered a host of measures of relative human superiority, with particular emphasis on nobility of aim and integrity of action (cf. James 1988a, 420; 1988b, 113, 479). As crisp as his response may be, the six pages James dedicates to explaining himself introduce a broad range of considerations to his listeners. For present purposes, it will be most helpful to deal first with the upshot of James's essay before parsing its finer points about what exactly he means by *college* education.

While James is now widely embraced as a pluralist liberal whose work lends itself to a robust defense of democracy (see, e.g., Miller 1997; Koopman 2005; Connolly 2005; Flathman 2005; Ferguson 2007; Throntveit 2014; Livingston 2016), he was not an enthusiastic partisan of the common man. This is nowhere better reflected than in his "Social Value" essay, which is written with an eye to saving America from the democratic rabble, who lack the discernment gained by those with college training. James is indeed friendlier to the people than his hero John Stuart Mill, who suggested a scheme of differential representation in which the educated held more votes than other citizens (Mill 1977b, 474), but this alone hardly makes James a visionary democrat. The point of college education is to develop a "critical sense"—a phrase whose variations are almost certainly included in any contemporary professor's "Statement of Teaching Philosophy," an odious genre of writing that the growth of the PhD Octopus has unfortunately necessitated. Whatever meaning this boilerplate phrase holds for us, for James this "critical sense" is

> a general sense of what, under various disguises, *superiority* has always signified and may still signify. The feeling for a good human job anywhere, the admiration of what is really admirable, the disesteem of what is cheap and trashy and impermanent . . . the sense for ideal values. It is the better part of what men know as wisdom. (James 1987, 108)

Colleges, he continues, "ought to have lit up in us a lasting relish for the better kind of man, a loss of appetite for mediocrities and a disgust for cheapjacks" (ibid.).

One might wonder how this critical sense squares with the moral and value pluralism of James's other writings highlighted by some recent commentators: James's cheapjacks might very well be *my* heroes. When it comes to the argument between Jeremy Bentham and J. S. Mill and the alliterative debate over the relative merits of pushpin and poetry,[3] James endorses the latter. This is in line with his praise of Mill at the outset of *Pragmatism*, which James dedicated "To the Memory of John Stuart Mill[,] from whom I first learned the pragmatic openness of mind[,] and whom my fancy likes to picture as our leader were he alive to-day" (James 1975, 3). In *On Liberty*, Mill's elitism is evident in his emphasis on enabling what he termed "genius." As Mill explains, the biggest problem facing democracy is not the tyranny of a minority ensconced in power, a traditional concern of democratically minded thinkers. Rather, Mill suggests that the tyranny of a majority demanding social conformity is of greater concern, lest the abridgement of freedom impede the development of those extraordinary individuals who "are, *ex vi termini*, *more* individual than any other people," and who enable social progress (Mill 1977a, 267). Mill therefore recommends "experiments in living" (Mill 1977a, 260) with the hope that the disruptions nonconformists bring to social life will ultimately lead to the betterment of humanity.[4]

James concurs to an extent with those contemporary critics of democracy who worry that "its preferences are inveterately for the inferior" and that it represents "vulgarity enthroned and institutionalized" (James 1987, 109). Indeed, in line with Mill's notion that great men uplift humanity, James offers a philosophy of history that "mankind does nothing save through initiatives on the part of inventors, great or small, and imitation by the rest of us—these are the sole factors active in human progress. Individuals of genius show the way, and set the patterns, which common people then adopt and follow" (James 1987, 109; cf. James 1979). James, of course, does not (at least not expressly) espouse the well-nigh metaphysical narrative of progress that Mill did, and he avidly countered the imperialism Mill supported (see Baker 2013; Livingston 2016; Pitts 2005, ch. 5). Moreover, James commits himself undeniably to the *idea* of democracy, describing it as "a kind of religion, and we are bound not to admit its failure" (James 1987, 109). Presumably, James's ostensible commitment to democracy stems from his conviction that all human beings have at least the capacity for greatness within themselves, and therefore the regime that governs them should allow for at least the possibility of their self-development; as James writes in "The Will to Believe," "the capacity for the strenuous mood"—his ethical ideal that gives meaning to life, "probably lies slumbering in every man" (James 1979, 160). If we are bound to accept democracy and yet cannot trust it to be self-regulating *as such*, the question accordingly becomes what can be done to enable us to maintain our faith. *This* is the purpose of higher education, to allow those within democracy to discern "the kind of men from whom our majorities shall take their cue" (James 1987, 110). That James does not appear to place himself within those majorities, but rather above them, is significant, for college training not only enables the ability to discern the superior with the critical sense, but makes its beneficiaries themselves superior to the masses. As James puts it, "we alumni and alumnae of the colleges are the only permanent presence that corresponds to the aristocracy in older countries"[5]; in what should be read charitably not as mockery of the proletariat but as a moment of self-deprecating irony, James exhorts his college-bred audience that "we ought to have our own class-consciousness. 'Les intellectuels!'" (James 1987, 110). In sum, James concludes that "if democracy is to be saved it must catch the higher, healthier tone" (111). Saved from what, or rather, from whom? From those of an inferior critical sense all around us. That only a small group of citizens have the privilege of attending college, moreover, makes no difference, for James allows that certain widely circulated magazines "constitute together a real popular university along this very line" (112).[6] Elite education, it seems, eventually trickles down to the hoi polloi.

It is important to note that James might have been searching for a new language with which to describe something that had *not* been around for ages: the "aristocracy" of democracy is not meant to suggest a structural nobility or something that intentionally excluded others, full stop. Rather, James was undoubtedly thinking of the original meaning of that term as "rule of the best," from *aristos* (ἄριστος, "best, virtuous") and *kratos* (κράτος, "power"). This conception of an aristocracy in the modern world is presumably also meant to supplement the ambiguity of democracy also taken in its original sense, as *demos* (δῆμος) denotes "the people," "the common," and "the mass"; indeed, the historical opposition that political philosophers have held toward this social formation stems in part from the concern that democracy inevitably shades into ochlocracy, or rule of the mob, democracy's traditionally conceived "degenerate" form (see Polybius 1972, 275). "Meritocracy," now carrying positive connotations, was coined in 1958 by the sociologist Michael Young, who meant it satirically, to mock "what he saw as the cold scientization of ability and the bureaucratization of talent" in modern societies.[7] Given James's aversion to routinization and conformity, the modern notion of meritocracy is not his aim. Instead, James is likely following Charles W. Eliot, the visionary President of Harvard (1869–1909) whose tenure practically spanned the entirety of James's time at that institution as both a student and teacher.[8]

Eliot had brought major reforms, introducing an elective system that freed undergraduates from rigid adherence to a single educational path, and Harvard blossomed under his guidance: the undergraduate population grew six-fold during his Presidency, from 100 in the 1860s to over 600 in 1904 (Deresiewicz 2015, 29). In his Inaugural Address, Eliot explained that the "worthy fruit of academic culture" was "an open mind, trained to careful thinking, instructed in the methods of philosophic investigation, acquainted in a general way with the accumulated thought of past generations, and penetrated with humility" (Eliot 1926a, 8).[9] Like James, Eliot hoped that higher education could create an aristocracy of sorts, but Eliot was clearer about its class-spanning composition. He argued for the need of poor and rich alike at Harvard, as "the country suffers when the rich are ignorant and unrefined. Inherited wealth is an unmitigated curse when divorced from culture." Continuing in this vein, Eliot noted that,

> Harvard College is sometime reproached with being aristocratic. If by aristocracy be meant a stupid and pretentious case, founded on wealth, and birth, and an affectation of European manners, no charge could be more preposterous: the College is intensely American in affectation, and intensely democratic in temper. But there is an aristocracy to which the sons of Harvard have belonged, and, let us hope, will ever aspire to belong—the aristocracy which excels in manly sports, carries off the honors and prizes of the learned professions, and bears itself with distinction in all fields of intellectual labor and combat; the aristocracy which in peace stands firmest for the public honor and renown, and in war rides first into the murderous thickets. (Eliot 1926a, 21)

While the pacifist James would have balked at the equation of manliness with combat readiness, searching as he did for a "moral equivalent of war" in his celebrated essay of the same name (James 1982), he shared Eliot's belief that higher education could create an aristocracy of culture that would save democracy from its lower impulses. Eliot goes further in an essay on education in democratic societies, wherein he described its object to "lift the whole population to a higher plane of intelligence, conduct, and happiness" (Eliot 1926b, 98). This is accomplished by firmly implanting in youthful minds "certain great truths which lie at the foundation of the democratic social theory" (ibid., 109) chief among which was "the intimate dependence of each human individual on a multitude of other individuals, not in infancy alone, but at every moment of life—a dependence which increases with civilization and with the development of urban life." It should also "inculcate in every child the essential unity of a democratic community, in spite of the endless diversities of function, capacity, and achievement among the individuals who compose the community" (ibid., 111). Above all, children should learn "what the democratic nobility is": "fidelity to all forms of duty which demand courage, self-denial, and zeal, and loyal devotion to the democratic ideals of freedom, serviceableness, unity, toleration, public justice, and public joyfulness. The children should learn that the democratic nobility exists, and must exist if democracy is to produce the highest types of character" (ibid., 113).[10] The roots of James's reflections on education are to be found in Eliot's notion of democratic education, according to which the beneficiaries of liberal education will redeem democracy from its worst excesses (cf. Townsend 1996, 168).

So much for James's considerations of the *ends* of a college education. What, however, does James mean by *college* itself? In a passage cited above, James mentions a "popular university," yet this is a misnomer, for he clearly means something much narrower than is expressed by the contemporary use of that term. James's titular descriptor of the "College-Bred" is significant, for it implies a distinction between types of institution of higher learning, the tensions between which help explain the development of the institution of the modern university that employs most of this volume's contributors (including the present author). Indeed, given what James says, it is evident that he would *not* be interested in the "University-Bred."

In the second paragraph of his essay, James distinguishes between college education and "the education which business or technical or professional schools confer" (James 1987, 106). The latter give one "a relatively narrow practical skill" such that "you are made into an efficient instrument for doing a definite thing." By contrast, colleges might leave one less efficient for any particular task, but they "suffuse your whole mentality with something more important than skill. They redeem you, make you well-bred; they make 'good company' of you mentally" (ibid., 106–07). What distinguishes colleges is the curriculum revolving around the humanities. James's understanding of the humanities is not, however, limited to the traditional liberal arts. Instead, the humanities refer to "the study of masterpieces in almost any field of human endeavor" (ibid., 107). As such, "geology, economics, mechanics, are humanities when taught with reference to the successive achievements of the geniuses to which these sciences owe their being" (ibid.). A Millian emphasis on genius is underlined by James's suggestion that training in the humanities should be oriented toward biography, as colleges should teach "biographical history . . . of anything and everything so far as human efforts and conquests are factors that have played their part" (James 1987, 108).[11] We learn to discern great men and (presumably) great women in the present by studying great men and (presumably) great women of the past, who can be taken as exemplary models for the integrity of our own aspirations.

The breadth of this pedagogical program notwithstanding, James's distinction between practical and college education suggests the exclusion of many disciplines that currently entice undergraduate minds. In particular, James implies that business studies, presently the most popular major in American higher education,[12] does not pass muster. Success in business neither impressed nor interested James, who held a patrician disdain for money-making as a purely instrumental pursuit. His concern was instead the success of great men who contribute to the diversity of human endeavors rather than the growth of bank balances. As noted at the outset of this essay, James wrote to H. G. Wells in 1906 that he was disinclined toward the "bitch-goddess SUCCESS" as an end in itself, and held special disdain for "the squalid cash interpretation put on the word success" which he claimed was "our national disease" (James 2003, 267). In this regard, it is possible that James's 1907 talk to the Radcliffe Alumnae Association reflects an unspoken element of internal criticism of Harvard, whose renowned business school opened its doors one year later, in 1908.[13] As James said in a 1903 speech at the Harvard Commencement Dinner, "the only rational ground for the pre-eminent admiration of any single college would be its pre-eminent spiritual tone" (James 1987, 75), where "spiritual" appears to signify "moral" (see James 1987, 744n75.33). Much of what passed for success at Harvard left James cold, for "to be a college man, even a Harvard man, affords no sure guarantee for anything but a more educated cleverness in the service of popular idols and vulgar ends" (James 1987, 76). Mammon and privilege presumably did not count for noble ends, as he identified the "true Harvard" with the "inner spiritual Harvard," comprised of men who "seldom or never darken the doors of the Pudding or the Porcellian," two of its exclusive student social clubs. In a line that he repeats in the "Social Value" essay, James explains that "the true Church was always the invisible

Church. The True Harvard is the invisible Harvard in the souls of her more truth-seeking and independent and often very solitary sons" (James 1987, 77). His preference is for its free-thinking nonconformists rather than those chasing mundane success: "our undisciplinables are our proudest product. Let us agree together in hoping that the output of them will never cease" (James 1987, 77).

These reflections on college education that keep instrumentalism at arm's length are reinforced by James's comments about Stanford University, at which he spent part of 1906 as a visiting scholar (see Simon 1990/1991). Reflecting on the ultimate ends of this then-fifteen-year-old institution, James begins by claiming "there is something almost pathetic in the way in which our successful business men seem to idealize the higher learning and to believe in its efficacy for salvation" (James 1987, 102). This is a dig at the aspirituality of the modern university as envisioned by many of its benefactors, who hold its physical space or organizational structure to be the telltale marks of quality. No, says James; these are irrelevant considerations, as "it is the quality of its *men* that makes the quality of a university" (James 1987, 104). "Spend money till no one can approach you," James allows, "yet you will add nothing but one more trivial specimen to the common herd of American colleges, unless you send into all this organization some breath of life, by inoculating it with a few men at least who are real geniuses. . . . [T]he alpha and omega in a university is the *tone* of it, and this tone is set by human personalities exclusively" (James 1987, 104). Because one cannot measure genius in cash terms, cash should be left largely out of the equation. Stanford, James urges, should aim to become a place "for training scholars; devoted to truth; radiating influence; setting standards; shedding abroad the fruits of learning; mediating between America and Asia,[14] and helping the more intellectual men of both continents to understand each other better" (James 1987, 106).

HIGHER LEARNING IN AMERICA

James's description of college education as primarily one of humanistic training stands in contrast to a model of higher education oriented toward scientific research and practicality. A tension between these models has long existed in the United States, which has tried to combine them in single institutions, with varying degrees of success. This tension runs deep in the nation's history: Thomas Jefferson's 1818 plan for the University of Virginia encapsulates these different demands, including as it does the need to develop something like the critical sense James lauds, as well as the practical needs of enabling the flourishing of a new nation in its physical and material constitutions. Jefferson explains the objects of his university so: "To harmonize and promote the interests of agriculture, manufactures and commerce, and by well-informed views of political economy to give a free scope to the public industry. . . . And, generally, to form them to habits of reflection and correct action, rendering them examples of virtue to others, and of happiness within themselves" (Jefferson 1975, 334–35). Here we see a rather capacious notion of higher education: a college based on a humanistic conception of broad learning indebted to the English system, a research university stressing specialization and the advancement of science indebted to the German system, and a practical mindset aimed at meeting the growing needs of a burgeoning nation, uniquely typified by the so-called land-grant institutions. These models boast not only different core educational aims, but also different students, with colleges concentrating on undergraduates and universities including large graduate student populations. By and large, the college model dominated American life until the late nineteenth century, and it should be no surprise that many of the great American thinkers of that era pursued graduate study in Europe rather than in their home country, where comparable research institutions were in short supply.[15]

It should be noted, of course, that the success of institutions of higher education—however measured—relies on something often beyond the remit of the institutions themselves: the willingness of students and faculty to engage in the endeavor. Even Harvard, the "best" institution of higher education on earth according to most tables, is plagued by this thorny problem. James's 1903 speech at the Harvard Commencement Dinner is a testament to this reality, as the "invisible church" he described there as its "true" self was, by definition, impossible to see (James 1987, 77). A flavor of college life in the era when James was himself studying at that august university[16] can be gleaned from the recollections of Henry Adams, four years James's elder and a graduate of Harvard College, class of 1858. As Adams reports, "any other education would have required a serious effort, but no one took Harvard College seriously. All went there because their friends went there, and the College was their ideal of social self-respect" (Adams 2000, 54). Adams further complained that "it taught little, and that little ill, but it left the mind open, free from bias, ignorant of facts, but docile. The graduate had few strong prejudices. He knew little, but his mind remained supple, ready to receive knowledge" (Adams 2000, 55). In Adams's own case, after his four years at the decidedly visible Harvard—the Harvard of the Pudding and the Porcellian that James derides—"as yet he knew nothing. Education had not begun" (Adams 2000, 69).

In any event, James's recommended college education must be distinguished from a *university* education. The names themselves already reflect an important difference: "college," like "colleague" and "collegial," derives from the Latin *collegium*, signifying a body of equals, a community or a fraternity. "University," by contrast, derives from *universitas*, signifying a totality or the whole of creation, and hence all possible knowledge. To be sure, both connote a community of inquirers, but the practical differences are considerable, especially in the American context. In simplest terms, the difference is between an emphasis on teaching or on research. Colleges emphasize the former, and universities the latter, with a concomitant distinction in degrees conferred: most colleges solely award bachelors' degrees, in contrast to universities that offer a gamut of graduate and professional degrees, and have advanced graduate students as appendages. As such, there is also a distinction between faculty members; unlike (historical) colleges, university faculties were staffed with certified professionals (Delbanco 2012, 79). The college life James supports is thus clearly distinct from the universities that we take to be our default. James railed against what he considered the unnecessary profusion of research degrees amongst the faculties of colleges, famously complaining in 1903 about the growing tentacles of the "PhD Octopus" (James 1987). Although it is now hardly imaginable, in 1884, only nineteen members of the Harvard faculty had earned their doctorates (Townsend 1996, 163). This was hardly a concern for James himself, who adamantly opposed fetishizing this highest degree and worried about a world in which "the standard, and not the candidate, commands our fidelity" (James 1987, 72). Anyone who has served on an admissions or hiring committee may understandably believe this regrettable situation has come to pass.

The historical roots of the institutions are also different. The college is an English invention, rooted in the scholastic seminaries of the middle ages and revolving around the classic liberal arts curriculum of the verbal arts' trivium (grammar, logic, rhetoric) and the numerical arts' quadrivium (arithmetic, geometry, music, and astronomy), and for which Oxford and Cambridge (both founded in the twelfth century) once served as models. The university, by contrast, is a German invention, and came to prominence in the nineteenth-century as an institution of primarily scientific research, for which Alexander von Humboldt's University of Berlin (founded in 1810) served as a model. As philosopher Jürgen Habermas has written, Humboldt (and Friedrich Schleiermacher, another intellectual architect of the University) had two notions in mind connected with the idea of a university: the first concerned the institutionalization of modern science and scholarship while remaining autonomous from state control, and the second concerned how it was in the state's interest to guarantee this intellectual freedom for the purpose of progress (Habermas 1989, 108–09). John Henry Newman's *Idea for a University*, often taken as the archetypal description of the institution, appeared in 1852, just as universities were rising. With Newman's express orientation toward humanities and religion, little space for scientific faculties, and his steadfast refusal to be informed by practical ends, his work was arguably immediately obsolete, and should have instead borne the title *The Idea of a College* (see Newman 1996, 81–82). Contrast Newman's account of a detached sanctuary promoting the "pure and clear atmosphere of thought" (Newman 1996, 77) with a 1963 manifesto by another college administrator, Clark Kerr, Berkeley's first chancellor from 1952 to 1957 and the president of the UC system from 1958 to 1967. The shift in emphasis away from pure knowledge and toward instrumentality is clear in Kerr's title, *The Uses of the University*. Kerr describes Newman as having written for the "cloister university," whilst the "Berlin model" broken down into departments was "a veritable organism" (Kerr 1982, 3). Johns Hopkins, the first American university built on the German model, introduced the idea of high academic standards driven by a strong graduate school (Kerr 1982, 13–14). For Kerr, the modern American university represents a third mode of higher education insofar as it incorporates professional schools like law, medicine, and business in addition to the liberal arts of the undergraduate college and the scientific research of the university. In Kerr's estimation, this "multiversity" works best when it acts like Oxford for undergraduates, Berlin for graduates, and American schools for the vocations (Kerr 1982, 18).

The history of American higher education is one of universities supplanting colleges.[17] As the historian Richard Hofstadter explained in his classic account of this development, from the colonial era until the nineteenth century, one could speak of "The Age of the College" in the United States, when seminarians (or their intellectual descendants) studied classical curricula at small liberal arts colleges (Hofstadter 1952, 18).[18] Jefferson's University of Virginia was meant to go beyond the ostensible narrowness and impracticalness of colleges by adding practical training to the idea of developing humanistic knowledge. It was only after the Civil War, however, that the scientific and practical universities came into their own. The growth of industry was essential for this development, as was the need to create a strong industrial basis for a newly (re)unified country. Two moments stand out in this process. The first is the founding of land-grant institutions by the Morrill Acts (1862 and 1890), which set aside public land for "the endowment, support, and maintenance of at least one college where the leading object shall be, without excluding other scientific and classical studies, and including military tactics, to teach such branches of learning as are related to agriculture and the mechanic arts" (Morrill Act of 1862, sect. 4). The Morrill Acts, first passed during the U.S. Civil War and later amended, saw the explosion of state universities, whose founding dates reflect their provenance: The Ohio State University (1862), University of Kentucky (1865), University of Maryland (1865), and University of California, Berkeley (1868), to mention but a few, have their origins in the 1362 Law. These schools, all of which had major agricultural components,[19] were meant to aid the newly reunified nation in generating itself, in line with Jefferson's idea of the University of Virginia as a comprehensive institution for the furthering of national interest. If land-grant institutions were fulfilling Jefferson's dream of agricultural-cum-civic higher education, the same post–Civil War era saw the foundation in 1876 of the first American university based on the Berlin model of the research university, Johns Hopkins, which offered the first graduate degrees in philosophy, among many other fields. Josiah Royce received his PhD there in 1878, and John Dewey followed shortly afterward in 1884; James's friend and the "founder" of Pragmatism, Charles S. Peirce, served on the Hopkins faculty (1879–1884) in his only formal stint as a professor.

MAKING DOCILE WORKERS, MAKING PRODUCTIVE CITIZENS

Colleges and universities thus differ dramatically, although in their contemporary guise the latter are supposed to incorporate the former, usually as a "college" of arts and sciences, albeit often alongside more practical "colleges" of nursing, business, and engineering. Insofar as universities are geared toward higher research in science and ultimately practical aims, the funding models and the expectations of outcome associated with each institution also differ. The late twentieth and early twenty-first centuries have seen the reinforcement of a particularly profit-oriented mode of existence at the university, which has had considerable impact on the colleges as well, which compete with universities for students (now sometimes considered "customers" first[20]). The entire ecosystem of higher education—the psychology of students included—has shifted away from the humanistic model James idealizes, with indirect instrumental social benefits but mainly aimed at giving the tools to direct one's own life, and toward a purely instrumental approach in which it becomes an (expensive) step on the path toward a socially productive and economically remunerative life. The profit orientation and managerialism of modern higher education has in effect obviated the distinction between colleges and universities James highlights, and undermined his hope of it being able to elevate democracy by offering its citizens the capacity to recognize greatness in themselves and others.

In 1918, less than a decade after James's death, sociologist Max Weber described American universities as "state capitalist" enterprises (Weber 1958, 131). The same year, sociologist Thorstein Veblen noted that transformations in higher education mirror transformations in society at large (Veblen 1918, 34). Foreshadowing the later Marxist philosopher Louis Althusser, who counted educational institutions among the "Ideological State Apparatuses" (Althusser 1971), Veblen wrote that, "the habits of thought induced by workday life impose themselves as ruling principles that govern the quest of knowledge; it will therefore be the habits of thought enforced by the current technological scheme that will have most (or most immediately) to say in the current systematization of facts" (Veblen 1918, 6). The worry about the profusion of degrees that James voiced in "The PhD Octopus" can be extended beyond the nature of the PhD to a generally conformist fixation on credentials and a concomitant loss of quality and aims of education itself. These transformations were already visible in James's own lifetime, and by 1923 Upton Sinclair expressed the new tendencies he perceived in education in the stark title of his study of the subject, *The Goose-Step* (Sinclair 1970).

In the century since James wrote his essays, higher education has exploded both in terms of students and money in a manner that undercuts the autonomy, meaning, and nobility of spirit he hoped college breeding could enable. The uniquely American vision of the modern university as an institution that could increase the country's productive power accelerated after World War II, as the United States government funded both private and public institutions for scientific endeavors, particularly in physics as the Cold War and the space race heated up (Leslie 1993; Aronowitz 2000, ch. 3; Newfield 2003, pt. 1). (One can imagine James especially ruing this militaristic development.) In tandem with the growth of universities' importance as "knowledge factories," in Stanley Aronowitz's phrase, the managerial revolution found its way into higher education, as faculty and curricula came to be seen primarily as inputs, and research findings and students primarily as outputs, for a productive society (see Ginsberg 2011). This bureaucratization and meritocratization of university life came literally, moreover, at the expense of the greater society (Newfield 2003, 78ff.). In terms of the products of university research, this process arguably reached its apex with the Bayh-Dole Act of 1980, according to which universities could obtain exclusive patents to the fruits of the research conducted within their walls. In effect, this law allowed public monies to fund private patents, upsetting the very notion of collaborative science—federal funding for a chemist at Stanford, say, can now be used to enrich that private institution, which has no legal obligation to share the profits of its endeavors with the public that enabled it (Washburn 2005, 61ff.; Newfield 2003, 179ff.). At the same time, the costs of attending university have skyrocketed as government funding has fallen—between 1980 and 2005, for example, tuition and fees at *public* universities increased at three times the rate of inflation (Washburn 2005, xiii)—and students have been increasingly led to take on debt (Kamanetz 2006; Eliot and Lewis 2015, especially pt. 1). The total load of student debt at universities in the United States is now $1.31 *trillion* and growing (Federal Reserve Bank of New York 2017, 2); in constant dollars, the annual borrowing of student loans more than quadrupled from $24 billion in 1990–91 to $110 billion in 2012–13 (Fry 2014). These figures are all the more stunning when one considers that over this same period enrollment increased 62 percent while the debt load tripled (Fry 2014).[21] Such figures have driven a general mentality of quantitative excellence, measured by university administrators and students alike, reflected both in mandates from administrators to add quantifiable "learning objectives" to syllabi (an arguably nonsensical exercise in the humanities that James so loved) and in the no-nonsense practicality of many students seeking fungible degrees. For many, the pursuit of knowledge and of the creation of open-minded democratic citizens has taken a backseat to abstract measures of success, and institutions of higher learning compete to provide the most extracurricular perks like plush gyms and butteries at the same time that faculty hiring is frozen and teaching increasingly casualized.[22] It is no wonder that the most popular major in the United States is now business,[23] a field that may very well militate against democratic citizenship by normalizing the self-seeking behavior at odds with the sense of social obligation and interdependency Eliot remarked (Frank, Gilovich, and Regan 1993; 1996; but cf. Yezer, Goldfarb, and Poppen 1996). In like fashion, the sheer quantity of faculty's academic production, regardless of quality, has become a crucial measure of scholarly success—a bitch-goddess indeed. English professor Stefan Collini wryly reminds his readers, "not everything that counts can be counted" (Collini 1999a, 240).[24] This congeries of transformation has led commentator Bill Readings, another English professor, to call the university "a ruined institution" (Readings 1996, 129) bent more on profit and perpetuating industry instead of its original missions of contributing to the life of the mind and even creating a democratic aristocracy as James and Eliot envisioned. If anything, while college of course remains a central rite of passage for a great number of American students, the current state of higher education in the United States reproduces and reinforces the nation's inegalitarian class structure far more than it challenges it.[25]

What are the results of these transformations? The opposite of the strenuous striving for meaning that James valorized. Former English professor William Deresiewicz has argued that today's college students are, as the title of his book has it, "excellent sheep." For Deresiewicz, "the system manufactures students who are smart and talented and driven, yes, but also anxious, timid, and lost, with little intellectual curiosity and a stunted sense of purpose: trapped in a bubble of privilege, heading meekly in the same direction, great at what they're doing but with no idea why they're doing it" (Deresiewicz 2015, 3). Put simply, the system "forces you to choose between learning and success" (Deresiewicz 2015, 4). This is contrary to the original point of the college experience: as Deresiewicz writes, the strength of college is that it is *not* the real world. Rather, it "is an opportunity to stand outside the world for a few years, between the orthodoxy of your family and the exigencies of career, and contemplate things from a distance" (Deresiewicz 2015, 81). Anyone who has taught at large universities has undoubtedly encountered students who seem to have never considered James's idealistic conception of education as remotely feasible. In my own experience, at elite universities as well as large state ones (albeit never at liberal arts colleges), a dismaying number of students exhibit a mix of apathy and banal ambition. In light of James's exhortations to find life meaningful as a result of active seeking and active struggle ("Life is worth living, no matter what it bring, if only such combats may be carried to successful terminations and one's heel set on the tyrant's throat" [James 1979, 47]), today's students' obsession with safety is notable. Deresiewicz notes the irony that "elite students are told that they can be whatever they want, but most of them end up choosing to be one of a few very similar things" (Deresiewicz 2015, 20). Many desire to have their lives mapped out long in advance, and demand precise guidelines for what will ensure them an A grade, regardless of the content of the learning itself. Not only is such a life plan ultimately meaningless insofar as it evinces an impossible striving for sovereign mastery of events far beyond one's control (Larmore 1999), it is also petty-minded, as if the tyrant to be conquered of which James metaphorically speaks is the chair of Yale Law's admissions committee. Yet as higher education has become fixated on quantitative measures of success, learning has become thought to be algorithmically related to particular outcomes.[26]

Curiously enough, I have been most struck by the attitudinal similarities between many elite university students and the incarcerated students I taught in a prison education program, both of whom desired in advance precise quantitative guides for success. The latter group's need was borne of a number of things, the most significant of which is an understandable adaptation to a confined world in which regulation promised predictability and the outside possibility of serving one's time in peace and safety. Ironically, despite the vast opportunities at their fingertips, university students seem to have placed themselves in mental prisons, in which the point of education is an instrumental predictability that will (in their minds, at least) ensure material success. Perhaps because they had not been regimented in their earlier usually less-than-stellar academic careers, perhaps because of the diversity of their life experiences in comparison to the relatively secure and safe upbringing of today's university students,[27] the incarcerated students exhibited more enthusiasm for and creativity in their studies.

REALIZING JAMES'S IDEAL, MOVING BEYOND JAMES

All of the above criticisms notwithstanding, James presents a splendid ideal for higher education. There are intrinsic and instrumental reasons for humanistic learning, not least of which is the fruitfulness of that endeavor for every individual's own conception of their own lives. James's pluralism rests on overcoming that certain blindness in human beings that he described (James 1983)—and from which he himself suffered on occasion—and the experience of encountering diverse modes of life that a humanistic education can provide may genuinely aid in that important pursuit of self. Democracies, furthermore, function better when their citizens can distinguish frauds from genuine articles among those who aspire to lead them. I have suggested, however, that the social value of college breeding James idealizes rings hollow today, given the vast changes in higher education since his own time. The world of the liberal arts colleges James embraced has been largely supplanted by research universities whose size, ambition, and cost far exceed their collegial cores, and which accordingly provide a vastly different experience for their students, teachers, and administrators alike. These transformations were already discernable in James's lifetime, and he very well may have felt compelled to write on the topic of college breeding as an opening salvo against the creeping commodification and bureaucratization of education he sensed on the horizon.

In a sense, James remains the hero of this tale, but there is another sense in which he is, if not its villain, a tragic figure struggling against the limits of his own thinking. Long ago, in one of the most incisive critiques of James ever penned, the philosopher M. C. Otto identified a blindness in James concerning his inability to see structural inequality as an obstacle to human flourishing (Otto 1943). As Otto put it, James was "all but oblivious to the character-forming significance of the economic conditions under which [humans] live and work" (Otto 1943, 185).[28] Otto hazarded that James was inattentive to these conditions for three reasons: (1) he was "strongly antipathetic to regimentation and control," (2) his "battleground was the cosmos, not society," and (3) he lived before the widespread understanding of "the vital interdependence of the individual and the environmental objects and procedures by means of which he lives and achieves" (Otto 1943, 189–90). The world had to await more socially minded pragmatists like John Dewey for the last point to be appreciated, or so Otto has it. The first two of these reasons appear more plausible than the third, not least because before James wrote his essays on education, Charles W. Eliot had already noted—in a passage cited above—the interdependence of all classes in democracy.[29]

Be that as it may, my aim here is not to relitigate earlier critiques of James (cf. Goldman 2012). What I do want to insist on, however, is that the world of James's college breeding has disappeared, overwhelmed by the combined forces of capital, ostensible national interest, and instrumental reason. The sort of leisure that James allows college students to discover their critical sense remains possible for a privileged few. To make it available for the bulk of our democratic co-citizens will require a sea change in attitude and educational funding; even in James's individualist framework, the profusion of debt throws the liberal assumptions of self-ownership into question. Such changes will require, as Otto espied, a willingness to use "bigness" in a manner unpalatable to the anarchic James, who proclaimed himself against all big organizations as such, national ones first and foremost; against all big successes and big results; and in favor of the eternal forces of truth which always work in the individual and immediately unsuccessful way, under-dogs always, till history comes, after they are long dead, and puts them on top. (James 2000, 546)

This purity of heart is indeed admirable, but most have neither the courage nor the time to wait for the truth to arrive after they are long dead. James embraced big thoughts, but rarely big actions. And yet big actions may be the only hope for realizing the collegial and pluralistic world of James's imagination: bigness in the form of a massive restructuring of funding for higher education, bigness in the form of increased taxes on those privileged enough (like James) to have won in the financial lottery of life, bigness in the form of a movement to reclaim learning from the mentality of managerialism. Dewey (along with Vico, Hegel, Marx, and others) taught a lesson that James ignores, namely that humans *working together* have made their own history, big and small.

NOTES

1. Radcliffe was incorporated into Harvard when the latter went coed in 1977.

2. James, incidentally, does not see a gendered difference here, as he immediately writes that "this is as true of women's colleges as of men's colleges" (1987, 106). At the time of this essay's composition, far fewer institutions of higher education in America were coeducational than today. The characteristics of a "good man" for James are unclear.

3. On the imputed equation of push-pin (a version of bowling) and poetry in Bentham, see Mill (1969a, 113). For Bentham's original (and less pithy) statement, see Bentham (1825, 207). Mill missed his chance for his own alliterative contribution to the history of ethics by declaring in *Utilitarianism* that "it is better to be a human being dissatisfied than a pig satisfied; better to be Socrates dissatisfied than a fool satisfied" (Mill 1969b, 211). In a more literary moment, and without doing any violence to the spirit of his argument, Mill might have remarked that it is better to be poor Plato than a pleased pig.

4. "Ultimately" is the operative word here, for Mill holds that our present estimation of social acceptability is a poor guide for condemning certain modes of conduct not patently harmful to others. Future generations might (and almost certainly will) have different valuations.

5. Cf. Emerson 1994, 111. Kim Townsend (168) links James's ideas here to Emerson's "The American Scholar," in which the scholar is society's "delegated intellect. In the right state, he is, *Man Thinking*" (1996, 54).

6. James mentions *McClure's Magazine*, *The American*, *Collier's*, and *The World's Work*.

7. See Young 1958; the description is cited from Khan (8). For reflections on the reproduction of privilege within elite education as antithetical to democracy, see Khan (196–99).

8. James was at Harvard from his matriculation at the Lawrence Scientific School in 1861 until his death in 1910.

9. In this way, Eliot continues in his inaugural address as president of Harvard College, "the university in our day serves Christ and the church" (1926a, 8).

10. Townsend (90) notes that these were new ideas at the time.

11. These pedagogical suggestions were not apparently followed by James himself. Kim Townsend, in his study of the Harvard of James's day, writes that James's students reported he showed "that learning not only need not but must not be pretentious or evasive, that it had to be grounded in the complex realities of everyday life at the turn of the century," not merely historical biographies (162). For a sobering account that suggests the sort of humanistic learning James espouses can lead to *anti*-democratic tendencies (albeit at the level of elite high school, not college), see chapter 5 in Khan.

12. See the breakdown from the National Center for Education Statistics at nces.ed.gov/programs/digest/d16/tables/dt16_322.10.asp?current=yes_

13. It seems that James had no interaction with Edwin Francis Gay, then an assistant professor of economics at Harvard and the first Dean of its business school, as the latter's name never appears in anything James wrote or in any of his letters. I thank Ermine Algaier for ascertaining the lack of connection between James and Gay.

14. Because of Stanford's location in California, James thought it could "mediate" between the United States and Asia, just as Harvard and other East Coast universities could do the same between the United States and Europe.

15. Josiah Royce and W.E.B. Du Bois, for example, both spent considerable time studying philosophy in Germany.

16. Albeit at the Lawrence Scientific School and Harvard Medical School, for while James had studied at Harvard, he made clear he was not an alumnus of its undergraduate college (1987, 74).

17. Many books have been written on the history of higher education in the United States. I have benefited particularly from three now-classic treatments: Veblen, Hofstadter, and Veysey. For more critical takes, upon which I draw later, see Readings, Aronowitz, Newfield, Washburn, Giroux, Donoghue, Nussbaum, Hacker and Dreifus, Ginsberg, Collini (2012), Delbanco, Giroux (2012), and Deresiewicz.

18. As the Ohio charter of 1787 states, in a phrase prominently displayed at the entrance to the campus of the present author's former employer, Ohio University (founded 1803), "Religion, morality, and knowledge, being necessary to good

government and the happiness of mankind, school and the means of education shall forever be encouraged."

19. Washington State University, Cornell University, and the University of Minnesota, all land-grant universities, for example, still boast important apple-breeding programs (see Seabrook, "Crunch: Building a Better Apple").

20. In her novel *Moo*, Jane Smiley hilariously satirizes the economese used at modern universities. See also Collini, "Against Prodspeak."

21. This disproportionate increase, moreover, probably understates the problem, as the past several decades have seen the explosion of for-profit institutions that often amount to little more than degree mills established for the loan money available from the federal government rather than for the sake of education (see Looney and Yannelis; Mettler).

22. In a story that seems directly from the pages of Jane Smiley's satirical campus novel *Moo*, the (state) University of Louisiana-Monroe recently announced that it was closing its Museum of Natural History, including a collection of 6 million fish and half a million plant species, in order to make room for the expansion of a running track, a greater revenue generator for the university (see Kaplan).

23. Inversely related to the growth of business majors from 1970 to 2015 (115,000 to 363,799) is the decline of education majors over the same period (176,307 to 91,623). See note 12 above.

24. See also Collini, "Company Histories," which describes the transformation of Cambridge University from "a federation of seventeen small private corporations which provided agreeable hotels for the sons of the landed classes, whilst offering to those from less prosperous, but still largely genteel, backgrounds an appropriate preparation for a career in the Church" (270–71) in the nineteenth-century into the billion-dollar entity he ironically calls "CamU PLC."

25. Deresiewicz cites a litany of figures about the privilege of contemporary college students: "in 1985, 46 percent of students at the 250 most selective colleges came from the top quarter of the income distribution. By 2000, it was 55 percent. By 2006 . . . , it was 67 percent. Only 15 percent came from [the] bottom half that year; a slightly older study put the share of the bottom quarter at all of three percent" (205–06). Unsurprisingly, college admission is also deeply shaped by privilege (see Golden; Karabel).

26. The complaint that universities now obsess over an indefinite notion of "excellence" is a driving theme of Readings's *The University in Ruins*.

27. Deresiewicz notes that today, moreover, the system is populated by the children of people who came through the system itself, unlike the 1970s and 1980s, when far fewer graduates of elite universities had backgrounds in those same schools (35).

28. I have emended this line to correct a certain blindness in M. C. Otto.

29. Otto does not consider, incidentally, that James's privilege as the scion of one of America's richest families may have limited his own vision. On this point, see Green.

REFERENCES

Adams, Henry. *The Education of Henry Adams*. New York: Mariner, 2000.
Althusser, Louis. "Ideology and Ideological State Apparatuses." In *Lenin and Philosophy and Other Essays*, 127–86. New York: Monthly Review Press, 1971.
Aronowitz, Stanley. *The Knowledge Factory*. Boston: Beacon Press, 2000.
Baker, Bernadette. *William James, Sciences of Mind, and Anti-Imperialist Discourse*. Cambridge, UK: Cambridge University Press, 2013.
Bentham, Jeremy. *The Rationale of Reward*. London: John and H. L. Hunt, 1825.
Collini, Stefan. "Against Prodspeak." In *English Pasts*, 233–251. Oxford: Oxford University Press, 1999a.
———. "Company Histories: CamU PLC and SocAnth Ltd." In *English Pasts*, 269–288. Oxford: Oxford University Press, 1999b.
———. *What are Universities For?* London: Penguin, 2012.
Connolly, William. *Pluralism*. Raleigh, NC: Duke University Press, 2005.
Delbanco, Andrew. *College: What it Was, Is, and Should Be*. Princeton, NJ: Princeton University Press, 2012.
Deresiewicz, William. *Excellent Sheep*. New York: Free Press, 2015.
Donoghue, Frank. *The Last Professors*. New York: Fordham University Press, 2008.
Eliot, Charles W. "Inaugural Address as President of Harvard College." In *Charles W. Eliot: The Man And his Beliefs*, Vol. 1, edited by William A. Neilson. New York: Harper and Brothers, 1926a.
———. "The Function of Education in Democratic Society." In *Charles W. Eliot: The Man and His Beliefs*, Vol. 1, edited by William A. Neilson. New York: Harper and Brothers, 1926b.
Eliot, III, William, and Melinda K. Lewis. *The Real College Debt Crisis*. Santa Barbara, CA: Praeger, 2015.
Emerson, Ralph Waldo. "Aristocracy." In *English Traits*, Vol. 5 of *The Collected Works of Ralph Waldo Emerson*. Cambridge, MA: Harvard University Press, 1994.
———. "The American Scholar." In *Emerson: Essays and Poems*, 51–71. New York: Library of America, 1996.
Federal Reserve Bank of New York. "Quarterly Report on Household Debt and Credit." 2017. www.newyorkfed.org/medialibrary/interactives/householdcredit/data/ pdf/HHDC_2016Q4.pdf
Ferguson, Kennan. *William James: Politics in the Pluriverse*. Lanham, MD: Rowman and Littlefield, 2007.
Flathman, Richard. *Pluralism and Liberal Democracy*. Baltimore, MD: Johns Hopkins University Press, 2005.
Frank, Robert H., Thomas Gilovich, and Dennis T. Regan. "Does Studying Economics Inhibit Cooperation?" *Journal of Economic Perspectives* 7: 159–71, 1993.
———. "Do Economists Make Bad Citizens?" *Journal of Economic Perspectives* 10

(1996): 187–92.

Fry, Richard. "The Growth in Student Debt." *Pew Research Center Social and Demographic Trends*. 2014. www.pewsocialtrends.org/2014/10/07/ the-growth-in-student-debt

Ginsberg, Benjamin. *The Fall of the Faculty: The Rise of the All-Administrative University and* Why it Matters. Oxford: Oxford University Press, 2011.

Giroux, Henry. *The University in Chains*. New York: Routledge, 2007.

———. *Education and the Crisis of Public Values*. New York: Peter Lang, 2012.

Golden, Daniel. *The Price of Admission*. New York: Three Rivers Press, 2006.

Goldman, Loren. "Another Side of William James: Radical Interpretations of a 'Liberal' Philosopher," *William James Studies* 8 (2012): 34–64.

Green, Jeffrey Edward. *The Shadow of Unfairness*. Oxford: Oxford University Press, 2016.

Habermas, Jürgen. "The Idea of the University: Learning Processes." In *The New Conservatism*, 100–127. Cambridge, MA: MIT, 1989.

Hacker, Andrew, and Claudia Dreifus. *Higher Education?* New York: Times Books, 2010.

Hofstadter, Richard. *Development and Scope of Higher Education in the United States*. New York: Columbia University Press, 1952.

James, William. *Pragmatism*. Vol. 1 of *The Works of William James*, edited by Fredson Bowers, and Ignas K. Skrupskelis. Introduction by H. S. Thayer. Cambridge, MA: Harvard University Press, [1907] 1975.

———. *The Will to Believe and Other Essays in Popular Philosophy*. Vol. 6 of *The Works of William James*, edited by Frederick H. Burkhardt, Fredson Bowers, and Ignas K. Skrupskelis. Introduction by Edward H. Madden. Cambridge, MA: Harvard University Press, [1897] 1979.

———. *Essays in Religion and Morality*. Vol. 11 of *The Works of William James*, edited by Frederick H. Burkhardt, Fredson Bowers, and Ignas K. Skrupskelis. Introduction by John J. McDermott. Cambridge, MA: Harvard University Press, [1884–1910] 1982.

———. *Talks to Teachers on Psychology; and to Students on Some of Life's Ideals*. Vol. 12 of *The Works of William James*, edited by Frederick H. Burkhardt, Fredson Bowers, and Ignas K. Skrupskelis. Introduction by Gerald E. Myers. Cambridge, MA: Harvard University Press, [1899] 1983.

———. *Essays, Comments, and Reviews*. Vol. 17 of *The Works of William James*, edited by Frederick H. Burkhardt, Fredson Bowers, and Ignas K. Skrupskelis. Introduction by Ignas K. Skrupskelis. Cambridge, MA: Harvard University Press, [1865–1909] 1987.

———. *Manuscripts, Essays and Notes*. Vol. 18 of *The Works of William James*, edited by Frederick H. Burkhardt, Fredson Bowers, and Ignas K. Skrupskelis. Introduction by Ignas K. Skrupskelis. Cambridge, MA: Harvard University Press, [1884–1910] 1988a.

———. *Manuscript Lectures*. Vol. 19 of *The Works of William James*, edited by Frederick H. Burkhardt, Fredson Bowers, and Ignas K. Skrupskelis. Introduction by Ignas K. Skrupskelis. Cambridge, MA: Harvard University Press, [1872–1907] 1988b.

———. Letter to Sarah Wyman Whitman, June 7, 1899. In *The Correspondence of William James*, Vol. 8, 545–46. Charlottesville: University Press of Virginia, 2000.

———. Letter to H. G. Wells, September 11, 1906. In *The Correspondence of William James*, Vol. 11, 267–68. Charlottesville: University Press of Virginia, 2003.

Jefferson, Thomas. "Report of the Commissioners for the University of Virginia, 1818." In *The Portable Thomas Jefferson*, edited by Merrill D. Peterson. New York: Viking, 1975.

Kamanetz, Anya. *Generation Debt*. New York: Riverhead Books, 2006.

Kaplan, Sarah. "A University Is Eliminating Its Science Collection—to Expand a Running Track." *The Washington Post*, March 29, 2017.

Karabel, Jerome. *The Chosen: The Hidden History of Admission and Exclusion at Harvard, Yale, and Princeton*. New York: Mariner Books, 2006.

Kerr, Clark. *The Uses of the University*. Cambridge, MA: Harvard University Press, 1982.

Khan, Shamus Rahman. *Privilege*. Princeton, NJ: Princeton University Press, 2011.

Koopman, Colin. "William James's Politics of Personal Freedom." *Journal of Speculative Philosophy* 19 (2005): 175–86.

Larmore, Charles. "The Idea of a Life Plan," *Social Philosophy and Policy* 16 (1999): 96–112.

Leslie, Stuart W. *The Cold War and American Science: The Military-Industrial-Academic Complex at MIT and Stanford*. New York: Columbia University Press, 1993.

Livingston, Alexander. *Damn Great Empires! William James and the Politics of Pragmatism*. Oxford: Oxford University Press, 2016.

Looney, Adam, and Constantine Yannelis. "A Crisis in Student Loans? How Changes in Characteristics of Borrowers and in the Institutions They Attended Contributed to Rising Student Loan Defaults." *Brookings Papers on Economic Activity*. 2015. www.brookings.edu/wp-content/uploads/2016/07/ConferenceDraft_LooneyYannelis_StudentLoanDefaults.pdf

Mettler, Suzanne. *Degrees of Inequality*. New York: Basic Books, 2014.

Mill, John Stuart. *On Liberty*. In *Essays on Politics and Society Part 1*. Vol. 18 of *Collected Works of John Stuart Mill*, edited by J. M. Robson. Toronto: University of Toronto Press, 1977a.

———. "Considerations on Representative Government." In *Essays on Politics and Society, Part 2*. Vol. 19 of *Collected Works of John Stuart Mill*, edited by J. M. Robson. Toronto: University of Toronto Press, 1977b.

———. "Bentham." In *Essays on Ethics, Religion, and Society*. Vol. 10 of *Collected Works of John Stuart Mill*, edited by J. M. Robson. Toronto: University of Toronto Press, 1969a.

———. "Utilitarianism." In *Essays on Ethics, Religion, and Society*. Vol. 10 of *Collected Works of John Stuart Mill*, edited by J. M. Robson. Toronto: University of Toronto Press, 1969b.

Miller, Joshua I. *Democratic Temperament: The Legacy of William James*. Lawrence: University of Kansas Press, 1997.

Morrill Act. "An Act Donating Public Lands to the Several States and Territories which may provide Colleges for the Benefit of Agriculture and the Mechanic Arts." Public Law 37–108, *U.S. Statutes at Large Enrolled Acts and Resolutions of Congress*, 1789–1996; Record Group 11; General Records of the United States Government: National Archives, 1862.

Newfield, Christopher. *Ivy and Industry*. Durham, NC: Duke University Press 2003.

Newman, John Henry. *The Idea of a University*. New Haven, CT: Yale University Press, 1996.

Nussbaum, Martha. *Not for Profit: Why Democracy Needs the Humanities*. Princeton, NJ: Princeton University Press, 2010.

Otto, M. C. "On a Certain Blindness in William James." *Ethics* 53 (1943): 184–91.

Pitts, Jennifer. *A Turn to Empire*. Princeton, NJ: Princeton University Press, 2005.

Polybius. *The Histories*. Cambridge, MA: Harvard University Press, 1972.

Readings, Bill. *The University in Ruins*. Cambridge, MA: Harvard University Press, 1996.

Seabrook, John. "Crunch: Building a Better Apple." *The New Yorker*, November 21, 2011.

Simon, Linda. "William James at Stanford." *California History* 69 (1990/1991): 332–41.

Sinclair, Upton. *The Goose-Step: A Study of American Education*. New York: AMS Press, 1970.

Smiley, Jane. *Moo: A Novel*. New York: Anchor, 1995.

Throntveit, Trygve. *William James and the Quest for an Ethical Republic*. London: Palgrave Macmillan, 2014.

Townsend, Kim. *Manhood at Harvard*. New York: Norton, 1996.

Veblen, Thorstein. *The Higher Learning in America: A Memorandum on the Conduct of Universities by Business Men*. New York: B. W. Huebsch, 1918.

Veysey, Laurence. *The Emergence of the American University*. Chicago: University of Chicago Press, 1965.

Washburn, Jennifer. *University, Inc.* New York: Basic Books, 2005.

Weber, Max. "Science as a Vocation." In *From Max Weber: Essays in Sociology*, edited by Hans Gerth and C. Wright Mills. Oxford: Oxford University Press, 1958.

Yezer, Anthony M., Robert S. Goldfarb, and Paul J. Poppen. "Does Studying Economics Discourage Cooperation? Watch What We Do, Not What We Say or How We Play." *Journal of Economic Perspectives* 10 (1996): 177–86.

Young, Michael. *The Rise of the Meritocracy*. London: Pelican, 1958.

CHAPTER 3

WHAT MAKES THE LIVES OF LIVESTOCK SIGNIFICANT?

ERIN MCKENNA

All humans are involved in a number of complex relationships with other animal beings, whether they are aware of those relationships or not. While many humans live with pets, and many others care about the well-being of wild animals (either to preserve these species or to hunt them), all of us are intricately intertwined with the lives of livestock. Humans are shaped by their relationships with horses who changed the possibilities of human transportation, war, and food. Chickens and turkeys have long eaten insects in gardens and provided eggs and meat for humans and other animals (dogs, cats, pigs) to consume. Pigs, often left to forage on their own and eat human waste, were a cheap and easy source of protein. Sheep and goats changed people's diets as cheese became a way to store milk prior to refrigeration. The hides and wool from these animals also provided clothing, storage vessels, and housing materials. Along with cattle, these animals also provided fertilizer so settled groups of humans could continue farming the same land. Cattle (along with horses) also helped plow those same fields and became a form of currency in many societies. Today, cows are used to make many common products: detergents, fabric softeners, toothpaste, mouthwash, lipstick, soap, shampoo, candles, marshmallows, chewing gum, jelly beans, gummy bears, mayonnaise, Jell-O, crayons, paint, wallpaper floor wax, cough syrup, lozenges, vaccines, and numerous medications (Hayes 2015, 26–28). The list goes on. Even vegans, especially if they eat organic produce, are eating food that has benefitted from the contributions of animals. There is no way for a human to remain separate from the lives and deaths of other animal beings—especially livestock.

Given human dependence on those animals commonly seen as livestock, one might expect humans to take good care of these animals and respect them. That has been the case from time to time. Cows and bulls have been (and are) worshipped in some societies, pigs have been noted for their intelligence, and horses are seen as majestic and spiritual. However, on balance, humans have more commonly seen livestock as just that—live stock. They are stock in at least two senses: (1) stored food and (2) stored assets. They are cared for with the purpose of using them as food or a unit of exchange. Prior to modern antibiotics, wormers, and vaccines, such care was often consistent with lives that fulfilled many of the natural needs and desires of these animals. Young animals needed to be left with their mothers until they were naturally weaned to build antibodies, learn where and what to eat, and establish their place in the social order of the herd or flock. The animals were fed foods consistent with their natural diets or left to graze and forage much as their wild cousins. Confinement was usually temporary—limited to the times of milking, shearing, or slaughtering.

For those animals used as transportation, however, more confinement and human intervention was necessary. Given the need for food and care, these animals were few in number and considered quite valuable. As people gained experience in keeping animals in confinement, their number grew. As developments in farming made hay and surplus grain available for feeding livestock, these numbers increased, but there was still a natural limit on how many could be kept due to the availability of food and the risks of disease. Modern agriculture changed all that with the reliance on chemical fertilizers to produce large amounts of surplus corn and soy, hormones to make the animals get to slaughter weight faster, and the use of antibiotics to keep the animals alive long enough to slaughter. These developments made it possible to confine large numbers of animals, grow them fast, kill them in large numbers, process them quickly, and distribute the meat and other products around the world. Today,

> the big-five global food species are cattle, sheep, pigs, goats, and chickens, and it is estimated that "the world has over 1.3 billion cattle—about one for every five people on the planet. The world's sheep population is just over one billion—one for roughly every six people. There are about a billion pigs, one for

every seven people, and 800 million goats, one for every eight people. And chickens outnumber humans by 3.5 to 1 worldwide; there are nearly 17 billion of them. (Wilkie 2010, 19)

These changes came at the expense of the well-being of the land, the human consumers, and the livestock animals themselves. Focused on the monocrops of soy and corn, U.S. farmland is increasingly depleted of topsoil and aquifers are drained. Humans who can afford to eat more meat than in the past (and more than any other primate) increasingly suffer from cardiovascular disease, cancer, and obesity. The livestock animals live lives of cramped confinement and have few, if any, opportunities for their natural social and physical behaviors. They suffer physically and psychologically. Their death entails further stress as they are transported long distances, crowded in holding pens, prodded, beaten, stunned (sometimes improperly), and killed. While a tiny fraction of the livestock animals in the United States get to live more natural lives in pasture-based production, this general description applies to the vast majority of the animals providing meat, dairy, and eggs today.

This short sketch does not do justice to the topic, but provides some context for considering what the work of William James might have to say about the pressing ethical issues of contemporary industrial farming of livestock animals. While most philosophers who write on issues of animal ethics and animal welfare fall into either utilitarian or deontological approaches, William James is neither of these. There are ecofeminists and ethics of care theorists who also write on these issues. William James is neither of these either. He can be seen as working out of the tradition of American pragmatism and so focused on amelioration. For most working in the pragmatist tradition, life, and so truth and ethics, are never fixed. Given that, moral theories that try to abstract one element of moral concern and apply it across different and changing circumstances miss important considerations. Thinking about possible ways to live out our social and ethical relationships (with other human or other animal beings) is important for James, but the most we can hope for is to make particular relationships better in particular ways at particular times. The lives of animals were never a strong focus in his own writings, but he does have some things to say about their nature and their lives. His philosophical views and commitments also suggest some possible positions that his work might be used to support. That is what will be explored here.

JAMES'S CONFLICTED VIEWS

William James often writes that humans need to be aware of their inability to understand the world as it is lived by others. He encourages humans to be tolerant of, and sympathize with, people positioned different from themselves. At times, he includes other animal beings in this call and asks humans to be aware that while other animal beings experience the world in different ways than human beings do, this does not make their lives meaningless or insignificant. At other times, however, James seems to suggest that animal lives have significance only in terms of the human use of those animals. These conflicting positions are important to explore and place in the context of the time when James was writing. I believe the positions that other animal beings have lives that are meaningful and significant is the position most consistent with his philosophy as a whole. Further, James's focus on meliorism is an important resource for those interested in calls for animal rights and animal welfare. Here I will explore how James's work can be used to provide a complex understanding of those animal beings commonly used as food (livestock) and ways to make their (and our) lives better.

To begin, it is important to know that James's work can be placed in the tradition of other American pragmatists who came to prominence in the late 1800s and early 1900s. This is important because these philosophers were writing after the publication of Darwin's *On the Origin of Species* in 1859 and took seriously the various theories of evolution that were in the air. For example, in his 1910 "The Influence of Darwinism on Philosophy," John Dewey noted:

> The conceptions that had reigned in the philosophy of nature and knowledge for two thousand years, the conceptions that had become the familiar furniture of the mind, rested on the assumption of the superiority of the fixed and final; they rested upon treating change and origin as signs of defect and unreality. In laying hands upon the sacred ark of absolute permanency, in treating the forms that had been regarded as types of fixity and perfection as originating and passing away, the "Origin of Species" introduced a mode of thinking that in the end was bound to transform the logic of knowledge, and hence the treatment of morals, politics, and religion. (Dewey 1998, 1)

Here Dewey is emphasizing a new way of seeing the world that is rooted in change. This new way of looking is a shift in metaphysics and epistemology that impacts morals—including the ethics of human relationships with other animal beings, as humans are more connected with all the other animals on Darwin's view of evolution. For Darwin, humans shared not just a physical evolutionary history, but one that includes emotion and intelligence as well.

Charlotte Perkins Gilman, more influenced by Lamarck than Darwin, focused on the ways that women's inequality had stunted the possibilities of human evolution. Writing in 1898, she said that male selection of mates, rather than female selection, had resulted in a focus on human competition over social cooperation and the diminished physical and mental capabilities of women (Gilman 1966). Women's economic dependence made her ability to attract a mate the only way to survive and so she became dependent on male taste for excessive sex characteristics such as small size and lack of physical vigor. This impacted human women, just as it had affected livestock animals such as the milk cow:

> To make clear by an instance the difference between normal and abnormal sex-distinction, look at the relative condition of a wild cow and a "milch cow," such as we have made. The wild cow is a female. She has healthy calves, and milk enough for them; and that is all the femininity she needs. Otherwise than that she is bovine rather than feminine. She is a light, strong, swift, sinewy creature, able to run, jump, and fight, if necessary. We, for economic uses, have artificially developed the cow's capacity for procuring milk. She has become a walking milk-machine, bred and tended to that express end, her value measured in quarts. The cow is over-sexed. (Gilman 1966, 43–44)

In addition to connecting the plight of domesticate animals and the plight of women, Gilman also noted the problematic impacts related to livestock. City streets were polluted by the manure from cart horses and meat animals being driven to the stockyards and slaughterhouses. There was also pollution caused by the stockyards and slaughterhouses themselves, as well as the spread of disease. There were also problems such as tainted meat and milk, food stored and shipped so long that it lost its nutritional value, and the general rise in cruelty (to humans and nonhumans) that resulted from using animals for meat, milk, and hides. These were pressing issues during James's lifetime as the railroads allowed for the increased confinement of livestock animals in feed operations before shipping them to centralized slaughter facilities.

In addition to Dewey and Gilman directly taking up Darwin and issues of evolution, Charles S. Peirce complicated the idea of evolution by finding problems with Darwin's view, which he said relied too much on chance, and with Spencer's view, which he said relied too much on mechanical necessity. Instead he too preferred Lamarck, who he thought bridged the other two approaches by making room for the passing on of acquired characteristics or habits. He argued that between the views of chance and necessity was the view that there was a continuity of minds in the universe (including the universe itself) that were not just passive objects of evolution but agents participating in evolution. Ideas become a kind of habit of the universe that impact the relationships and possibilities within the universe. Importantly, his view led him to take human continuity with the rest of life very seriously, as all beings were kinds of minds or personalities, and sympathy is what should guide our relationships. He argued that communication and personality were characteristic of all life, not just human life.

James was influenced by Peirce. Along with the idea of continuity, though, James also focused on difference. Continuity does not mean sameness, and it is important to take account of difference and make room for different points of view and different ways of experiencing the world. James himself often failed to remain positively open to the differences of others (women, the Irish, dogs, and other animals). But his theory focuses on embracing pluralism and working to understand multiple points of view. In his 1900 "On a Certain Blindness in Human Beings," James famously argues that humans need to remain open to the experiences of other human and animal beings (James 1983b). While his main point is about how humans need to be careful about judging the value of the lives and experiences of other humans, he also argues that this applies to human judgments about the lives of other animals. He notes that humans are often blind to the smells that capture the attention of dogs and that dogs enjoy bones more than books. He thinks humans should try to remain open to appreciating what makes life significant for dogs:

> Take our dogs and ourselves, connected as we are by a tie more intimate than most ties in this world; and yet, outside of that tie of friendly fondness, how insensible, each of us, to all that makes life significant for the other!—we to the rapture of bones under hedges, or smells of trees and lamp-posts, they to the delights of literature and art. As you sit reading the most moving romance you ever fell upon, what sort of a judge is your fox-terrier of your behavior? With all his good will toward you, the nature of your conduct is absolutely excluded from his comprehension.

To sit there like a senseless statue when you might be taking him to walk and throwing sticks for him to catch! What queer disease is this that comes over you every day, of holding things and staring at them like that for hours together, paralyzed of motion and vacant of all conscious life? (James 1983b, 132–33)

Here James recognizes that human and other animal beings often have different interests, feelings, and behaviors. While this can result in miscommunication, it does not mean mutual understanding is not possible. For such understanding to be possible, though, humans must remain open to the differences and not limit our perspective by assuming difference in another is always some kind of lack. James believes that once we are aware of our tendency to fail to fully see the lives of others, this "absolutely forbids us to be forward in pronouncing on the meaninglessness of forms of existence other than our own; and it commands us to tolerate, respect, and indulge those whom we see harmlessly interested and happy in their own ways, however unintelligible these may be to us" (James 1983b, 149).

Similarly, in 1895, in "Is Life Worth Living?" he pointed to the failure of humans to consider the experience of cattle (James 1979). People dining on beef rarely think about the experiences of the cattle who have ended up on their plate. At the time he was writing, it would have been common for those cattle to have spent some time on the range, but most of their time confined. First, they would have been confined to fatten on corn, then confined as they shipped by railroad to the slaughterhouse, and then confined in the pens at the slaughterhouse. They would then have been killed and slaughtered in ways that did little to alleviate pain and suffering. He wrote: "When you and I, for instance, realize how many innocent beasts have had to suffer in cattle-cars and slaughter-pens and lay down their lives that we might grow up, all fattened and clad, to sit together here in comfort and carry on this discourse, it does, indeed, put our relation to the universe in a more solemn light" (ibid., 47).

From James, we ultimately learn that since we are continuous with the rest of nature and nature is changing, continuous, uncertain, and developmental, we need to stay open to many possibilities—including the perspectives of other animal beings. But this view of animals took some time to develop. In 1878, he published "Brute and Human Intellect," in which he denies the capacity for abstract and reasoned thought to all but human beings (James 1983a, 1–37). For James, other animal beings are limited by having only immediate experience and interests. He contradicts

Darwin's attribution of intelligent reasoning to arctic dogs who scatter when they hear the sound of cracking ice. Instead, James says, for the dogs, it's just a matter of associating the sound of cracking ice with getting wet and associating the sound stopping with their scattering. On the other hand, he asserts that humans from the tropics, with no experience of ice, would immediately recognize the sound as indicating breaking ice and so scatter to relieve pressure on the ice. James offers no support for his assertion of this difference between the dogs and the humans from the tropics other than his assumed perspective of the limited ability of nonhumans. He goes on to dismiss other accounts of animal intelligence as mere association of contiguous things, though they *might* entail some recognition of a property or characteristic. He also denies animals the capacity for humor and laughter, for language, and for self-consciousness.

In his 1890 *The Principles of Psychology* James repeated many of the ideas in this earlier article. For instance, he reiterated that animals

> are enslaved to routine, to cut-and-dried thinking; and if the most prosaic of human beings could be transported into his dog's mind, he would be appalled at the utter absence of fancy which reigns there. . . . To wonder why the universe should be as it is presupposes the notion of its being different, and a brute, which never reduces the actual to fluidity by breaking up its literal sequences in his imagination, can never form such a notion. He takes the world simply for granted, and never wonders at it at all. (James 1981, 977)

Here James himself seems unable to see or appreciate the ways that another animal might experience the world. Further, he then uses this to argue that they lack imagination and insight, thereby pointing toward common justifications for the human use of such animals in experiments and as food.

But there is no basis for him to assume the absence of fancy rather than a different focus of fancy. There is no evidence that these "brutes" are "enslaved to routine." James further denigrates the reasoning abilities of other animal beings when he says, "The results of reasoning may be hit upon by accident. . . . Cats have been known to open doors by pulling latches, etc. But no cat, if the latch got out of order, could open the door again, unless some new accident of random fumbling taught her to associate some new total movement with the total phenomenon of the closed door. A reasoning man, however, would open the door by first analyzing the hindrance" (1981, 965). But there are numerous examples of inventive play, insight, communication, learning, and problem solving by a variety of species. We tend to think animals who play and solve problems are "smart." Mammals and birds are among such animals. Birds tease dogs, solve food puzzles, remember where they store food, and use tools to obtain food. Cats and dogs play with each other and engage in play behavior with the human beings in their lives. Who can share a home with other animal beings and not have many examples of play and pretending? Most farmers who know their livestock animals individually tell similar stories. Pigs are good cause-and-effect thinkers who solve complex problems and are used as retrievers, truffle hunters, and service animals. Sheep have preferences for the company they keep and learn to outwit herding dogs (and humans). Cattle and horses form deep relationships and losing a friend can affect their moods and performance. Chickens and goats often befriend horses and humans. Usually maligned as "birdbrains," even chickens show remarkable abilities, as they can add, subtract, "understand geometry, recognize faces, retain memories, and make logical deductions. . . . Some of these cognitive abilities equal or surpass those of assorted primates, and it is possible that the chicken possesses a primitive self-consciousness." They have good memories and numerous calls that correlate with specific behaviors (Lawler 2014, 240–42). None of this is considered in the living conditions of most industrially farmed birds and mammals. Livestock animals are interactive and empathetic social creatures who find value in things that help with cooperation, cohesion, and harmony. While they may or may not wonder at the nature of the universe, these are not beings without fancy and imagination.

In yet another shortsighted moment, James argued that humans are much more complex and varied than other animal beings. While "the dog singles out of any situation its smells, and the horse its sounds, because they may reveal facts of practical moment, and are instinctively exciting to these several creatures," "man" has more varied instincts, wants, and feelings and so is "sure to dissociate vastly more characters than any other animal; and accordingly we find that the lowest savages reason incomparably better than the highest brutes" (James 1981, 970). And yet, this same logic is used to argue for the superiority of European men over "savages" and women. "Since nature never makes a jump, it is evident that we should find the lowest men occupying in this respect an intermediate position between the brutes and the highest men, and so we do" (James 1983a, 29). He goes on to write that "savages" and primitive humans reason by analogy and are unable to move to reason by abstraction. "The primeval man will say not 'the bread is hard,' but 'the bread is stone'" (33). This carries over to ethical matters as well, and without abstract analysis humans cannot justify their positions. "Ask the first Irish girl why she likes this country better or worse than her home, and see how much she can tell you" (34).

James concludes that nonhuman animals, and some humans, are governed by fixed habits while true humans are "the *educable* animal." He says that instinctual humans, such as Italians, have an immediate sense of the world that the "untutored German" lacks. While the German must be taught what the Italian finds innate, the German's ability to learn sets him on the path of reasoned thinking that James believes the Italian cannot achieve. Similarly, women's character is ahead of men's around the age of twenty because she is finished developing. Men of this age seem to be undeveloped but "this absence of prompt tendency in his brain to set into particular modes is the very condition which insures that it shall ultimately become so much more efficient than the woman's" (James 1983a, 37).

The inherent racism, sexism, and speciesism present in these works by James contradicts the openness and tolerance James calls for in his 1896 essay "On a Certain Blindness in Human Beings." In that essay, discussed above, James acknowledges the intimacy between humans and dogs and shows deep understanding and sympathy for them. He does not assume that dogs have no interests, plans, or purposes, but just that dogs' interests, plans, and purposes often differ from those of humans. James argues that this difference does not make the dog's existence meaningless, and that humans should respect the meaning of dogs' existence on their own terms. Many writing on animal cognition today make the same basic claim that humans need to stop trying to measure and understand other animals only in terms of human intelligence, sensation, and emotions. Each species has its own kind of experience of the world that results in its own kind of intelligence and meaning. As Stephen Budiansky says, "modern cognitive science and evolutionary ecology are beginning to show that thinking in animals can be complex and wonderful in its variety, even as it differs profoundly from that of man" (1999, xxvii).

THE POSSIBILITIES OF JAMES'S VIEW

James's denigration of the abilities of other animal beings is not beyond question given the observational and experimental evidence available to us today, nor is it consistent with his call for tolerance and respect. It also fails to pay attention to his own call for understanding and respecting pluralism. A consistent Jamesian perspective suggests, instead, that human beings should seek to understand the motivations and actions of other animal beings. There is no reason to try to reduce their being to the simplest explanation, or to measure their intelligence only by a human standard. Such reductionist approaches may, in fact, get in the way of productive understanding and successful relationships. Successful and respectful relationships require that we are open to a plurality of ways of being and experiencing the world.

Just as James's view of animal worth evolved over time, so have the views of many others. Today there are approximately 7.3 million vegetarians and 1 million vegans in the United States. Worldwide there are an estimated 375 million vegetarian/vegans. Many more who do not remove animals from their diets still object to using them for fur and less than vital experimentation. Many who eat them object to the conditions in which they live and die in industrial farms and slaughterhouses. I think there is need for more thinking about these issues, and James's philosophy can play a role.

First it is important to consider the evolving view of animal consciousness, intelligence, emotion, and their expression of pain and pleasure (physical and psychological). The Cambridge Declaration on Consciousness, issued in 2012 by a group of prominent scientists, states: "Convergent evidence indicates that non-human animals have the neuroanatomical, neurochemical, and neurophysiological substrates of conscious states along with the capacity to exhibit intentional behaviors. Consequently, the weight of evidence indicates that humans are not unique in possessing the neurological substrates that generate consciousness. Non-human animals, including all mammals and birds, and many other creatures . . . possess these neurological substrates" (2). There is research documenting empathetic responses in chickens, pleasure when learning a task in cows, anticipation of pain and stress in pigs, joy and depression in fish. All these animals have signals and forms of communication that allow them to navigate their social settings.

This leaves just philosophy as the discipline holding out with more or less official separation of human beings from other animal beings. As Matthew Calarco says, "while philosophy's historical reputation for being a leading voice of critical thought is often wholly deserved, on the issue of the distinction between humans and animals and the ethical worth of animals, it has unfortunately and frequently failed to live up to its more admirable ideals. In fact, in many ways, philosophy in the Western tradition has been one of the chief architects in constructing the traditional philosophical and ethical dogmas we have inherited concerning animals" (2015, 7). As a discipline, philosophy has long distinguished itself as focusing on what was supposed to be the uniquely human ability to reason and use language. While James, too, denied them language, he did admit that they used signs and that some of their use of signs could be complex. Given his willingness to go that far over a hundred years ago, I suspect that he would be impressed with more recent language studies with other animal beings. Some of these focus on teaching other animals some form of human language (spoken, sign, lexigrams), but many others focus on human beings learning how the other animals communicate (body, vocal, and chemical). This is exactly the kind of study that would have interested James. He would also be interested in the experiments that try to determine which parts of the brain are involved in language and problem solving. Unfortunately, some of these experiments involve invasive surgery to implant equipment in the animals' brains, restraint and deprivation to take readings, and often the death of the animals in order to examine the brain itself. I think James would have supported such experimentation, as he saw vivisection as a "painful duty" (James 1987, 11). While he wanted ethical consideration and regulation of animal experiments, his desire to understand the brain would outweigh any concern for the animals involved.

That said, however, the results of such experiments (and others) have over time established the complex nature of other animals' brains, and their "training" has shown that they have great capacity for language and problem solving. Ironically, their use in such experiments provides the grounds for many to question the ethics of using them in such experimentation. I think James would have struggled with this irony as the evidence for animals' complexity and intelligence mounted. Again, though, I think he'd support limited use of animal experimentation for medical and psychological research. For good research, though, one needs to make sure the animals are well cared for. This goes beyond clean living conditions and a healthy diet. It includes attention to noise levels, light, and odors. It also includes good social relationships and enriching environments that help prevent boredom, loneliness, and stress. This would be both an animal welfare concern and a matter of getting good research results. This requires understanding the world from the other animals' point of view, as James tried to do with his dog in "On a Certain Blindness in Human Beings."

As more researchers come to take the point of view of the Other, more ethical questions arise. As handling and socialization of the research animals become part of good research, so does the researcher's attachment to the animals. In good research settings, these animals are not seen or treated as objects, but this makes harming them and/or killing them much harder. Some labs have bereavement counselors available in the lab—especially those working with dogs or cats, since researchers may live with dogs and cats in their homes. Some of the research is done to benefit dogs and cats themselves, but this doesn't make killing them any easier. Given this, I think James would be concerned, and support the use of live animal research only in very limited cases.

Using animals for cosmetic testing, and repeated product testing, would be harder for him to justify as the pain and suffering, plus the waste of intelligent life, is for no vital purpose. Of course, people argue about what is vital or necessary for human life. Is eating meat necessary for humans? James expressed concern for the suffering of the cattle on the train only in order to further fatten humans. If he was able to see the current obesity crises and the health conditions related to high meat diets, I think he would further question the necessity for meat—or at least the amount of meat many in the United States eat. While he did express concern for the animals themselves, he would also be concerned about the health of human consumers. Current industrial farming practices can spread diseased and tainted meat, eggs, and dairy products across the nation (or the world) in short order. Mad cow, e.Coli 0157H7, salmonella, listeria, and campylobacter bacteria are just the most publicized examples of such concerns. Most of these can be traced back to the conditions in which the livestock animals live and die.

While James says he wants a world with real risk, his focus is on risks individuals can face and potentially overcome. Tainted meat, milk, and eggs are not such risks. They don't make life more meaningful for humans or the livestock animals themselves. Given the advances in what we know about the intelligence and suffering of animals, I do think James would move beyond the human health concerns to focus on the livestock animals themselves. I think he'd find the moral questions related to raising, killing, and eating animals interesting and complex. At a minimum, it seems he does not condone animals suffering for the sake of human food (especially luxury food). This sounds like a standard utilitarian concern. But utilitarians are clear that prevention of pain is the main focus. That may now include emotional and psychological pain, as well as physical, but it remains committed to pain and suffering as things to be avoided. James, however, thinks a life without some pain and suffering is a life not worth living. Given his own life experiences, he took an approach that found physical and psychological pain and suffering as opportunities for personal growth and change. James found his time at the Chataqua boring and numbing. He wrote that "sweat and effort, human nature strained to its uttermost and on the rack, yet getting through alive, and then turning its back on its success to pursue another more rare and arduous still—this is the sort of thing the presence of which inspires us" (1983b, 153). While his privileged position might have made him more than a little romantic regarding real suffering, there is some evidence in animal studies to back up his view.

Life without any fear or stress can compromise and weaken an animal's immune system and overall health. Some zoos try to respect the prey and predator nature of animals by housing them in ways that prey experience some amount of threat and predation, and predators have a chance to express stalking and hunting behavior. It is now seen as part of animal enrichment to have animals work for food, compete with each other, and solve problems. Given what we now know, keeping livestock animals can be done in ways that respect their needs and natures. For example, weaning is a stressful but natural event, and so weaning young animals, which is part of most livestock farming, is not inherently bad. But weaning offspring too young (as is commonly done in dairy operations) is morally problematic and can cause health problems. Similarly, death is part of life, but being hauled hundreds of miles in crowded containers (with no attention to social bonds) in hot and cold weather is not. Living in one's feces is not natural or healthful for livestock animals and fails to respect what makes life acceptable, much less meaningful, for them. James saw and lamented such suffering during his lifetime.

To live meaningful lives would not only include the need to respect the physical needs and preferences of the various livestock beings—temperature, air quality, noise level, bedding, food (content and delivery), water, ability to move, and more. It would also require people to respect the animals' social and psychological needs. Relationships are important to all the animals commonly seen as livestock—sheep, goats, cows, pigs, chickens, and turkeys. Flock and herd size would need to be of a size that allowed varied relationships but did not exceed their ability to get to know each other. Once friendships are formed they should be respected when handling and housing the animals—don't force together animals who don't like each other and don't unnecessarily separate friends.

Those working with livestock must know and understand the animals with whom they work so they can respect what makes life significant for them. Like James's understanding of his dog's interest in hedges and bones, livestock handlers should know what interests the animals, what scares them, what challenges them (mentally and physically), and what generally enriches their lives. This is very much in line with what Temple Grandin calls for in her work on handling livestock and designing slaughterhouses with the perspective of the animal in mind (e.g., Grandin 2008). With such knowledge, the handlers themselves should come to respect the animals with whom they work. As with lab animals, this can have the consequence of making it harder to kill and eat them. In fact, many ranchers who raise livestock in a manner that allows them to know the animals individually do not eat as much meat, milk, and eggs as the typical U.S. citizen.

This is like James's idea, discussed in *Pragmatism*, of knowledge or "truth" growing like a grease spot (1975, 83). Thinking doesn't change wholesale, but grows out of old ideas and experiences. It changes slowly and gradually by building on previous "truths." This nicely describes the general societal view of human relationships with other animal beings—livestock, in particular. It is possible to see such gradual change in James's own thinking about animals, and it is possible to use his ideas to promote such growth and change in human thinking about, and treatment of, other animal beings today. This is what can make meaningful amelioration possible.

REFERENCES

Budiansky, Stephen. *Covenant of the Wild: Why Animal Chose Domestication*. New Haven, CT: Yale University Press, 1999.

Calarco, Matthew, "On the Separation of Human and Animal," *Stanford University Press* (blog), 2015. stanfordpress.typepad.com/blog/2015/09/on-the-separation-of-human-and-animal.html.

Dewey, John. "The Influence of Darwinism on Philosophy." [1910] 1998. www.iupui.edu/~arisbe/menu/library/aboutcsp/dewey/Darwin.htm

Dewsbury, Donald A. "Early Interactions Between Animal Psychologists and Animal Activists and the Founding of the APA Committee on Precautions in Animal Experimentation." *American Psychologist* 45 (1990): 315–27.

Gilman, Charlotte Perkins. *Women and Economics: A Study of the Economic Relation Between Men and Women*. New York: Harper Torchbooks, 1966.

Grandin, Temple, and Mark Deesing. *Humane Livestock Handling*. North Adams, MA: Storey Publishing, 2008.

Hayes, Denis, and Gail Boyer Hayes. *Cowed: The Hidden Impact of 93 Million Cows on America's Health, Economy, Politics, Culture, and Environment*. New York: W.W. Norton, 2015.

James, William. *Pragmatism*. Vol. 1 of *The Works of William James*, edited by Fredson Bowers, and Ignas K. Skrupskelis. Introduction by H. S. Thayer. Cambridge, MA: Harvard University Press, [1907] 1975.

———. *The Will to Believe and Other Essays in Popular Philosophy*. Vol. 6 of *The Works of William James*, edited by Frederick H. Burkhardt, Fredson Bowers, and Ignas K. Skrupskelis. Introduction by Edward H. Madden. Cambridge, MA: Harvard University Press, [1897] 1979.

———. *The Principles of Psychology*. Vols. 8–10 of *The Works of William James*, edited by Frederick H. Burkhardt, Fredson Bowers, and Ignas K. Skrupskelis. Introductions by Rand B. Evans and Gerald E. Myers. Cambridge, MA: Harvard University Press, [1890] 1981.

———. *Essays in Psychology*. Vol. 13 of *The Works of William James*, edited by Frederick H. Burkhardt, Fredson Bowers, and Ignas K. Skrupskelis. Introduction by William R. Woodward. Cambridge, MA: Harvard University Press, [1878–1906] 1983a.

———. *Talks to Teachers on Psychology; and to Students on Some of Life's Ideals*. Vol. 12 of *The Works of William James*, edited by Frederick H. Burkhardt, Fredson Bowers, and Ignas K. Skrupskelis. Introduction by Gerald E. Myers. Cambridge, MA: Harvard University Press, [1899] 1983b.

———. *Essays, Comments, and Reviews*. Vol. 17 of *The Works of William James*, edited by Frederick H. Burkhardt, Fredson Bowers, and Ignas K. Skrupskelis. Introduction by Ignas K. Skrupskelis. Cambridge, MA: Harvard University Press, [1865–1909] 1987.

Lawler, Andrew. *Why Did the Chicken Cross the World? The Epic Saga of the Bird that Powers Civilization*. New York: Atria, 2014.

Wilkie, Rhoda M. *Livestock/Deadstock: Working with Farm Animals from Birth to Slaughter*. Philadelphia: Temple University Press, 2010.

CHAPTER 4

SIGNIFICANT LIVES AND CERTAIN BLINDNESS
William James and the Disability Paradox

NATE JACKSON

Disability is pervasive. We are, if fortunate, only temporarily "able," as life's precariousness makes us susceptible to some form of disability. Most of us, as we age, experience greater degrees of impairment. This fact should spawn reflection on what it means to live well as a disabled person, to imagine a flourishing human life as a disabled individual.[1] Our conceptions of disability often do not square with our ideas about a good human life, as evidenced by the phenomenon of "disability anxiety," broadly, anxiety at the prospect of becoming disabled.[2] As disabled, I am puzzled, trying to articulate a conception of flourishing compatible with my experiences and apparent limitations. I find a sympathetic resource in William James. James wrestles with the experience of impairment—his own and his sister, Alice's—while also striving to specify what makes life worth living. Beyond the biographical and historical reasons to include James as a resource for disability scholarship, however, are philosophical ones. He embraces pluralism, which, regarding value judgments, allows a range of moral ideals and conceptions of a good life.[3] This pluralism motivates a melioristic attitude: embracing the promise that, through our efforts, we can alleviate suffering in a variety of forms and realize more inclusive conceptions of these ideals.

Given James's biography and his commitments to pluralism and meliorism, we should not be surprised to find him offering epistemological and ethical perspectives friendly to contemporary projects in disability scholarship. However, James's work has not yet been brought to bear overtly on issues surrounding disability. In part, I would hazard, this quietude stems from the fact that James did not offer a theory of disability, although he makes use of the testimony of disabled individuals in his works. Nonetheless, his work and experiences suggest that he was at least aware of some of the realities of living with impairment. Reading James's corpus, one finds a persistent struggle to appreciate individuals' testimony and to give voice to an account of life's significance over and against the ideal of a life free from strain.

In particular, James's work can help to confront the so-called "disability paradox." Disabled persons experiencing a wide range of forms of disablement report surprisingly high levels of life-satisfaction, but nondisabled individuals often think of disability as necessarily contrary to well-being (Albrecht and Devlieger 1999). For instance, if you asked expecting parents whether they would rather their child be born nondisabled or disabled, you would likely find overwhelming agreement in their preferences. People tend to dismiss disabled persons' testimony regarding positive life-satisfaction, re-interpreting it as evidence of their resilience or a lack of knowledge of nondisabled life. These kinds of treatments of the paradox pose an epistemological problem: disabled persons' testimony about their own circumstances is considered to lack justificatory force. Responding to this problematic tendency requires a more fundamental thesis: disability need not be contrary to flourishing. As such, treatment of the problem of testimony intertwines with substantive questions about the nature of well-being and its possible compatibility with disability.

James provides elements of a response to these related challenges to disability-positive testimony. His critique of "medical materialism" can be applied to the tendency to disregard disabled persons' self-reported levels of life-satisfaction. And in his popular lectures, wherein he confronts questions of what makes life significant and our (in)ability to readily appreciate those judgments from alternative perspectives, James provides resources for defending disabled persons' testimony as a source of justification. While we ought to acknowledge that disabled persons do not make *uniformly* positive assessments regarding life-satisfaction, Jamesian theory affords a rejoinder to the tendency to dismiss the authority of disabled persons who do offer such evaluations. If we take seriously the idea that to acknowledge prospects for flourishing in the lives of disabled persons can help to mitigate their marginalization, then we will be glad to find an ally in James.

DISABILITY AND WELL-BEING

Recently, disability scholars have turned to questions concerning the relationship between disability and well-being. Disability is a broad category, including a variety of persistent limiting conditions—mental, physical, and psychological. The lack of ability, opportunity, or diminished capacity characteristic of a disability is often understood as causally related to a physical or mental *impairment*—"a pathological condition of an organism that has a certain chronicity" (Schramme 2014, 73–74). Different models of disability place lesser or greater emphasis on the causal role individual impairments play in those restrictions. "Medical" or "individual" models of disability locate the cause of these restrictions in medical impairments experienced by individuals, while "social models" delineate limitations in terms of restrictions imposed by the interplay between characteristics of individuals and features of their social environments.[4]

Mike Oliver writes that "models are ways of translating ideas into practice and the idea underpinning the individual model was personal tragedy, while the idea underpinning the social model was that of externally imposed restriction" (2004, 19). Appreciation for the strengths of social models of disability has implications for conceptions of the relationship between disability and well-being. Specifically, the social account challenges the evaluative implications of the individual model, what Guy Kahane and Julian Savulescu call the "everyday concept" of disability:

> [In addition to a descriptive dimension,] the everyday use of disability also has an evaluative dimension. People are often described as suffering from a disability. Disability is taken to be a misfortune, something that makes life worse, and thus something that gives us reasons to try to avoid or correct it. In other words, the concept of disability is a thick evaluative concept. (2009, 17)

Broadly, the social model construes restrictions imposed by disabilities as products of social organization and opportunity, redirecting our gaze toward sites of socially imposed limitations.

The revitalized concern for accounts of flourishing compatible with disability stems from recognizing that underlying our designed structures and institutions is a conception of the individual navigating them, and that our conception of this person is often one of "normal" ability. The disparity between this "idealized" individual and the realities of disability can further entrench disabled persons' social isolation. For instance, we might imagine a building inaccessible to someone using a wheelchair as indicating that intended users of the building lack mobility impairment. Or, as educators, we might be familiar with students with learning disabilities for whom accommodations and resources are available, although accessing those resources demands their navigating a bureaucracy inimical to how they process information. Even a hopeful narrative study of the experiences of university students with learning disabilities revealed a pattern in which students had to be "caught" and guided through the process of applying for institutional support (Fullerton and Duquette 2016). The disability advocacy movement suspects that such examples are pervasive.

Analyses of well-being that are compatible with forms of disablement promise to help mitigate marginalization. Carol Breckenridge and Candace Vogler contend that "concepts of citizenship, the economy, and the body are embedded in understandings of what constitutes well-being, understandings that generally exclude or marginalize the forms or realities of disability" (2001, 351). Insofar as operative conceptions of a flourishing individual are incompatible with disability and yet manifest in our designs, this can create deleterious effects such as isolation or even discrimination. Breckenridge and Vogler argue that we impute unity to a concept through the function it serves. In the case of disability, we tend to consign the concept to a limiting role; it clarifies the nature of flourishing by illustrating its limiting case. Limiting cases delineate the meaning of a concept by defining its boundaries. To illustrate, and moving beyond examples from architecture and the structure of bureaucracies, we can point to barriers facing disabled people in democratic deliberation. In this instance, cognitive disabilities seem incompatible with the demands of rationality and independence underlying democratic citizenship, forming what Stacy Clifford Simplician characterizes as a challenge to a "capacity contract" that underlies democracy. Such a contract "bases political membership on a threshold level of capacity and excludes anyone who falls below" (2015, 27). That is, disability supposedly defines capacities needed for democratic participation by illustrating the point at which one's abilities are insufficient to participate. Conceived this way, disability appears to be necessarily inimical to well-being.

While the social model promises to explain barriers to flourishing in terms of malleable social forces, the intuition persists that disability generally makes one's life "go worse." However, disabled persons' rates of reporting a high level of life-satisfaction are generally and perhaps surprisingly high. This tension drives the so-called "disability paradox." On one hand, the pull of disability's conceptual role as a limit case motivates construing it as necessarily contrary to well-being. On the other, it is easy to find disabled persons who attest that they take pride in their identity as disabled, and that being disabled enables valuable expressions of their identity and opportunities for meaningful relationships.[5] Gary Albrecht and Patrick Devlieger found that 54.3% of respondents to their survey who identified as having a serious disability reported having an excellent or good quality of life (1999, 981). The survey respondents included 153 people with a variety of impairments, including but not limited to mobility impairment, paralysis, perceptual impairments, mental illness, HIV/AIDS, and substance addiction (ibid.). Reviewing their findings, Albrecht and Devlieger phrase the paradox in the form of a question: "Why do so many people with serious and persistent disabilities report that they experience a good or excellent quality of life when to most external observers these people seem to live an undesirable daily existence?" (1999, 977). Thus articulated, the paradox invites consideration of the nature of well-being and its compatibility with conditions of disability. These self-assessments, at face value, should motivate reconsideration of the relationship between disability and human flourishing.

That said, it is important to acknowledge the variety of responses amongst disabled people to their disability status. For example, a more fine-grained analysis of self-reported levels of life-satisfaction reveals disparities between disabled persons with different kinds of impairments. Tom Shakespeare highlights such differences, showing that people who become disabled in adulthood typically, though not uniformly, have a more negative view of disability than those who are born disabled (2014, 140–42). There is also variation among persons with different kinds of impairment. A 2004 survey suggests that few people with bipolar disorder, for example, have a positive assessment of life-satisfaction (Morselli, Elgie, and Cesana 2004). Such research resonates with the idea that disability can negatively impact one's life, especially once overlaid with a variety of social factors that intensify isolation (ibid.).

While recognizing such variety in the testimony that disabled people offer regarding their well-being, interpreting and responding to the tendency to dismiss disability-positive testimony presents a challenge. Importantly, a defense of the justificatory merit of disability-positive (or even disability-neutral) testimony need not imply that disability-negative testimony lacks force. We should at least be sensitive to the possibility that people with a variety of impairments can offer insightful, though not infallible, testimony regarding their own levels of well-being. Taking these narratives as evidence of the possibility that well-being is compatible with forms of disablement promises to bolster the larger project of disclosing how various conceptions of flourishing can negatively impact disabled persons.

A tendency to construe disability as a tragedy contrary to a good human life, and to focus on individual impediments, creates problems when we turn to understanding why disabled persons might offer disability-positive or disability-neutral testimony. Prompted by the disability paradox, an all-too-common response is to dismiss the testimony of disabled persons. Even Albrecht and Devlieger hypothesize that the reported levels of life-satisfaction might reflect a " 'secondary gain' that occurs when individuals with impairments adapt to their new conditions and make sense of them" (1999, 987). As a "secondary gain," a sense of well-being is a product of coming to appreciate the new social position and its possibilities that one has in virtue of impairment. Put another way, disabled persons' self-reports might not actually conflict with the idea that disability is contrary to well-being, since one's life would have been better off had one not been in a position to realize these secondary gains.

For example, disabled persons sometimes report that their disability facilitates development of a sense of identity or membership of a unique culture. However forceful these claims might be—and they can be very forceful: "If I were given the choice of a new life without a disability I would not take it. My disabling condition is one of the many characteristics which has contributed to the person I have become" (quoted in Brown 2002)—the suspicion is that the life-satisfaction experienced is a response to a situation that "counts against" well-being. We should not give much weight to these self-reported levels of satisfaction, so the thinking goes, because these preferences are coping mechanisms formed in response to nonideal circumstances.

In response to the surprising degree to which disabled persons report a high degree of well-being or life-satisfaction, then, the paradox might be resolved by dismissing or reinterpreting the meaning of their testimony. Instead of regarding it as evidence that disabled lives can indeed be flourishing, or for the contingency of disability's impact on life-satisfaction, nondisabled individuals preserve the intuition that well-being and disability are at odds. Here, I argue, James provides avenues of response, enabling a defense of the prima facie justificatory force of first-person testimony that disability can be compatible with well-being.[6] He endorses an ethic of tolerance and a perspectivalist epistemology that demand sympathetic attentiveness to others' positions. Further, James's biography reveals that he was sensitive to (if sometimes inarticulate regarding) experiences of disability and the testimony to which they give rise.

DISABILITY IN JAMES'S EXPERIENCE

Personally and professionally, James was familiar with physical and psychological disability. Various references to impairment appear in his work, including his deferring to the experiences of a visually impaired individual to bolster key points in his *Principles of Psychology* (1981, 256). Additionally, James's life was affected by the experience of impairment in various ways. Not only did precarious health interrupt his own life, but his family members too bore marks of disability. His father, Henry, was an amputee, his leg having been badly burned in a childhood accident. His sister, Alice, an intellectual powerhouse in her own right, was diagnosed with "neurasthenia," and experienced multiple breakdowns. Her diaries reveal something of her experience of disability and its impact on her relationship with the rest of the family through years of deteriorating health until her death from cancer in 1892. Although James's reactions to his sister's condition were not uniformly supportive or sensitive, the familiarity and apparent sympathy with which James treats disability nonetheless should motivate further inspection of his corpus as a potential resource for disability scholarship.

James's work in psychology reveals both a knowledge of disability and an implicit acknowledgment that accounts of human nature must square with the realities posed by impairment.[7] James frequently uses the language of deafness and blindness (and occasionally "idiocy" and "madness") in *The Principles of Psychology*.[8] More than quiet nods to disability, disabled figures serve a crucial role in his arguments. In his discussion of the "Stream of Consciousness," for instance, James argues that

> a deaf and dumb man can weave his tactile and visual images into a system of thought quite as effective and rational as that of a word-user. The question whether thought is possible without language has been a favorite topic of discussion among philosophers. Some interesting reminiscences of his childhood by Mr. Ballard, a deaf-mute instructor in the National College at Washington, show it to be perfectly possible. (1981, 256)

By relying on Mr. Ballard's testimony to establish that thought is possible without language, James accords the report of a disabled person prima facie authority, and encourages deference to that perspective.[9] Moreover, James anticipates a central call of the project of contemporary disability studies by treating Mr. Ballard's testimony as something an adequate psychology must countenance.

James was personally familiar with the realities of impairment and their demands on his time and energy. His biographers have highlighted his history of disruptive physical and psychological impairments. Robert Richardson draws attention to these moments in relation to their effects on James's work. For example, James's medical studies left him in such a state of overexertion that in 1866 back spasms nearly incapacitated him, leading to a prolonged period of depression. Later in his career, he was forced to postpone his Gifford Lectures because of a heart ailment, leading him to write to Harvard administrators, "I regret to inform you that since last June I have been affected with a serious infirmity of the heart which has so increased as to unfit me for any work at present" (Richardson 2006, 399).

In terms of his own psychological states, James reports bouts of depression and melancholy, even describing his own experiences of a "sick soul" in *Varieties of Religious Experience,* and vaguely attributing them to a French correspondent (1985, 133–36). Ralph Barton Perry argues that these depressive episodes led James to see philosophy as a kind of analgesic: "James required a philosophy to save him" (1976, 122). Perry links James's 1870 depression with a therapeutic vision of his work, observing that, "he *was* a strong man, overtaken by weakness—a man of action cut off from action by bodily incapacity" (ibid.), and asking "what is the strong man's medicine, diluted to suit his disabled condition? *The gospel of belief.* For belief is action, and yet a sort that may be demanded even of a sick man; and belief may have action as its object" (ibid.). Though he resists offering a *diagnosis* of James's psychological characteristics, Perry in a chapter titled "Morbid Traits" lists melancholy, mood swings, hallucinations, and hypochondria as generic features of William James's personality (ibid., 368–69).

Further to these encounters with disability, his sister, Alice, had a long history of depression and anxiety. Alice James's biographer, Jean Strouse, recounts an episode from 1866–67 when Alice lived apart from her family, residing instead with an "orthopedic surgeon with a particular interest in nervous disorders and the diseases of women" (Strouse 1980, 106). During this time, Alice became prone to "nervous attacks," experiencing a series of psychological breakdowns, and her diaries reveal her ongoing efforts to make sense of them. Strouse notes Alice's recollection of her response to William's 1890 essay, "The Hidden Self": "Alice endorsed William's description of this process [the splitting of consciousness into "personages"]: he used (she wrote) an 'excellent expression' in saying that the nervous victim 'abandons certain portions of his consciousness'" (ibid., 117).

Strouse discloses that William's relationship with his sister as she endured breakdowns and therapy was at times paternalistic, and Erin McKenna offers a helpful synopsis of their interactions, revealing a complex relationship in which William was sometimes self-absorbed (ignoring Alice's instructions and requests) and masculinist (imploring his father to see to Alice's education for the sake of "woman's charms"). As McKenna summarizes it, "William liked strong women, but didn't want them stronger than himself" (2015, 85). Without diminishing this criticism, we can still appreciate that James knew something of the lived experience of disability, and was extraordinarily concerned for his sister. Toward the end of Alice's life, as she was coping with breast cancer, William offered several sympathetic comments on her life, affirming that she was "the most remarkable member of the family" (Strouse 1980, 308). In his relationship with Alice, too, William encountered disability first-hand, and, although his responses were sometimes deficient, he still bore sympathetic witness to her experiences.

Although James does not directly confront the tendency for reports by disabled people regarding their life-satisfaction to be dismissed, two aspects of his work seem helpful for doing so. First, his argument against medical materialism calls into question easy inferences from a speaker's physical or "organic" condition to the credibility of their testimony. Second, in his *Talks to Students on Some of Life's Ideals* (1983), James critiques conceptions of life's "significance" that are incompatible with various forms of disablement. Since these conceptions could undergird arguments that derogate disability-positive testimony, his criticisms can be leveraged in defense of such self-reported levels of life-satisfaction.

ADAPTIVE PREFERENCES, MEDICAL MATERIALISM, AND SELF-REPORTS

We might understand the tendency to discredit self-reports by disabled people regarding happiness or life-satisfaction as symptomatic of a broader phenomenon. Disabled persons do not encounter barriers just when making claims about levels of happiness. Rather, they often feel ignored as "real" participants in social activity and conversations. Particularly vicious instances of such disregard paradigmatically fit Miranda Fricker's account of testimonial injustice, where prejudice "results in [a speaker's] receiving less credibility than she otherwise would have" (2007, 17). But even as the early literature on the disability paradox suggests, the story is complex. The temptation to diminish the word of disabled persons seems to stem from the idea that they just don't know what they are missing, such that unexpectedly high levels of self-reported life-satisfaction are taken to be symptomatic of adjusting one's preferences to diminished options. These "adaptive preferences" are coping mechanisms, and we should hesitate to afford them credibility. James confronts a similar problem in a different context, the challenge of medical materialism undermining the legitimacy of reports concerning religious experience. Before drawing analogies from his argument, a glance at disability narratives will reveal the apparent pervasiveness of feeling dismissed or unacknowledged as potential knowers and conversation partners.

A common theme of these narratives is the experience of being dismissed or ignored, even in interactions with well-intentioned neighbors. For instance, reporting on the experience of blindness, John Hull writes,

> at church, one of the vergers approached Marilyn as she was standing with me, and said to her, "Marilyn, is it John's wish to go forward to the Communion Rail?" Marilyn made no reply, I turned towards him and said with a smile, "Yes, thank you very much, I will be going forward." . . . Why not tap me on the elbow, and ask me whether I intended to go forward, and whether I would need any assistance? I would appreciate this thoughtful gesture. To speak *about* me, in the third person, to someone else, is another matter. (2009, 71)

Disabled persons experience a variety of communication barriers, even where their impairments make no relevant difference. In her characterization of disability as a disruption of the "lived body," or one's schema of orientation toward the world, S. Kay Toombs reveals how even simple interpersonal interactions can leave a disabled person feeling diminished in relation to the social environment. Toombs uses a wheelchair because of the progression of multiple sclerosis, and finds that even this change in bodily comportment diminishes her interactions with others. She is no longer considered a viable conversation partner:

> Loss of upright posture . . . causes others—those who are still upright—to treat one as dependent. Whenever I am accompanied by an upright person, in my presence strangers invariably address themselves to my companion and refer to me in the third person. "Can *SHE* transfer from her wheelchair to her seat? Would *SHE* like to sit at this table?" (1995, 17)

Nondisabled individuals often "read" impairment as suggesting that someone is largely dependent, failing to conform to whatever standards of interaction or speech might be at work in the background.[10] We might understand the tendency to dismiss disabled persons' self-reports as not just a product of the intransigent belief that disability is antithetical to well-being, but as a particular problematic instance of this more general phenomenon.

Common images of disability further undermine the idea that disabled persons can function as viable imparters of testimony. Rosemarie Garland-Thomson writes that "public representations of disability have traditionally been contained within the conventions of sentimental charity images, exotic freak show portraits, medical illustrations, or sensational and forbidden pictures" (2002, 23). These images and framing devices reinforce the notion of disability as dependence, or a kind of limiting case. We should not be surprised, then, in acknowledging the narratives of disabled individuals or reflecting on the ways in which disability images are used, to find that prejudice infects appreciation of the testimony of disabled individuals.

Applied to reports of life-satisfaction, though, the dismissal tends to have a unique structure. Elizabeth Barnes remarks that

> when a disabled person says that they value being disabled, or that being disabled can be just as good as being non-disabled, it doesn't match our view of disability as a misfortune. And so we re-interpret what disabled people are saying. They're so brave that they don't even think of themselves as facing hardship. They've had to overcome so much that they don't even realize what they're missing. And so on. In short, we don't take them at their word, because of our stereotypes of what disability and disabled people are like. (2016, 139)

To preserve the stereotypical view that disability is always a tragedy to be overcome, there is a tendency to redescribe what the testimony reveals, sometimes in terms of it evidencing the "resilience" of the individual. This well-meaning re-interpretation is an instance of testimonial injustice since "prejudice causes a hearer to give a deflated level of credibility to a speaker's words" (Fricker 2007, 1). Further, such re-interpretation can manifest in what Bill Hughes calls "the emotional infrastructure of abilism," whereby "attitudes to bodily and intellectual difference . . . harden into aversive emotions like fear and disgust and into the conviction that impairment is a tragedy" (2012, 68).

One common way of preserving such stereotypes or intuitions regarding disability is to dismiss disability-positive testimony as an effect of "adaptive preference." Jon Elster illustrates the concept using the fable of the fox and the grapes (1985, 110). Finding that he is unable to reach some grapes, the fox proclaims that they "are too sour for foxes anyway." The fox's distaste for grapes is a coping mechanism, and although he convinces himself that grapes are too sour, we should not trust his consequent claim. While Elster uses the fable to argue that preference change in response to a desire to not experience frustration or challenge is irrational, the basic point of his argument can be used in other contexts to study the reliability of people's testimony regarding their own well-being.

Writing on adaptive preferences and gender roles, Martha Nussbaum considers the possibility that women in a patriarchal society might come to prefer submissive roles. We would hesitate in that case to acknowledge this preference as evidence for the quality of a life devoted to submission, or as justification for political and social structures that entrench such roles (2001). Since the preferences seem to have been formed in response to diminished or constrained options, we should not rely on them to make inferences about quality of life or well-being. Likewise, if disabled persons' self-reported levels of well-being are mere coping mechanisms formed in response to less than ideal options, perhaps we should not endorse this testimony as evidence regarding quality of life.[11]

Applied to disability, the problem of adaptive preference compounds the tendency to dismiss the word of disabled people.[12] The condition of the speaker, as disabled, calls into question the justificatory force of her claims rather than bolstering them. Instead of considering disabled people as being in the best position to attest to the value of life *as* a disabled person, their testimony is interpreted such as to invert the ordinary structure of testimonial justification.

Recall that even Albrecht and Devlieger's early formulation of the paradox hints at an explanation of the testimony that degrades its justificatory force, subtitling their article, "High Quality of Life Against All Odds." They offer the hypothesis that self-reports are products of "secondary gains," whereby disability creates hardships that count against flourishing but encourage dispositions, relationships, valuable life-projects, and so on that promote a sense of life-satisfaction. This treatment suggests that we ought to be suspicious of disabled persons' claims to well-being, insofar as whatever gains one experiences come in virtue of an initial loss.

James's work can help to counter such a suggestion by disclosing the illegitimacy of the inference from a speaker's condition to the worthiness of her word. He outlines an avenue of response in his criticism of "medical materialism" in *The Varieties of Religious Experience*, where he confronts a tendency to dismiss claims regarding mystical experience as products of some disabling condition. Medical materialists point to the conditions of the speaker to denigrate the value of testimony to a mystical experience. James writes:

> Medical materialism finishes up Saint Paul by calling his vision on the road to Damascus a discharging lesion of the occipital cortex, he being an epileptic. It snuffs out Saint Teresa as an hysteric, Saint Francis of Assisi as an hereditary degenerate. George Fox's discontent with the shams of his age, and his pining for spiritual veracity, it treats as a symptom of a disordered colon. Carlyle's organ-tones of misery it accounts for by a gastro-duodenal catarrh. All such mental over-tensions, it says, are, when you come to the bottom of the matter, mere affairs of diathesis (auto-intoxications most probably), due to the perverted action of various glands which physiology will yet discover. And medical materialism then thinks that the spiritual authority of all such personages is successfully undermined. (1985, 20)

The medical materialist's response to religious experience is to offer a causal story from the malfunctioning of a speaker's physical or mental abilities to the unreliability of her testimony. Although testimony regarding life-satisfaction exhibits some salient differences from the kinds of report considered here by James (for instance, it is not understood as being directly caused by the disability, but rather as an assessment of one's state caused by an adjustment in preferences), there are also some important similarities. In particular, rejection of testimony on the basis of medical materialism resembles cases of testimonial injustice in how it victimizes individuals. James highlights how a speaker can *feel* slighted by its application:

> When other people criticize our more exalted soul-flights by calling them "nothing-but" expressions of our organic disposition, we feel outraged and hurt, for we know that, whatever be our organism's peculiarities, our mental states have their substantive value as revelations of the living truth. (1985, 19)

Just as disabled persons might reasonably respond negatively to being dismissed as knowers or conversation partners, as Toombs suggests, so too James thinks dismissals based on bodily or "organic" dispositions can have this effect. But James's account of the source of the distress is telling. Recognition by others of the value of one's reports about one's own mental states is not just a matter of being appreciated as a knower. Such reports are "revelations of the living truth," and so, when our testimony is not recognized appropriately, we feel hurt or outraged. Having one's testimony treated as a matter merely of one's preference is a kind of dismissal. In the disability case, we feel hurt, offended, or ignored because we are told that our sense of life-satisfaction is a product, at least in part, of "our organism's peculiarities," and the charge of adaptive preference diminishes them as "nothing but" coping mechanisms.

More pointedly, James argues that the inference from one's physiological state to the invalidity of an experience or testimony is suspect "unless one has already worked out in advance some psycho-physical theory connecting spiritual values in general with determinate sorts of physiological change" (1985, 21). James argues that without such a theory, every belief and doubt becomes suspect, as all of them accompany some bodily change. Thus, to make the medical dismissal work, some account of *which* bodily conditions imply illegitimate testimonies must be at work in the background. Absent such an account, we have no reason to believe that medical materialism undermines the weight of testimony regarding mystical experiences. James states, "when we speak disparagingly of 'feverish fancies,' surely the fever-process as such is not the ground of our disesteem—for aught we know to the contrary, 103° or 104° Fahrenheit might be a much more favorable temperature for truths to sprout and germinate in, than the more ordinary blood-heat of 97 or 98 degrees" (1985, 21). Similarly, when we disparage the testimony of disabled people as a product of physical or mental atypicality, the "organic antecedent" of the belief is generally not the source of suspicion.

James calls on the reader to investigate *why* we regard some states of mind as "superior." He offers two reasons: we might take "immediate delight" in the belief, or else "we believe them to bring good consequential fruits for life" (1985, 21). Regarding the latter, James famously privileges the "fruits" rather than the "roots" of belief:

> When we praise the thoughts which health brings, health's peculiar chemical metabolisms have nothing to do with determining our judgment. . . . It is the character of inner happiness in the thoughts which stamps them as good, or else their consistency with our other opinions and their serviceability for our needs, which makes them pass for true in our esteem. (James 1985, 21–22)

Unable to cite the particular bodily conditions that gave rise to a reliable belief, James offers forward-looking criteria for the evaluation of experience (specifically, religious experience): immediate luminousness, philosophical reasonableness, and moral helpfulness. Thus, while calling into question the quick inference from bodily qualities to mistake, James does not leave us resourceless in judging the value of religious experience. Instead, he offers criteria concerning the lived effects of such experience or belief.[13] While a criterion like "immediate luminousness," for instance, might not be readily applicable to the case of disability, it does point toward a way forward: what are the fruits of treating first-person testimony regarding quality of life from disabled persons as having justificatory force?

James's response to medical materialism suggests that, unless we have already established disability as *necessarily* contrary to well-being, the charge of adaptive preference just will not stick. Looking to the organic roots of self-assessment does not provide solid ground for dismissing testimony without committing testimonial injustice. However, we can imagine a rejoinder built on the premise that disability is necessarily inimical to well-being. Even focusing upon the fruits rather than the roots of the experience of being disabled, it would seem, we might suppose that there is something wrong with testimony from a disabled person that they have a high quality of life. James's work provides materials for a rejoinder here, too, by proposing that we might be unable to easily appreciate "significance" from perspectives other than one's own. As James observes in his comments on "moral blindness," we tend to have a limited appreciation for the value judgments and ideals of others. Countering such "blindness" motivates his championing a more hands-off approach to judging the worthiness of other's lives and projects.

SIGNIFICANT LIVES: DISABILITY AND WELL-BEING

Regarding religious experience, James argues that without establishing a causal connection between a bodily state and subsequent experiences and testimony, we lack reason to discredit that testimony. In the context of disability, the analogue would be a theory of well-being that is incompatible with disability: we might believe that disability just is contrary to well-being. If the concept of disability functions necessarily as a limit case on flourishing, then we would have such a connection. And it seems as though being disabled will indeed involve trials that might otherwise have been avoided. Tom Shakespeare calls into question the notion that all restrictions experienced by disabled persons are products of natural or social environments, contending that "while many limitations experienced by disabled people are externally imposed restrictions arising from inaccessible environments and social discrimination, there are also often intrinsic limitations to individual functioning that can only be overcome through the assistance of others, and sometimes not even then" (2014, 101). To bolster the claim that we should take disabled persons' self-reports at face value, then, we need an account of flourishing compatible with conditions of disability. An effective response to the problem of dismissing disabled persons' self-reports demands that disability's relationship to well-being be an open question.[14]

Again, James provides a fruitful starting point. While not offering a full-blown account of human flourishing, his *Talks to Teachers on Psychology; and to Students on Some of Life's Ideals* provides some helpful ideas, particularly when they are read with disablement in mind. The first lecture, "The Gospel of Relaxation," was written to an audience of young women shortly after Alice's death. Commenting on James's apparent awareness of the overstressed condition of women students, Megan Craig speculates that "James's sensitivity to the plight of women in 1895 may have been tied to the history of his sister [who had died in 1892]. . . . Alice's fate must have been on James's mind as he stood facing a class of young women, their futures before them, in Boston a few years later" (2015, 173). While Craig highlights the historical significance of these lectures with an eye toward disclosing feminist themes, it is hard to ignore connections to disability, particularly with Alice's presence in mind. "The Gospel of Relaxation" warns of the disabling effects of "the need of feeling responsible all the livelong day" and offers a therapeutic exhortation to ease "moral tensions" (James 1985, 131).

In two other essays in *Talks to Teachers*, "On a Certain Blindness in Human Beings" and "What Makes a Life Significant," James calls for an ethic of tolerance based on the recognition of our limited ability to comprehend and assess the values of others. In the former, James offers reasons to assess as suspect our ability to fully appreciate others' judgments of value; in the latter, he questions accounts of flourishing that are incompatible with various forms of impairment. He opens the latter this way:

> In my previous talk, "On a Certain Blindness," I tried to make you feel how soaked and shot-through life is with values and meanings which we fail to realize because of our external and insensible point of view. . . . It has the most tremendous practical importance. . . . It is the basis of all our tolerance, social, religious, and political. . . . The first thing to learn in intercourse with others is non-interference with their own peculiar ways of being happy, provided those ways do not assume to interfere by violence with ours. No one has insight into all the ideals. No one should presume to judge them off-hand. (1985, 150)

These two essays undergird a case for prima facie deference to disability-positive testimony. Such authority might be defeated by consideration of the particular form of disablement or its effects, of course—substance addiction's often deleterious effects might give us pause regarding the word of some disabled persons as ultimately authoritative, for instance. But generally, James's proposals help to counter the tendency to disregard disabled individuals' testimony regarding quality of life.

The idea that disability is inimical to flourishing might be motivated by the apparent hardships associated with impairment. Insofar as disability bears a connection to impairment and demands effort to "overcome hardship," living with disability supposedly involves extraneous exertion, apparently contrary to reports by disabled people of a high quality of life. But in "What Makes a Life Significant," James argues that a life of ease might in fact be contrary to well-being rather than necessary for it. Reflecting on his time at a retreat center at Lake Chautauqua, he recounts that "you have no zymotic diseases, no poverty, no drunkenness, no crime, no police. You have culture, you have kindness, you have cheapness, you have equality, you have the best fruits of what mankind has fought and bled and striven for under the name of civilization for centuries" (1985, 152). Yet, having enumerated the amenities, diversions and entertainment, and the freedom from stress and struggle, James laments rather than celebrates. He proclaims a kind of longing for a world with imperfections, writing that "there are the heights and depths, the precipices and the steep ideals, the gleams of the awful and the infinite; and there is more hope and more help a thousand times than in this dead level and quintessence of every mediocrity" (1985, 153). Chautauqua embodies a life free from struggle and strain, but it fails to engage at least some of those facets that make us human.

For James, the need for struggle is a necessary part of *human* life. The failure of Chautauqua is its inhumanity. Summarizing James's ethics in terms of energy, Sergio Franzese helpfully elaborates that "good . . . is neither the ideal nor the active effort in itself, but rather the active tension (the effort) toward the ideal. . . . [H]aving finally achieved its goals, the culture at its perfect ergonomical equilibrium is utterly boring and unheroic; it is the *tedium vitae* as a social institution" (2008, 186). Although we might question whether James has the right account of life's significance and meaning, his comments on life at Chautauqua call into question the ideal of a life free from struggle as emblematic of well-being.

Some such intuition seems sometimes to be at work in derailing the testimony of disabled people. Disability's relationship to variegated challenges and struggles motivates the view that disability and well-being are in tension. This intuition rings of the empty Chautauquan ideal of the well-lived life as free from pain or inconvenience. If such a life is devoid of essentially human energies, as James suggests, then we should be incredulous when some version of this view is leveraged to devalue the testimony of disabled people.

Of course, struggle for the sake of struggle is not an adequate conception of well-being either, and James's comments on this matter confront another potential root of the intuition that disability is incompatible with flourishing. Later in "What Makes a Life Significant," James considers a conception of a good human life on the opposite pole, as a life of energetic action, labor and effort:

> I was speeding with the train toward Buffalo, when, near that city, the sight of workingmen doing something on the dizzy

edge of a sky-scaling iron construction brought me to my senses very suddenly. And now I perceived, by a flash of insight, that I had been steeping myself in pure ancestral blindness, and looking at life through the eyes of a remote spectator. Wishing for heroism and the spectacle of human nature on the rack, I had never noticed the great fields of heroism lying round about me (1985, 154)

James finds and extolls in work the exercise of virtue: "the demand for courage is incessant, and the supply never fails" and "there, every day of the year somewhere is human nature *in extremis* for you" (ibid., 154–55). Even at first glance, this vision of the good human life seems contrary to at least some aspects of the well-being of disabled people, insofar as disability can make it difficult to sell one's labor freely in the marketplace.[15] Moreover, even in the workplace, disabled people face such barriers as prejudicial attitudes, lack of access to accommodations, and problems linked to one's impairments, such as fatigue.[16]

James goes on to resist the temptation to see idyllic life in terms of work, citing Tolstoy and Stevenson at length before commenting, "if it is idiotic in romanticism to recognize the heroic only when it sees it labelled and dressed-up in books. it is really just as idiotic to see it only in the dirty boots and sweaty shirt of someone in the field" (ibid., 159). Mere laboring cannot be constitutive of human flourishing. Exploring the economic relationship between laborers and their employers, one finds that market conditions frequently subvert working in the service of an ideal. Instead, wage-slavery and economic forces constitute external, rather than internal, pressures to perform labor. James cites sociologist Walter Wyckoff: "[W]e have sold our labor where we could sell it dearest, and our employer has bought it where he could buy it cheapest. . . . From work like ours there seems to have been eliminated every element which constitutes the nobility of labor" (quoted in James 1985, 160). Disconnected from an "ideal" served by one's labor, the activity is inhuman, routine, and mechanical.

Each of these bases for human flourishing—life as freedom from struggle and as energetic laboring—is unsatisfactory, and might be used to justify denigrating the testimony of disabled people. If life free from toil is considered optimal, and disability (in virtue of its connection to impairment and the associated difficulties) involves toil, then we can read self-reported levels of well-being as adaptive preferences. But if the life of work and economic engagement is considered ideal, and disability prevents people from freely exchanging their labor in the marketplace, then we seem to have located another reason for disregarding positive testimony.

In fact, James maintains that life's significance rests on a "chemical combination" of culture, will and aspiration, and ideals to which one aspires (1985, 165). No one of these alone is sufficient for well-being, he contends; they must operate together. This realization is relevant to the question of whether disability might be compatible with well-being because there is a tendency to focus myopically on one element over and against others. Being unable to locate and explain the precise dynamics of James's "chemical combination" does not mean that we ought to resort to such one-dimensional explanations of well-being as freedom from exertion or as the capacity to work. The point is that to dismiss the testimony of disabled people based on an a priori account of well-being is deeply suspect. It is not suspect because we can imagine living incredibly comfortably as a disabled person, but because, on James's view, the account of well-being on which it trades is unsustainable.

THE REVELATIONS OF SICK ROOMS

Having gleaned from James some basic elements of a response to the disability paradox, we can extend the arguments of his *Talks to Students* in service of promoting epistemic humility toward the testimony of disabled people regarding the quality of their lives. James concludes "On a Certain Blindness in Human Beings" by writing that the evidence on which he draws

> forbids us to be forward in pronouncing on the meaninglessness of forms of existence other than our own. . . . Hands off: neither the whole of truth nor the whole of good is revealed to any single observer, although each observer gains a partial superiority of insight from the peculiar position in which he stands. *Even prisons and sick-rooms have their special revelations.* (1985, 149; emphasis added)

Having reviewed criticisms of accounts of life's significance incompatible with disability, turning to James's ethic of tolerance in this essay provides reason for prima facie deference to the word of disabled persons in at least some cases of disability-positive testimony.

James argues that judgments of value "depend on the feelings the things arouse in us" (1985, 132). Given the dependence of these judgments on feelings, and feelings on the particularities of one's perspectives, we face barriers (he uses the term "blindness") in appreciating life's significance from the point of view of others. In James's opening example, he cannot conceive of the beauty or value of aspects of life in Appalachian North Carolina. The landscape of half-cleared forests and log cabins seemed to him dreary and dismal. Asking his driver for an explanation, James learns that the clearing was to locals "a symbol redolent with moral memories and sang a very pæan of duty, struggle, and success" (1985, 134). Jeff Edmonds helpfully explains James's account of "mental blindness" (or "asymbolia") as stemming "from a problem of association, in which the link between sensations and mental images is broken down," and in James's moral work, the problem is "a disconnect between impressions and ideas, between in this case feelings and judgments, that creates a certain type of social and political blindness" (2011, 135). Proposing ways for repairing the connection so that different perspectives on the same phenomenon can be imbued with shared feelings of significance is the task of James's lecture.

James's conception of the relational character of value judgments is central to this task. José Medina argues that James affirms an account of "relationality according to which nothing can be understood in and by itself, but rather in relation to other things, in a network of relations" (2010, 124). This commitment implies that "validity [of value judgments] . . . is conceived as something relational that emerges from normative engagements among different perspectives" (2010, 131). As an epistemic negotiation, James's reconsideration of the value of the Appalachian countryside is a product of engaging with an alternative perspective, revealing his own previous insensitivity in the process. Crucially, James's pragmatism precludes recourse to any absolute or extra-experiential arbiter of value, relying on our relational engagements to alert us to alternative judgments. As Heidi White puts it, for James, "we only have access to our own horizon and we rely on the individualism of others to fill in the blanks. If one can't turn to an absolute, to a grand rational spirit that unifies the world as a whole, and if one can't depend on a solipsistic self engaged in a skeptical stance, then one can only rely on oneself and one's neighbor" (2010, 10).

Such insistence on our reliance on others' perspectives further bolsters the argument for deference to the testimony of disabled individuals. James's ethics presses that whatever the operative conception of well-being, our inability to appreciate feelings of significance in others' lives should spur us to try and appreciate the situation from an alternative perspective.[17] In the case of disablement, such an optimistic project carries the promise that nondisabled and disabled people might cultivate shared feelings about an experience's significance so that they might come to appreciate something of the other's perspective.[18]

Returning to the disability paradox, we see that aspects of James's theory enable responses to both its epistemic and axiological dimensions. His response to medical materialism calls attention to mistakes inherent in the tendency to dismiss testimony based on its roots as a supposed coping mechanism. Just as the materialist challenge demands a psychological theory in the background, so the tendency to dismiss disability-positive testimony as a mere product of adaptive preference demands preconceptions regarding life's significance and meaning that are sometimes in tension with the experience of living with impairment. James's analyses of the value inherent in lives of ease and labor further question some accounts of a good human life that might bolster those preconceptions. Then, having described our "blindness" toward appreciations of life's significance from the perspective of others, he provides reason to hope that the inherent relationality of value judgments entails the promise of an ethics of tolerance. By considering others' positions sympathetically, we encourage new relational links between what we experience and the value that we attribute to it. In this sense, to defer to the testimony of others is to encourage shared feelings and values.

A James-inspired response to the disability paradox has the potential to encourage a melioristic attitude toward disability, affirming that we might, with effort, improve the experience of disabled persons without insisting on "cures" for disabling conditions. Laura Hershey, who turned from being a poster child for the Jerry Lewis MDA Labor Day Telethon to a disability activist protesting that very event, writes that "with the stated goal of 'helping' his 'kids,' Jerry Lewis is helping to keep alive the most pernicious myths about people who have disabilities. *He ignores our truth, substituting his distorted assumptions*" (1993; emphasis added). For Hershey, a myopic focus on cure, compounded by fundraising strategies, motivates portrayals of disabled persons as totally dependent, and their families and caretakers as "courageous."[19] Such conceptions exacerbate the problem of failing to respect the testimony of disabled people. Anticipating Hershey's criticism of adopting an outsider's view, James asserts that "the spectator's judgment is sure to miss the root of the matter and to possess no truth. The subject judged knows a part of the world of reality which the judging spectator fails to see, knows more where the spectator knows less" (1985, 133). James's attentiveness to *feelings* regarding life's meaning and significance encourages appreciation for the testimony of disabled people regarding their quality of life. His proposal that we ought to give sympathetic consideration to the perspectives and values of others encourages reappraisal of our own value judgments. In effect, as an ally in the philosophy of disability, James reminds us to pay attention. The revelations of sickrooms can disclose modes of life and significance that must figure into our empirical analysis of the full meaning of variegated human lives.

NOTES

1. Regarding the debate over whether to use the phrase "people with disabilities" or "disabled people," I opt here for the latter. It resonates with my own relationship to disability, and, in this context, I do not sense a need to remind the reader that disabled people are people whose lives are not entirely understood by taking account of our various impairments.

2. Harlan Hahn distinguishes between "existential" and "aesthetic" anxiety. Aesthetic anxiety refers to the apparent inability of physically "atypical" bodies to approximate dominant standards of beauty, while existential anxiety tracks the intuition that disability is incompatible with the demands of a flourishing life because it involves diminished capacities (42–43). More recently, Margrit Shildrick offered an analysis of disability anxiety in terms of the loss of recognition as a sexual subject.

3. For a helpful account of the varieties of pluralism in James's work, see Slater.

4. Other social models include the human variation model, which conceive of impairments as a result of bodily or mental characteristics that do not "match" well with an environment, and the minority group model, which theorizes disability identity in terms of membership in a stigmatized or excluded group. See Wasserman et al.; Mitchell and Snyder; Barnes.

5. For an excellent overview of the role of disability in terms of group identity and pride in that identity, see Brown.

6. Importantly, there can be cases where such testimony is defeated by other considerations. For instance, we might imagine the testimony on offer as that of a pathological liar. In such a case, we would have reason to think that the testimony lacks credibility.

7. Daniel Brunson offers a thorough synopsis of James's use of sensory impairments in his arguments for cognition without language.

8. In discussing the rise of comparative psychology, for example, James writes, "So it has come to pass that instincts of animals are ransacked to throw light on our own; and that the reasoning faculties of bees and ants, *the minds of savages,*

infants, madmen, the deaf and blind, criminals and eccentrics, are all invoked in support of this or that special theory of the mental life" (1981, 193; emphasis added).

9. Hustwit offers a nuanced investigation of some of the curiosities of this testimony. For instance, "Ballard says that he could convey his thoughts and feelings to his parents by natural signs or pantomime. But if we suppose that had a sign language to convey these thoughts, then we are unable to understand why Ballard would present himself as one thinking without language or why James would present him as such" (60). Hustwit hypothesizes that a sympathetic understanding of Mr. Ballard's testimony would indicate he had "some prelinguistic occurrences to which he later attached his new language" (66).

10. Simplician helpfully extends this criticism to show how standards of public rationality can assume forms incompatible with conditions of disability and provides an alternative model of political action (118–35).

11. Jessica Begon attempts to articulate an approach to adaptive preference that does not impugn the rationality of disabled persons, while simultaneously providing grounds for ignoring these preferences in considering questions of distributive justice. In a different vein, Clémence Thébaut worries about trusting deaf-positive testimony from hearing-impaired parents in deciding whether Cochlear replacements are appropriate for their children. If such testimony is an effect of adaptive preference, it would seem to be inappropriate to regard it as evidence against some medical interventions.

12. In a telling example of testimonial injustice, repeated dismissal of a woman's testimony as a product of "hysteria" might eventually lead to a hysterical outburst (Fricker, 88). This episode then provides justification for the prejudice, entrenching the injustice. In the disability case, it is not hard to imagine that pervasive and repeated instances of epistemic injustice create the conditions that lend this denigration some apparent credence.

13. Ruetenik offers a helpful synopsis and extension of James's evaluation of religious experience according to its "fruits" rather than its "roots" (383–85, 392).

14. As Barnes argues, to sustain the view that self-reports are indicative of "adaptive preferences" requires showing that they are responses to constrained and less-than-ideal circumstances.

15. According to the 2010 U.S. census, only 40.1% of working-age disabled persons were employed, compared to 79.1% of their nondisabled counterparts (www.census.gov/prod/2012pubs/p70-131.pdf).

16. See, for instance, Gupta.

17. Charlene Haddock Siegfried also emphasizes James's account of the uniqueness of each person's perspective:

> According to [James's] pluralistic and finitist conception of the way we come to understanding, every person has a unique and irreplaceable angle of vision because she or he is differently situated and has a varied ensemble of needs and desires and a characteristic temperament. (92)

18. Sarin Marchetti argues that James's emphasis on individual growth demands attention to the ways in which our social and political milieu constrains our individual "vision": "The contrast James is remarking is one between an unengaged and detached as opposed to an engaged and committed view of subjectivity, of its potentiality for improvement and of its relationship with the larger environment in which it necessarily moves." Individual growth, on this reading, demands engagement with and re-working of one's environment to facilitate new avenues of growth (224).

19. Similarly, theorist Joseph Shapiro famously critiqued the visual rhetoric of the "poster child," holding that "the poster child image oppresses" and quoting disability activist Cyndi Jones, who argues that "the poster child says it's not OK to be disabled" (14). Instead, Shapiro argues that "people with disabilities are demanding rights, not medical cures" (ibid.).

REFERENCES

Albrecht, Gary, and Patrick Devlieger. "The Disability Paradox: High Quality of Life Against All Odds." *Social Science and Medicine* 43, no. 8 (1999): 977–88.

Barnes, Elizabeth. *The Minority Body: A Theory of Disability*. New York: Oxford University Press, 2016.

Begon, Jessica. "What are Adaptive Preferences? Exclusion and Disability in the Capability Approach." *Journal of Applied Philosophy* 32, no. 3 (2014): 241–57.

Breckenridge, Carol, and Candace Vogler. "The Critical Limits of Embodiment: Disability's Criticism," *Public Culture* 13, no. 3 (2001.): 349–57.

Brown, Steven. "What is Disability Culture?" *Disability Studies Quarterly* 22, no. 2 (2002): 34–50.

———. "Disability Culture and the ADA." *Disability Studies Quarterly* 35, no. 3 (2015). dx.doi.org/10.18061/dsq.v35i3 4936

Brunson, Daniel. "Disability, Neurodiversity and Philosophical Problems." Paper presented at the Annual Meeting of the Society for the Advancement of American Philosophy, Birmingham, AL, March 2017.

Craig, Megan. "Habit, Relaxation and the Open Mind: James and the Increments of Ethical Freedom." In *Feminist Interpretations of William James*, edited by Erin C. Tarver and Shannon Sullivan. University Park: Pennsylvania State University Press, 2015.

Edmonds, Jeff. "Towards an Ethics of Encounter: William James's Push Beyond Tolerance." *Journal of Speculative Philosophy* 25, no. 2 (2011): 133–47.

Elster, Jon. *Sour Grapes: Studies in the Subversion of Rationality*. New York: Cambridge University Press, 1985.

Fullerton, Stephanie, and Cheryll Duquette. "Experiences of Students with Learning Disabilities in Ontario Universities: A Case Study." *International Journal of Special Education* 31, no. 1 (2016): 55–66.

Franzese, Sergio. *The Ethics of Energy: William James's Moral Philosophy in Focus.* Piscataway, NJ: Transaction Books, 2008.

Fricker, Miranda. *Epistemic Injustice: Power and the Ethics of Knowing.* New York: Oxford University Press, 2007.

Garland-Thomson, Rosemarie. *Extraordinary Bodies: Figuring Physical Disability in American Culture and Literature.* New York: Columbia University Press, 1997.

———. "Integrating Disability, Transforming Feminist Theory." *NWSA Journal* 14, no. 3 (2002): 1–32.

Gupta, Jyothi. "An Issue of Occupational (In)justice: A Case Study." *Disability Studies Quarterly* 32, no. 3 (2012). dx.doi.org/10.18061/dsq.v32i3.3280

Hahn, Harlan. "The Politics of Physical Differences: Disability and Discrimination." *Journal of Social Issues* 44, no. 1 (1988): 39–47.

Hershey, Laura. "From Poster Child to Protester." *Crip Commentary*, 1993. www.cripcommentary.com/frompost.html

Hughes, Bill. "Fear, Pity and Disgust: Emotions and the Non-Disabled Imaginary." In *Routledge Handbook of Disability Studies*, edited by Nick Watson, Alan Roulston, and Carol Thomas. New York: Routledge, 2012.

Hull, John. "Touching the Rock: An Experience of Blindness." In *Disability: The Social, Political, and Ethical Debate*, edited by Robert Baird, Stuart Rosenbaum, and S. Kay Toombs. Amherst, NY: Prometheus Books, 2009.

Hustwit, Ronald E. "The Curious Case of Mr. Ballard." *Philosophical Investigations* 17, no. 1 (1994): 59–66.

James, William. *The Principles of Psychology.* Vols. 8–10 of *The Works of William James*, edited by Frederick H. Burkhardt, Fredson Bowers, and Ignas K. Skrupskelis. Introductions by Rand B. Evans and Gerald E. Myers. Cambridge, MA: Harvard University Press, [1890] 1981.

———. *Talks to Teachers on Psychology; and to Students on Some of Life's Ideals.* Vol. 12 of *The Works of William James*, edited by Frederick H. Burkhardt, Fredson Bowers, and Ignas K. Skrupskelis. Introduction by Gerald E. Myers. Cambridge, MA: Harvard University Press, [1899] 1983.

———. *The Varieties of Religious Experience.* Vol. 15 of *The Works of William James*, edited by Frederick H. Burkhardt, Fredson Bowers, and Ignas K. Skrupskelis. Introduction by John E. Smith. Cambridge, MA: Harvard University Press, [1902] 1985.

Kahane, Guy, and Julian Savulescu. "The Welfarist Account of Disability." In *Disability and Disadvantage*, edited by Kimberly Brownlee and Steven Cureton. New York: Oxford University Press, 2009.

Marchetti, Sarin. *Ethics and Philosophical Critique in William James.* New York: Palgrave Macmillan, 2015.

McKenna, Erin. "Women and William James." In *Feminist Interpretations of William James*, edited by Erin C. Tarver and Shannon Sullivan. University Park: Pennsylvania State University Press, 2015.

Medina, José. "James on Truth and Solidarity: The Epistemology of Diversity and the Politics of Specificity." In *100 Years of Pragmatism: William James's Revolutionary Philosophy*, edited by John J. Stuhr. Bloomington: Indiana University Press, 2010.

Mitchell, David, and Sharon Snyder. "Minority Model: From Liberal to Neoliberal Futures of Disability." In *Routledge Handbook of Disability Studies*, edited by Nick Watson, Alan Roulston, and Carol Thomas. New York: Routledge, 2012.

Morselli, P. L., R. Elgie, and B. M. Cesana. "GAMIAN-Europe/BEAM Survey II: Cross-National Analysis of Unemployment, Family History, Treatment Satisfaction and Impact of the Bipolar Disorder on Life Style." *Bipolar Disorders* 6, no. 6 (2004): 487–97.

Nussbaum, Martha. "Adaptive Preferences and Women's Options." *Economics and Philosophy* 17 (2001): 67–88.

Oliver, Mike. "The Social Model in Action: If I Had a Hammer." In *Implementing the Social Model of Disability: Theory and Research*, edited by Colin Barnes and Geof Mercer. Leeds, UK: Disability Press, 2004.

Perry, Ralph Barton. *The Thought and Character of William James*. Nashville, TN: Vanderbilt University Press, 1976.

Richardson, Robert D. *William James in the Maelstrom of American Modernism*. New York: Houghton Mifflin, 2006.

Ruetenik, Tadd. "Fruits of Health; Roots of Despair: William James, Medical Materialism and the Evaluation of Religious Experience." *Journal of Religion and Health* 45, no. 3 (2006): 382–95.

Schramme, Thomas. "Disability (Not) as a Harmful Condition: The Received View Challenged." In *Disability and the Good Human Life*, edited by Jerome Bickenbach, Franziska Felder, and Barbara Schmitz. New York: Cambridge University Press, 2014.

Shakespeare, Tom. *Disability Rights and Wrongs Revisited*. 2nd ed. New York: Routledge, 2014.

———. "Nasty, Brutish and Short? On the Predicament of Disability and Embodiment." In *Disability and the Good Human Life*, edited by Jerome Bickenbach, Franziska Felder, and Barbara Schmitz. New York: Cambridge University Press, 2014.

Shapiro, Joseph. *No Pity: People with Disabilities Forging a New Civil Rights Movement*. New York: Three Rivers Press, 1994.

Shildrick, Margrit. "Dangerous Discourses: Anxiety, Desire, and Disability." *Studies in Gender and Sexuality* 8, no. 3 (2007): 221–44.

Siegfried, Charlene Haddock. "James: Sympathetic Apprehension of the Point of View of the Other." In *Classical American Pragmatism: Its Contemporary Vitality*, edited by Sandra Rosenthal, Carl Hausman, and Douglas Anderson. Urbana: University of Illinois Press, 1999.

Simplician, Stacy Clifford. *The Capacity Contract: Intellectual Disability and the Question of Citizenship*. Minneapolis: University of Minnesota Press, 2015.

Slater, Michael R. "William James's Pluralism." *Review of Metaphysics* 65 (2011): 63–90.

Strouse, Jean. *Alice James: A Biography*. New York: New York Review Books, 1980.

Thébaut, Clémence. "Dealing with Moral Dilemmas Raised by Adaptive Preferences in Health Technology Assessment: The Example of Growth Hormones and Bilateral Cochlear Implants." *Social Science and Medicine* 99 (2013): 102–09.

Toombs, S. Kay. "The Lived Experience of Disability." *Human Studies* 18, no. 1 (1995): 9–23.

United States Census Bureau. *Americans With Disabilities, 2010: Current Population Reports*, by Matthew W. Brault. US Department of Commerce, Economics and Statistics Administration. 2012. www.census.gov/prod/2012pubs/p70-131.pdf

Wasserman, David, Adrienne Asch, Jeffrey Blustein, and Daniel Putnam. "Disability: Definitions, Models, Experience." *Stanford Encyclopedia of Philosophy*. Summer 2016 ed. plato.stanford.edu/archives/sum2016/entries/disability

White, Heidi. "William James's Pragmatism: Ethics and the Individualism of Others." *European Journal of Pragmatism and American Philosophy* 2, no. 1 (2010): 1–11.

CHAPTER 5

PRAGMATISM AND PROGRESS

*Has There Been Progress in
Race Relations in the United States?*

DAMIAN COX AND MICHAEL P. LEVINE

> The reasonable man adapts himself to the world: the unreasonable one persists in trying to adapt the world to himself. Therefore all progress depends on the unreasonable man.
>
> —George Bernard Shaw, *Man and Superman*

If Shaw is right, then the idea that pragmatists are practical and reasonable is as mistaken as it is common. On Shaw's account, pragmatists should be seen as movers and shakers—as those who refuse to adapt themselves to the world (isn't there too much of that?), but seek instead to refashion the world to themselves. This refashioning is not "to himself" (themselves) in a selfish, narcissistic mode, but in terms of making things "better"—where "better" ranges across practical as well as ideal personal, social, and political improvements. And insofar as a belief that things can be made better (meliorism) is an essential aspect of pragmatism, then perhaps, bucking a common perception, it is better seen as utopian albeit not revolutionary, rather than as "down to earth" and merely adaptive. Or perhaps pragmatism's insistence on slow change should itself be seen as revolutionary—but both smart and cautious.

But what is meliorism? Colin Koopman says, "Despite [an] increase of interest in pragmatist meliorism and the near universal acknowledgment that meliorism is somehow central to pragmatism, it remains to be spelled out exactly *how* meliorism contributes to pragmatism . . . [and so Koopman] undertake[s] the project of explicating the philosophical significance of pragmatist meliorism" (2006, 16). We will examine his account in relation to hope and optimism later. Meliorism, along with truth, indeed more than truth (not in Charles Sanders Peirce, but in William James, John Dewey, and Richard Rorty), is essential to pragmatism, and is in some ways its driving force. But it is also an idea that needs to be examined.[1] What is meant by progress? Can it be measured, and if so, how?[2] Perhaps because he was more socially active and engaged, Dewey is better with examples than James or Rorty. But if we are going to investigate the idea of progress from pragmatism's point(s) of view, we could use an example. Here is one. Has there been progress with regards to race relations in the United States since "legally" sanctioned segregation allegedly ended in the 1960s? We will return to this question at the end of the chapter.

Where one has a robust notion of truth, the idea of cognitive progress can be teleologically conceived of and perhaps even measured as asymptotically approaching such truth. This vision of progress can take hold even if truth as a goalpost (telos) about some things in particular (for example, those outside the natural sciences and questions of value) seems to either always recede or remain disputed. Philip Kitcher for example says, "In the scientific case . . . [unlike the case with mathematics, ethics, politics, and religion] there's a strong—realist—temptation to think that progress involves some prior notion of truth. What explains the fact that progressive inquiry settles on *p* is that *p* corresponds to the way the world is" (2015, 477). He continues:

> I see truth as heterogeneous. *Realist* domains are those in which correspondence truth enters into the explanation of the stability of propositions in progressive inquiry. *Constructivist* domains (ethics, for example) are those in which correspondence truth is generated from, and partially explained by, the stability of propositions under progressive inquiry. *Non-realist* domains (like mathematics and religion) are those in which there is only stability of propositions in progressive inquiry (no correspondence). (477)

Nonetheless, the attraction of realist conceptions (and domains) of truth is strong. With regard to what Kitcher describes as non-realist domains of truth: why, one might ask, would mere stability in progressive inquiry apart from some alleged, perhaps imperfect, correspondence be indicative of truth at all? Propositions may remain stable, even throughout progressive inquiry, for reasons that have nothing to do with their alethic status. A proposition may be difficult to shift because so much else depends upon it and because, by itself, it causes little trouble for progressive inquiry. Not causing trouble is not the same thing as being true, it would seem.

Kitcher has a more ambitious purpose regarding his pragmatic notion of truth and progress. He is interested in finding a way to prove what he terms the "Entanglement Thesis. A full understanding of the concept of factual/scientific truth presupposes concepts of ethical truth and of social progress" (492). Insofar as this thesis is intelligible, and it is unclear that it is, it is not only no part of pragmatism, it may even be antithetical to it. Julian Barnes has something like the "entanglement thesis" in mind when in his novel *Flaubert's Parrot,* he says, "[Flaubert] didn't just hate the railway as such; he hated the way it flattered people with the illusion of progress. What was the point of scientific advance without moral advance? The railway would merely permit more people to move about, meet and be stupid together" (Barnes 2009, 108).

Although John Lachs (2001) does not explicitly defend the "entanglement thesis," he supports a related thesis. He argues that material and moral progress are intertwined; the former making the latter more likely. His principal thesis is that *unquestionably* there has been progress made in both areas. While he stops short of claiming that one has to be a moron to believe that little if any moral progress has been made over the last few centuries, he does say that while

> only fools would deny that, on the whole, there has been striking material progress . . [and] many believe, quite wrongly, that there is no connection between material and moral advancement . . . yet one can deny its [progress's] reality only by selective inattention, by the application of unreasonable standards, or by astonishing ignorance of history. (2001, 173–74)

But saying it does not make it so, and that is not the only way one can deny the "reality of progress." As our discussion will soon make clear, Lachs's extravagant claims are driven by a non-pragmatist idea of progress—one that does not take its contextualist nature into account. Moral progress itself is most readily affirmed through "selective inattention."

When it comes to progress Lachs appears to be an essentialist, believing that there are necessary and sufficient conditions for progress. More than this, he is *also* asserting (and believing) that these conditions have been/are being increasingly met. Clearly, he is optimistic. But isn't he also conflating or confusing (1) "good things happening" with (2) "progress?"[3] In any case, nothing remotely approaching either his optimism—his case for the world becoming a morally better and more compassionate place—is to be found in James, Dewey, or Rorty. Indeed, Lachs refers to neither these nor any other pragmatists in his essay (2001).

Pragmatist notions of truth regarded as effervescent or "relativistic" appear to remove goalposts altogether. Not all pragmatists abandon a correspondence theory of truth (with some it is hard to tell), though such an abandonment is at times taken as a pragmatist hallmark. Nevertheless, a common and pointed criticism of pragmatism's abandonment of truth as correspondence, as well as of its meliorism (progress is incremental, provisional and relative) is the charge of relativism. The claim is grounded in what critics see as pragmatism's unacceptable alternative notions of truth—unacceptable because they are either unclear or incoherent. The most famous of these criticisms was provided by Bertrand Russell, who charged James with a commitment to the truth of "Santa Claus exists" (1946, 772). The charge of unacceptable relativism is also closely related to the view that pragmatism is unable to adequately explain or define what progress or pragmatic meliorism is.

The question, then, is whether pragmatism can maintain a coherent and workable notion of progress—not only, or even primarily, philosophical or cognitive progress, but also social progress and progress more generally. Can it do so despite its various conceptions of truth, and just what it is that pragmatists mean when they speak of progress? If we are making progress, socially, politically, personally, and philosophically, then what, if anything, are we progressing toward and on what grounds can such claims be sustained? And if we are not progressing toward anything, no *telos* such as truth or a utopian ideal (even a vague one), then how is the pragmatist's conception of progress to be explained?

Furthermore, and disconcertingly, if the idea of progress is philosophically problematic, or no sense can be made of it, then can there be anything toward which we can and should strive that might come justifiably to be seen as progress? Can the notion of progress in ethics, politics, education, or even science and technology, be made sense of? Science and technology may be "advancing," but does it make sense to say they are progressing? If so, then in what sense are they progressing from a pragmatist's point of view?

PHILIP KITCHER: PROGRESS AND PRAGMATISM

Kitcher draws a distinction between "two concepts of progress. One of them is teleological: we make progress by decreasing our distance from a goal. The other . . . is *pragmatic*: progress consists in overcoming some of the problems of the current state" (2015, 475). As pragmatically conceived, Kitcher thinks that progress is *originary* rather than teleological (2105, 478). It is measured "in terms of the distance from the starting point." The distinction between Kitcher's two types is, at first glance, cogent and convincing. However, we think it is misleading. There is, we will argue, always an element of teleology in claims to progress. The task is to understand the nature of this teleology.

The examples Kitcher gives of "pragmatic" or originary progress are (1) "the financial progress of some commercial enterprise: here, progress is measured by the increase in profits. . . . [I]t would be absurd to measure progress in terms of the approximation of maximum profit—if only for the reason that any attempt to specify the 'goal' would be wildly speculative." And (2), "the development of musicians. We assess the progress of a young pianist in terms of the accumulation of technical and interpretative skills. Here, there is no ideal of the 'Complete Pianist' for the musician to approximate, but rather the acquisition of greater abilities to achieve sensitive performances of musical works. In cases like these, progress is measured in terms of the distance from the starting point." (Kitcher 2015, 478)

Kitcher's examples are revealing. The financial progress of a commercial enterprise might seem to be purely originary in character. To progress is to move further away from insolvency. But this is too simple a characterization of financial progress. A firm that piled on profits without regard for its long-term financial health, for the sustainability and the integrity of its business, need not really be making financial progress at all, despite appearances. A well-sorted firm is aiming at something: at the very least, a profitable, long-term future doing roughly the sort of thing it is doing now, or perhaps a set of related things. (Businesses are happy to grow, diversify and adapt, but they are not characterless profit machines—at least not all of them.) Again, pianists do not develop without an idea of what would constitute musical success for them. This idea may not be singular or very precise. There are various ways of developing, various ways of getting better at piano playing. And the idea of a musical future can change: one might move on from one aspiration to another. Thus, Kitcher is right to say that there is no singular ideal of the "Complete Pianist" toward which a developing pianist must progress. There are many kinds of excellent piano playing, but they function as exemplars nonetheless. A pianist does not characteristically measure herself by how much better she is at piano playing than she used to be. Of course, she might, but it would be a hollow kind of exercise if not supplemented by an account of the ways in which she is getting closer to pianistic excellence of one kind or another.

Kitcher seems to be advancing a false dichotomy, perhaps encouraged by the visual character of his metaphors. On his account, progress is either measured by movement away from a point or it is measured by closeness to a singular, complete, predetermined end (or movement along a strategically organized journey toward that end). In complex cases, and both his initial examples are like this, neither of his versions of progress is satisfactory. In these cases, progress is a matter of getting closer to the realization of some goal, even if that goal is plural, underdetermined, and vague, even if it is contingent and readily altered or discarded along the way. Even where there is no solid conception of a final end of a practice, progress is teleological in character.

The teleological character of progress is everywhere in evidence. Consider a person who measures "progress" through life by nothing more than birthdays accrued. They get older. Their life is not, for all that, a progressive phenomenon. To progress is to get better in a way that matters, and matters in context. If getting better in one respect entails getting worse in another, then we must have a clear sense that the tradeoff is worth it overall. And this requires a robust sense of what is better overall. To realize progress in something like pianism, we need both a sense of how our piano playing might be made better overall and a sense of what matters for piano playing. Say we decide that we are too right-hand dominant as a piano player. We decide that this is a problem, and its solution would constitute progress in our piano playing. Still, we should be able to account for why right-hand dominance is a problem for us (it isn't always). Problems are not self-identifying. They emerge as problems through comparison with how things can be better. This is to say, the very idea of what constitutes a problem that needs solving is itself riven through with teleology. To know that we progress in something, we must know what is meaningfully, relevantly, better for that thing and we must know that we are making progress toward what is better. We may also have a sense of how the betterment of a thing would go on until we have a clear sense of a singular, final end, but this is unnecessary. The teleological character of progress can be observed in the move to meaningful betterment itself.

Kitcher's principle concern is to argue for what he takes to be the surprising conclusion that "originary progress, specifically pragmatic progress, is the appropriate concept for thinking of progress in the most obvious case of all: progress in factual knowledge, and scientific knowledge in particular" (2015, 480–81). But if we are right about pragmatic progress, this claim is unconvincing. It might be that there is no final end of scientific inquiry—no one true theory of the world for us to approximate—but that doesn't mean that scientific progress isn't teleological. Science inquiry is—or should be—aimed at getting a better understanding of things that matter to us.

All of Dewey's practical projects aimed to make life better for people, but explicit and grandiose teleological philosophy was largely out of the picture. Like Peirce, though, we find remnants of teleology in the respect that Dewey had for science: the view that scientific enterprise aims at providing a better picture of the world than we had available to us before. How could Dewey maintain this view without buying into teleology specifically or progress generally? Even if progress is inherently teleological, a final goal or *telos* needn't be emphasized. One merely has to be headed in the right direction for progress to be made. Meliorism envisages slow progress, step by step, subject to revision and always checking and reassessing its direction and its goals in view of new knowledge, alerted beliefs, modified desires and expectations.[4]

In an account of pragmatism's notion of progress that appears to support Kitcher's nonteleological view, John McGowan says,

> Progress . . . is not about moving the world, or a whole society, toward a certain substantial good. Rather, goods are plural, and progress involves creating the conditions for the pursuit by individuals within varying social associations of those multiple goods. . . . Shorn of global narratives of progress or of inevitable decline, we are left with the daunting task of trying out how we can make things better here and now, right in front of our noses first, more widely second. (2008, 40)

Yet the claim that the concept of progress is inherently teleological entails neither the view that the world is moving "toward a certain [single] substantial good," nor that the goods toward which we may be progressing are not plural.

If pragmatist conceptions of progress are not characterized by a lack of teleology, then what else might characterize them? There are at least four things that mark out pragmatic progress and meliorism. The first is that sought-for improvements are seen as incremental. The second is that any claim of progress (or truth) is seen as provisional. The third, one of the most important, is that progress is to be understood contextually. "Progress" is progress in a certain context—understood within certain parameters. A bigger or smaller (or different) picture may reveal what seems like progress to not be progress. Thus, the answer—obviously—to the question of whether there has been progress with regards to U.S. race relations is that it all depends on what is meant by the question. The question entails a search for an appropriate context for judgment. The fourth thing that defines pragmatic progress, as James stressed in *Pragmatism*, is that meliorism is inherently conservative. There is a strong and natural presumption in favor of current beliefs, values, and knowledge in the face of the allegedly new and improved. It takes a great deal to "shake up" one's worldview and ethos. Meliorism slowly erodes current and long-abiding conceptions of reality and an associated ethos.

Clifford Geertz describes a people's ethos as

> the tone, character, and quality of their life, its moral and aesthetic style and mood—and their world view . . . [as] the picture they have of the way things in sheer actuality are, their most comprehensive idea of order. . . . [A] group's ethos is rendered intellectually reasonable by being shown to represent a way of life ideally adapted to the actual state of affairs the world view describes, while the world view is rendered emotionally convincing by being presented as an image of an actual state of affairs peculiarly well-arranged to accommodate such a way of life. This confrontation and mutual confirmation has two fundamental effects. On the one hand, it objectivizes moral and aesthetic preferences, by depicting them as the imposed conditions of life implicit in a world with a particular structure. . . . On the other, it supports these received beliefs about the world's body by invoking deeply felt moral and aesthetic sentiments as experiential evidence for their truth. . . . [There is] a basic congruence between a particular style of life and a specific (if, most often, implicit) metaphysic. (1973, 89–90)

This congruence, the fact that we are rooted in our ways, explains why we tend to hold on to our beliefs and values, and also why change is slow and incremental.

Kitcher describes the contextualist character of progress in somewhat different terms, as multidimensionality (2015, 479): "Multidimensionality allows for gains on one dimension to combine with losses on another." But for a number of reasons, contextualism (i.e., "progress in what regard"?) is a more accurate description. It is broader in that it encompasses multidimensionality but recognizes other kinds of tradeoffs and considerations as well—those that we naturally take into consideration when we talk about progress. Kitcher seems to recognize this as well. "Pragmatic progress thus has to face up to the difficulties involved in weighing the relative importance of problems" (2015, 479). Kitcher continues: "Sometimes that can be done. But not always—there are genuinely hard cases. Thus arises a new challenge to concepts of progress (particularly pragmatic ones): such concepts must impose a decision about the relative quality of states that can't reasonably be compared." This seems to be a fundamental and important truth about progress embodied in pragmatic meliorism.

Pragmatists like James and Dewey in particular recognize that any claim to progress is to be taken and understood contextually and sometimes with the incommensurability Kitcher calls attention to.[5] Not only does Kitcher's claim that "pragmatic progress consists in overcoming problems in the current state" tell us very little—it is after all a truism—but it also leads one away from both the four defining features of pragmatic progress outlined, as well as Kitcher's insights regarding incommensurability (2015, 478). Kitcher says: "I've suggested that pragmatic progress is a useful notion for pragmatists, one that enables them to avoid the demand to settle hard cases and to eschew teleology" (2015, 480). On the account offered here, this is a misunderstanding of pragmatists' account of progress, and progress generally. Pragmatists' account of progress cannot eschew teleology. And while it may postpone the demand to settle hard cases, its meliorism won't tolerate ignoring the demand to settle, or rather provisionally decide, hard cases for long.

HAS THERE BEEN PROGRESS IN RACE RELATIONS IN THE UNITED STATES?

Our chapter is not primarily about racial injustice in the United States; it is about pragmatist conceptions of progress. Nonetheless, we wish to briefly examine race relations in the United States to put into focus the conceptual issues we raise. Has there been progress in race relations in the United States since legally sanctioned segregation allegedly ended in the 1960s? Pragmatist meliorism, we claim, is characterized by its incremental, provisional, contextual, and conservative nature. Viewed in these terms, the question at hand is remarkably difficult to answer. It is a matter of accounting for incremental changes for the better alongside changes for the worse. It is a matter of judging what is lost as much as what has been gained; and it is a matter of understanding shifting, provisional, conceptions of what race relations ought to be that characterize the period from the 1960s until now. Overall judgment requires odious comparison between one thing of value and another.

A pragmatist answer to the question is likely to be just what one would expect from James and Dewey: "yes" and "no." Both answers are provisional, both represent shifting contexts, and both are resounding. One implication of this, not the most important, is that pragmatists who claim that progress has been or is being made and those who appear to claim the opposite are not necessarily in disagreement. Given that the nature and scope of what they mean by progress in the circumstances differs, the partial or absolute equivocation of the term "progress" as each is using it means that their disagreement as to whether progress is being made is neither as stark or absolute as it may appear. A pragmatist may point to the fact that people of color no longer have to use different bathrooms and that they can vote as signs of progress in race relations and a diminution of racial prejudice. Another pragmatist, or the same pragmatist at a different time, may point to the incarceration rate and gross economic inequities among races (let alone genders), or the killing of people of color by mostly white police officers, as grounds for saying that there has been no progress in race relations. Or they may be thinking of Julian Beck, co-founder of The Living Theatre in New York City, who is supposed to have said "I'm not free until the man who picks my bananas is free."[6]

This ambiguity does not disallow meaningful discussion about which perspective or claim is the more appropriate or correct in the circumstances. Although the contested claims may not fully conflict given the different notions of progress involved, this does not mean they are necessarily incommensurable and that there is no resolvable issue between them. In the case of race relations, a case can and should, we think, be made for claiming that very little, if any, progress has been made in race relations in the United States. This is because the measure that determines overall judgment must be made in context, and in a contemporary context what is most striking in race relations is the level of lifelong security of non-Caucasian Americans. And this has gone backward. Freedom from unjust incarceration; freedom from intrusive judicial oversight and control; freedom from police violence:

these matters have contemporary prominence and tend to push judgment against the idea that real progress has been made in U.S. race relations. The so-called "war on drugs" and the consequent mass incarceration of people of color in the United States undermines the very idea that, in the most important and fundamental areas of contemporary life, race relations in the United States have progressed overall since the 1960s. They may have become much worse.

This judgment about progress in race relations can be contrasted with judgment of progress in understanding the nature and source of varieties of racism. Consider Cornel West's work. Although West's treatment of the notion of progress regarding racial injustice is undoubtedly polemical, political, and rhetorical, it would be a mistake to treat it only in those terms. It is also theoretically, socially, ethically, and religiously grounded. For West, the question of progress in race relations is largely beside the point—an otiose and ill-formed question. This is because it takes one away, theoretically and practically speaking, from the real issues, and from an understanding of just how bad and how central things are regarding racial injustice and inequality.

A reviewer of *Race Matters* says that Cornel West "is consistently effective at pointing out how the intellectual frameworks used by both whites and blacks as well as by liberals and (neo)conservatives impede true progress and understanding" (*Kirkus Reviews*, 1993). Nevertheless, West would be justified in regarding his own work as pointing to progress in at least the limited sense of better understanding the problems of racism.

If asked whether any progress in race relations has been made, West might well deny it. But there are places in which, from a different vantage point, it seems that such a response on West's part is at least not unequivocal. "Cornel West: I think human history for the most part has been a cycle of hatred and revenge and indifference and callousness to the weak and vulnerable. But we're experiencing an awakening. That's what happens in America. Right when America's about to go under, you get a spiritual and moral awakening" (West 2016).

JOHN LACHS: PROGRESS AS DETRIMENTAL TO THE "ACTIVE LIFE" AND MELIORISM

We earlier discussed Lachs's optimism about progress and his view of the connection between material progress and moral progress. In more recent work, his attitude appears to have changed. Lachs is the only pragmatist—a leading one at that—we know of who appears to denigrate the notion of progress and its centrality to pragmatism, claiming that it is antithetical to the active life that pragmatism recommends. However, his notion of progress, along with what he takes it to imply, is peculiar and neither consistent nor consonant with that of pragmatism generally. Lachs says that

> [p]rogress is a kind of motion: It is motion in the direction of some desirable goal. What differentiates progress from mere movement or change is its directionality. Direction, in turn, implies a fixed point of reference: some state of affairs for which we strive, an objective that is deemed worthwhile. . . . Progress, in fact, is a movement, not a product, and its sole importance derives from the importance and the value of its goal. (2014, 307)

Lachs claims that "progress makes no sense at all without the possibility of fulfilment or attainment" (2014, 308). But we have seen this isn't true. Not only isn't it the case in pragmatism, it isn't true of the idea of progress in ordinary discourse either. One can make progress playing the piano with no possibility whatsoever of achieving fulfillment let alone some final goal.

The goals of some forms of progress, some of the most important kinds, will never be reached, and it is widely recognized that their fulfillment is impossible in a practical sense. Progress in playing the piano, to consider the example we introduced earlier, might conceivably aim at a perfection that is simply impossible because it requires powers of control, movement, and concentration that are not within the range of a person. This diminishes neither the importance of the goals toward which the progress aims, nor the progress itself. Indeed, it may make both more important. Social progress—and perhaps even progress in medicine and science—is not like striving for a moon landing. It is directional, but without any "fixed point of reference." There are objectives that are deemed worthwhile, but the idea of progress in these areas does not involve a supposition or belief that goals will be fulfilled or attained in any final sense.

The real objection that Lachs has to pragmatism's emphasis on progress is as follows:

> [A]ny society committed to progress is at once also committed to the future, and whoever is committed to the future ceases to

live in the present. But it is impossible to live in anything but the present. The person who attempts to live in the future ends up by not living at all: his present is saturated with a heavy sense of impermanence, worthlessness, and longing for the morrow. His concentration on what is yet to come blinds him to the satisfactions that are possible now. (2014, 308)

Even as a broad generalization this is false. What does Lachs mean by attempting to "live in the future"? Why would the pursuit of progress inhibit a concern with the present? If anything it would seem to be indicative of concerns with the present. There is no meaningful way of living in the present without a concern for the future—not for long at any rate. In general, it is not those who are concerned with progress that show a lack of regard concerning the present. Nor is such concern with the future indicative of trying to live in the future. It is those who claim, like Lachs, that a concern with the future and progress is indicative of a neglect to live in the present, that fail to live in the present or understand it. To seek a better, more just democracy is to be concerned with both the present and the future. If one sought to point to a predicament of the age, our age, it is certainly not peoples' concern for the future. Rather it is our immersion in the present—what one wants now with little regard for what is to become of oneself or others.

Lachs says: "I will call the belief, fostered by our veneration of progress, that the means and the end must be distinct and separated by time, the Fallacy of Separation. . . . If we are satisfied with what we do and are, it becomes unnecessary to look to the future and hope for improvement and progress" (2014, 308–09). It is difficult to imagine a claim less consonant with a pragmatist worldview. A certain level of satisfaction with the present should never lead one to abandon "look[ing] to the future and hope for improvement and progress." Although in some cases it may, a concern with progress need not and generally does not lead to this alleged fallacy. A (healthy) concern with progress toward future goals is generally integral to how we live in the present insofar as one can choose (or at least make choices as to) how to live. From a pragmatist's point of view, it is always (or often) necessary to look to the future for hope and improvement—though not before one's morning coffee. From a pragmatist's point of view, one should never be "satisfied with what we do and are" except provisionally. If meliorism is as essential to pragmatism as most pragmatists think, then one should always (well, often at any rate) act in the present with one eye toward the future. A denial for the separation thesis (the means and the end must be distinct and separated by time) does not entail the view that it is unnecessary and unwise to look to the future.

If all that Lachs means is that an unhealthy preoccupation with progress and the future can have terrible consequences for how one chooses to live in the present, then this is a truism. We need not be reminded (or do we?) that we can and often do strive for worthless or unworthy (or even worse) things and ends? We need hardly be reminded that those who plan *only* or even primarily for the future, those who are inordinately preoccupied with their futures, are failing to live in the present. That "reminder" is not a part of pragmatism—meliorism is.

PRAGMATISM, MELIORISM, HOPE

Pragmatism is often characterized as America's (i.e., the "United States'") home-grown, philosophical movement. It is regarded as embodying a hopefulness that reflects and is ingredient in the spirit of democracy in the United States—the optimism and spirit of Walt Whitman, Ralph Waldo Emerson, and Henry David Thoreau. And according to some, it also reflects an imaginary, wish-fulling, undeserved, and unjustified self-image. Let's leave this characterization to one side, though it is something pragmatists must address. What then are the relations among pragmatism, meliorism, optimism, and hope?

McGowan says: "James introduces 'meliorism' as 'midway between the two' positions of 'optimism,' which sees progress as inevitable, and 'pessimism,' which sees progress as impossible" (2008, 41 n.10). Others, however, see a much closer connection. Pragmatism's meliorism is not only optimistic, but essentially hopeful as well. Hope is not the same thing as optimism. "Hope" if not "hopefulness" is also compatible with pessimism. Nor is optimism necessarily ingredient in meliorism. Roberto Frega says: "Pragmatism is committed to the thesis that we can create better world[s] and selves. This, according to Colin Koopman [2006], is the central thesis of the pragmatist tradition" (2009, 136). But the idea "that we can create better worlds" is neutral with respect to the question of whether we will do so or are doing so.

Hope and optimism not only differ, they belong in opposite categories. To hope for something is to be open to, attentive toward, and welcoming of both its goodness and its genuine possibility. (Anything noncontradictory is possible in a sense, but what we are calling "genuine possibility" resides in the fact that a thing could be brought about without miracles or bizarre coincidence—without, for example, human nature spontaneously altering its character.) To have hope that a thing will occur is not to expect it to occur. By contrast, to be fully optimistic about a future outcome is to expect it. It is to be closed off—at least to a degree—to the possibility of its not happening. The optimist's default attitude toward a sought-for good is expectation. An optimist expects good things to happen; a person who hopes is attentive to and welcoming of the possibility of good things happening. Optimism can breed complacency (it needn't), but hope tends not to. Much (some?) optimism, like pessimism, is grounded in narcissism rather than a rational assessment of future prospects. Optimism and pessimism are at times the result of elevated, pathological self-esteem: in the first case perhaps because one's self-satisfaction obscures the awful realities, and in the second case because of one's contempt for the world.[7]

This relatively clear contrast between optimism and hope is disrupted by the concept of hopefulness. It is a difficult concept to come to terms with. "Hopefulness" doesn't simply mean "full of hope." It includes a measure of optimism. To be a hopeful person is not just to be a person in possession of hope, it is also to be a person who is at least mildly optimistic. It is to be a person who expects at least some good things to happen. One cannot be a hopeful person and fully pessimistic. (Of course, one can be hopeful and yet pessimistic about certain things and wary of naïve and unbridled optimism.)

Koopman claims that "hopefulness, which in its more philosophically robust moments can be called *meliorism*, combines *pluralism* and *humanism*, two central themes in the pragmatist vision" (2006, 107). If we are right about the meaning of "hopefulness," then this must be interpreted as equating at least mild optimism with meliorism. But it is unclear why Koopman promotes this equation, or that he is justified in so doing. It is hard to see why one might think that in general meliorism and hopefulness imply one another. One can be a meliorist in the pragmatist sense of viewing improvement as incremental, local, full of setbacks and the like, without being particularly hopeful. These are independent attitudes that, like emotion generally, color the way we see, interpret, and feel about the world.[8] Rorty, we think, was not particularly optimistic or hopeful despite at times linking meliorism to hope, and despite his politics (bygone liberalism) having at least the façade of optimism.[9] We say "bygone" because the ideal citizenry he seemed to have in mind was neither neoliberal nor neoconservative—the two types of citizens that have largely displaced Rorty's, Dewey's, and the traditional "liberal's" liberal. Rorty says, "both pragmatism and America are expressions of a hopeful, melioristic, experimental frame of mind" (1994, 24). He seemed to believe that if only the United States could return to its liberal democratic roots (arguably now defunct), all would be better—if not well.[10] There is no clear path between progress conceived as expected achievement, evident in Dewey's politics and less so in Rorty's, and progress conceived as a simple motivating attitude (as in James)—even though it is a theme that runs throughout pragmatism.

Koopman says that "Rorty offers neither bland optimistic reassurance nor pessimistic suspicion, but a unique hopefulness that we can create better selves and worlds without "prophecy and claims to knowledge," but with only "generous hope" that "sustain[s] itself without such reassurances" (2006, 110). But even if Koopman is right about Rorty placing hope at the center of his philosophy, this should not be taken as also claiming he is optimistic or hopeful. As we have argued, possessing a "generous hope" does not equate to being hopeful. To be hopeful is not just to be open to the possibility of progress; it is to expect progress—to a degree and of a limited kind perhaps, but progress nonetheless.

Koopman has better grounds for his claim that in pragmatism—though not only in pragmatism—meliorism combines pluralism and humanism: "James's pluralism and humanism ultimately lead to meliorism" (2006, 108). But even here Koopman's claim is troubling. He says:

> [M]eliorism, holding together pluralism with humanism, is the thesis that we are capable of creating better worlds and selves. Pluralism says that better futures are possible, humanism that possibilities are often enough decided by human energies, and meliorism that better futures are made real by our effort. Meliorism, then, is best seen as humanism and pluralism combined and in confident mood. Melioristic confidence offers a genuine alternative to both pessimism and optimism. These two moods, almost universally proffered by modern philosophers, share a common assumption that progress or decline is inevitable. Meliorism, on the other hand, focuses on what we can do to hasten our progress and mitigate our decline. (Koopman 2006, 107)

The problem here is that the concept of melioristic confidence is equivocal. Does it mean confidence that progress *can* be made or confidence that it *will* be made? As a concept, it seems not to escape the conceptual bounds of pessimism/optimism duopoly. The better term is "hope," distinguished from "hopefulness." James says, "meliorism treats salvation as neither necessary [a radical form of optimism] nor impossible [a radical form of pessimism]. It treats it as a possibility" (1975, 137). This means, we think, treating it as a very real possibility: one toward which we are attentive and open and welcoming. It is a thing we can hope for without being especially hopeful about.

Even if one can defend and pursue meliorism in the current political and social climate, pessimism (both cognitive and affective) may seem to many the most realistic stance regarding long term prospects for substantive progress. While themes of hope and prospects for progress are characteristic of *parts* of pragmatist thought, a case can be made for the claim that James, Dewey (despite his activism), and Rorty combine a quiet pessimism with their meliorism. Hope is what quiets their pessimism. Pragmatism's meliorism is often ambiguous between on the one hand (first and foremost) a view about how progress is made—incrementally, slowly. But on the other hand, notably in Dewey, it may segue into a view about what progress actually is. It is the incremental betterment or improvement of people's living conditions in various material and nonmaterial ways.

Emerson might seem to be an exception to our claim that pragmatists are, at least in some moods, quietly pessimistic. In his essay "Self-Reliance," Emerson says, "if the American artist will study with hope and love the precise thing to be done by him, considering the climate, the soil, the length of the day, the wants of the people, the habit and form of the government, he will create a house in which all these will find themselves fitted" (1842, 150). The opening "if" looms large here, and so even Emerson's statement is compatible with pessimism. In any case, it is unlikely that the conditions outlined in the "if" have even remotely come to pass. Even the most optimistic may acknowledge that they have not. Emerson's Americanism or nationalism is also a cause for concern if it is read as a kind of American "exceptionalism." Some (not all) other nations and people want the kinds of freedoms, equality of opportunity, and well-being that the United States claims, disingenuously perhaps, to want for its own.

Though particular pragmatists may hold one view or the other, the claim that progress is or is not being made is no part of pragmatism's meliorism. A great deal of pragmatist writing suggests that they are unsure and ambivalent—sometimes in the same work, as to whether progress is being made—though not about what would constitute progress. There are times, for example, where James and Dewey lean first one way and then the other. In James's writing in particular (e.g. *Pragmatism*) the ambivalence is a hallmark.

Gale says of James:

> At the root of the clash between his Promethean and mystical self is James's ambiguous attitude toward evil, his both wanting and not wanting to believe that we have absolute assurance that we are safe because all evils are only illusory or ultimately conquered. When James was in his healthy Promethean frame of mind he tingled all over at the thought that we are engaged in a Texas Death Match with evil, without any assurance of eventual victory, only the possibility of victory. This possibility forms the basis of his religion of meliorism. But there is a morbid side to James's nature, a really morbid side, that "can't get no satisfaction" from the sort of religion that his Promethean pragmatism legitimates. In order to "help him make it through the night" he needs a mystically based religion, which gives him a sense of absolute safety and peace that comes through union with an encompassing spiritual reality. (Gale 1999, 16)[11]

On Gale's account, James was of (at least) two minds about many things and so it would be a mistake to claim either that he was optimistic or pessimistic, hopeful or unhopeful.[12] Rather, James alternated between the two throughout his life—and, at times, moment to moment.

Aside from the idea that progress involves the incremental improvement of people's living conditions (and so the improvement of people), there is relatively little said in pragmatist writings about just what progress is, and whether any progress is being made. An answer to this latter question presupposes an answer to the prior one. If the contextualist or perspectival account of "progress" given above is correct (i.e., "it all depends . . ."), then there are good grounds for pragmatism's ambivalence concerning whether progress is being made. When contextualized in one way, it might be claimed that progress is being made; and yet in some other and perhaps broader context, it can be claimed without contradiction that there has been no progress. As we argued in the case of U.S. race relations, the question of whether progress has been made since the 1960s requires a difficult judgment of context. In one context—the one that is urgent to us today—progress has proved elusive. In others, progress is apparent. The question of progress turns on our capacity to judge the appropriate context from which to make an overall judgment. We have suggested that that context is just what motivates contemporary anxiety about race relations in the United States: freedom from the threat of incarceration, police violence, and all that follows from a bogus war on drugs.

NOTES

1. Koopman argues for a close connection between pragmatist meliorism and the concept of truth. As Cliff Stagoll puts it: "truth is (lots of different kinds of) agreement between a belief or a proposition on the one hand and the world as we conceive of it on the other, but commitment to such agreement is always in the cause of action, or progress." It is "in the cause of action, or progress" that makes it pragmatism (pers. comm.).

2. James writes that "design, free-will, the absolute mind, spirit instead of matter, have for their sole meaning a better promise as to this world's outcome. Be they false or be they true, the meaning of them is this meliorism" (1975, 63).

3. Lachs says: "To demand decency even, or especially, from the high and mighty is a stunning breakthrough in morality. These remarkable developments came about as a result of growth of concern for human beings simply because they are human and not on account of their being of the same race or religion or nationality as we are. . . . One can readily suppose that there have been pockets of caring throughout human history, but nothing ever existed that comes even close to the magnitude, the reach, and the institutional support of benevolence today. . . . [O]n the whole, humans today are not only better off but also better than previous generations. And by 'better' I mean not only that we do good things more often, but also that we are, on the whole, morally more admirable people" (2001, 180, 182).

4. Our thanks to Cliff Stagoll for these points.

5. Kitcher writes: "Pragmatists like Dewey, keenly interested in social progress, aren't interested in being able to compare any two societies, asking whether (say) the twentieth century USA has made progress over fifth century Athens. Their primary concern is with specific transitions they envisage as possible: would we make social progress by doubling the minimum wage (for example)?" (479).

6. We are unable to find the source of the quotation.

7. Our thanks to Tamas Pataki.

8. Wollheim describes the function of emotion—what emotion does, as well as (broadly) how it does it: "The role of emotion is to provide the . . . person—with an orientation, or an attitude to the world. If belief maps the world,

and desire targets it, emotion tints or colours it: it enlivens it or darkens it, as the case may be" (15).

9. See Koopman (113 n. 6): "Recent attempts to address Rorty's meliorism are usually circuitous and uncomfortable with taking hope seriously; cf. Festenstein; Marshall; Peters; and Talisse."

10. Cliff Stagoll remarks: Rorty's "is a politics of hope in a strictly pragmatist sense: 'things can just be better for people if we only . . . returned to traditional progressive politics'" (pers. comm.). Is there a politics of hope in a strictly pragmatist sense? Is that part of pragmatism?

11. Gale: "For a good account of James's rejection of meliorism, see John Smith's splendid introduction to *VRE*, especially pp. xxvi, xxx, and xxlv" (18 n.12).

12. Gale says: "The clashes between James's Promethean and mystical selves, therefore, cannot be explained away as diachronic ones, since he was a highly divided self throughout his life. The clashes, rather, are synchronic. At every moment in his career James was of several minds about everything, and that is why his philosophical writings are like a philosophical wheel of fortune. Whatever doctrine it stopped on and temporarily illuminated reaped a rich payoff, for every one of his many philosophies was espoused with incredible brilliance and passion. Whether James would defend pragmatism or mysticism on any given day depended on his mood, whether he was in a healthy- or a sick-minded one" (258).

REFERENCES

Barnes, Julian. *Flaubert's Parrot*. London: Vintage, 2009.

Emerson, Ralph Waldo. *The Essential Writings of Ralph Waldo Emerson*, edited by Brooks Atkinson. New York: Modern Library (1841/1844) 2000.

Festenstein, Matthew. "Pragmatism, Social Democracy, and Political Argument." In *Richard Rorty: Critical Dialogues*, edited by Matthew Festenstein and Simon Thompson. Cambridge: Polity, 2001.

Frega, Roberto. Review of *Pragmatism as Transition: Historicity and Hope in James, Dewey, and Rorty*, by Colin Koopman. *European Journal of Pragmatism and American Philosophy* 1, no. 1 (2009): 135–41.

Gale, Richard M. *The Divided Self of William James*. Cambridge: Cambridge University Press, 1999.

Geertz, Clifford. "Ethos, World View, and the Analysis of Sacred Symbols." In *Interpretation of Cultures: Selected Essays*, 126–41. New York: Basic Books, 1973.

James, William. *Pragmatism*. Vol. 1 of *The Works of William James*, edited by Fredson Bowers, and Ignas K. Skrupskelis. Introduction by H. S. Thayer. Cambridge, MA: Harvard University Press. [1907] 1975.

Kirkus Reviews, review of *Race Matters*, by Cornel West, February 15, 1993. www.kirkusreviews.com/book-reviews/cornel-west/race-matters

Kitcher, Philip. "Pragmatism and Progress." *Transactions of the Charles S. Peirce Society* 51, no. 4 (2015.): 475–94.

Koopman, Colin. "Pragmatism as a Philosophy of Hope: Emerson, James, Dewey, Rorty." *Journal of Speculative Philosophy* 20, no. 2 (2006): 106–16.

Lachs, John. "To Have and to Be." In *Freedom and Limits*, edited by Patrick Shade. New York: Fordham University Press, 2014.

———. "Both Better Off and Better: Moral Progress amid Continuing Carnage." *Journal of Speculative Philosophy* 15, no. 3 (2001): 173–83.

Latour, Bruno. *Politics of Nature: How to Bring the Sciences into Democracy*. Cambridge: Harvard University Press, 2004.

Marshall, James D. "On What We May Hope: Rorty on Dewey and Foucault." In *Richard Rorty: Education, Philosophy, and Politics*, edited by Michael A. Peters and Paulo Ghiraldelli Jr. Lanham, MD: Rowman and Littlefield, 2001.

McGowan, John. "The Possibility of Progress: A Pragmatist Account." *The Good Society* 17, no. 1 (2008): 33–42.

Peters, Michael A. "Achieving America: Postmodernism and Rorty's Critique of the Cultural Left." In *Richard Rorty: Education, Philosophy, and Politics*, edited by Michael A. Peters and Paulo Ghiraldelli Jr. Lanham, MD: Rowman and Littlefield, 2001.

Read, Rupert. "Wittgenstein and the Illusion of 'Progress': On Real Politics and Real Philosophy in a World of Technocracy." *Royal Institute of Philosophy Supplement* 78 (2016): 265–84.

Rorty, Richard. *Truth and Progress: Philosophical Papers*, Vol. 3. Cambridge: Cambridge University Press, 1998.

———. "Hope in Place of Knowledge: A Version of Pragmatism." In *Philosophy and Social Hope*, edited by Richard Rorty. New York: Penguin. [1994] 1999.

———. *Philosophy and Social Hope*. New York: Penguin, 1999.

Russell, Bertrand. *A History of Western Philosophy*. London: George Allen and Unwin, 1946.

Sorrell, Kory. "Pragmatism and Moral Progress: John Dewey's Theory of Social Inquiry." *Philosophy and Social Criticism* 39, no. 8 (2013): 809–24.

Talisse, Robert B. "A Pragmatist Critique of Richard Rorty's Hopeless Politics." *Southern Journal of Philosophy* 39, no. 4 (2001): 611–26.

Taylor, Paul W. *Principles of Ethics: An Introduction*. Encino: Dickerson, 1975.

Uffelman, Mark. "Jamesian Self-Cultivation: Meliorism in the Double-Barrelled Stream of Experience." Paper presented at the 41st Annual Meeting of the Society for the Advancement of American Philosophy, Denver, CO, 2014.

West, Cornel. *Race Matters*. Boston: Beacon Press, 1993.

———. "Reviving a Grand Tradition of 'Black Prophetic Fire,'" National Public Radio, November 1, 2014. www.npr.org/2014/11/01/360452483/reviving-a-grand-tradition-of-black-prophetic-fire

———. "Cornel West on State of Race in the US: 'We're in Bad Shape,'" interview by James Brown, *60 Minutes*, CBS, March 20, 2016. www.cbsnews.com/news/60-minutes-cornel-west-on-race-in-the-u-s

Wollheim, Richard. *On the Emotions. The Ernst Cassirer Lectures, 1991*. New Haven, CT: Yale University Press, 1999.

PART 2

THEORY: CLEARING THE WAY

CHAPTER 6

APPLYING JAMESIAN PRAGMATISM TO MORAL LIFE
Against "Applied Ethics"

SAMI PIHLSTRÖM

> As [Peter] Winch says, morality would be a strange guide around obstacles. But for morality there would be no obstacles. Means and ends come under a common moral scrutiny. Moral advice may be given, but only when morality already is constitutive of what faces one. It is constitutive of the accounts we give of the situations and actions facing us.
>
> —D. Z. Phillips, "Ethics, Faith and 'What Can Be Said'" (2001, 352)

INTRODUCTION

"Applied ethics" is often regarded as a welcome practical concretization of ethical inquiry, bringing moral philosophy down to earth from abstract theorization (both metaethical and normative theorization) and seeking to illuminate genuine moral problems and dilemmas we encounter in our personal, social, and professional lives. It might seem that William James's pragmatism encourages us to develop something like applied ethics in this sense, that is, pragmatic applications of ethical ideas and theories in different areas of concrete moral life, or perhaps to develop "applied philosophy" in a broader sense extending beyond ethics. According to such a picture, philosophers—particularly moral philosophers—could offer others moral guidance, help them to solve moral problems. James, after all, wants philosophy to be relevant to human life, individual and social, and most pragmatists have followed him (and the other classical pragmatists, especially John Dewey) in this regard.

This impression of James's pragmatism as a defense of applied philosophy and applied ethics might seem to be supported by the well-known way in which he characterizes the core principle of his pragmatism, the pragmatic method (which he originally derived from his friend Charles Peirce, who formulated the principle in the 1870s, though James was the first to use the term "pragmatism" in print in 1898):

> To attain perfect clearness in our thoughts of an object . . . we need only consider what conceivable effects of a practical kind the object may involve—what sensations we are to expect from it, and what reactions we must prepare. Our conception of these effects, whether immediate or remote, is then for us the whole of our conception of the object, so far as that conception has positive significance at all. (James 1975, 29)

When James says that the importance of this method, "Peirce's principle," can be "take[n] in" by getting accustomed to "applying it to concrete cases" (ibid.), and when he opens the third lecture of *Pragmatism* on "some metaphysical problems pragmatically considered" by claiming to illustrate the pragmatic method through "its application to particular problems" (ibid., 45), he does seem to be advancing something like a pragmatic conception of applied philosophy. However, it can be argued that the true applications of the pragmatic method—and hence the true applications of Jamesian pragmatism to moral life—are fundamentally different from what is usually meant by applied philosophy. I will, more strongly, try to show that they are actually *opposed to* the basic idea (or at least the received view) of applied ethics, insofar as the latter presupposes a sharp distinction between moral theories on the one side and their practical applications on the other. Rather than developing anything like applied ethics (or, more broadly, applied philosophy) in this sense, the Jamesian pragmatist ought to start from the rejection of the theory versus practice dichotomy itself, a dichotomy without which the very idea of applied ethics makes little sense. Ethical theorization, in a properly Jamesian pragmatism, is practical all the way down, and practice informs even our most abstract theories—or should do so, at least. Thus, for example, the applications of the pragmatic method are in fact ways of considering traditional metaphysical disputes about, for example, substance, determinism and free will, theism, or monism and pluralism (see ibid., Lectures III and IV); what it means to explore these issues by means of applying the pragmatic method is to be thoroughly practically concerned with one's being in the world in general, within human practices that make these and other issues significant to us.

Arguing along these lines, I will not only show how the pragmatic method urges us to explore all theoretical concepts in relation to ethics but will also suggest toward the end of the chapter that Jamesian moral philosophy is comparable to the loose tradition known as Wittgensteinian moral philosophy (represented by thinkers such as Rush Rhees, Peter Winch, D. Z. Phillips, and Raimond Gaita), roughly analogously to the way in which Jamesian pragmatist philosophy of religion can be regarded as parallel to such thinkers' Wittgensteinian-inspired views in the philosophy of religion (cf. Pihlström 2013). Moreover, no foundational distinctions between metaethics, normative ethics, and applied ethics can therefore be maintained in Jamesian pragmatism. Very simply, pragmatist ethics need not be, and need not even accommodate, applied ethics in its conventional sense.[1]

WHAT IS APPLIED ETHICS (AND APPLIED PHILOSOPHY)?

Let me first introduce the notion of applied ethics—in the context of the broader notion of applied philosophy—and offer some tentative critical remarks.[2] When considering what "applied philosophy" is, we may first just look around in university libraries. There are learned journals dedicated to applied philosophy, such as the *Journal of Applied Philosophy* and the *International Journal of Applied Philosophy*. In addition, an ever-increasing number of more specialized journals focus on relatively new academic fields such as bioethics, medical ethics, environmental ethics, business ethics, and many others. Anthologies in which philosophers apply their doctrines and arguments to crucial concrete issues have also been published (e.g., Almond and Hill 1991). Conferences are continuously organized in such fields of inquiry. The kind of articles that have appeared in these journals and collections over the past few decades provide us with paradigmatic examples of what might be called the *received view* of applied philosophy. This view may be changing, of course; there is now a growing body of very interesting "applied" and interdisciplinary work enhancing our philosophical understanding of grand challenges such as (say) migration, the global climate change, and social transformations related to digitalization. Nothing in what I will say in this chapter is intended to dismiss the importance of that kind of applied philosophy. Nevertheless, I do believe that we can employ Jamesian resources in a criticism of the rather thin received view of applied ethics and applied philosophy in such a way that this critique has relevance to a vitally needed assessment of more sophisticated contributions to these fields, too. My critical remarks will thus primarily focus on the received view.

Indeed, some philosophers remain puzzled about the very existence of applied philosophy as an area of research. For example, already three decades ago John Passmore (1988) worried about the lack of rigor in much of what is (or was then) called "applied philosophy," urging that applied philosophy properly so called should not be just "lay sermonizing." On the other hand, a number of writers have questioned the view—arguably a typical dogma among traditional analytic philosophers—that philosophy should be practically useless, as it is preoccupied with abstract problems of conceptual clarification. They remind us that philosophy ought to be reconnected with the practical problems of human life and that philosophers' work should not be detached from urgent issues of wider social concern.[3]

In a way, some lack of clarity regarding the status of applied philosophy and applied ethics should be welcomed, because philosophy should continuously be a problem for itself, and philosophers, moral philosophers in particular, ought to worry about their tasks, possibilities, and cultural role. If some contemporary thinkers claim to be doing "applied philosophy," it is worthwhile for others to investigate what their intellectual activity actually amounts to. Even if we find the contemporary methods and results of applied philosophy, especially applied ethics, unclear or otherwise problematic, it by no means follows that the investigations taking place under the rubric of applied philosophy should be abandoned; on the contrary, they should be seen as attempts to explore some inescapable problems of humankind—or what Dewey (1946) called "problems of men." Such attempts should, of course, be encouraged. What we may be skeptical about, however, is the possibility of literally "applying" a philosophical theory to some practical, concrete subject-matter drawn from ordinary human life. I will suggest that the difficulties surrounding applied philosophy lie in the non-pragmatic dichotomy between theory and practice that most applied philosophers still assume.

The problem concerning the status of applied philosophy cannot be solved by simply listing all instances of "philosophy of X," such as philosophy of art, philosophy of science, philosophy of religion, philosophy of medicine, philosophy of sport, and so on (or some subareas of these focusing on applied ethics). Some of these realms of philosophical reflection do not count as applied philosophy simply because they constitute much of what is known as "philosophy." Although applied philosophy, in the form in which we know it today, is perhaps not a perennial area of philosophical reflection, there is something like a traditional concept of applied philosophy, that is, the straightforward view, drawn from Aristotle's and Kant's distinctions between theoretical and practical reason and, correspondingly, theoretical and practical philosophy, according to which applied philosophy (as well as, more specifically, applied ethics) amounts to an application of theoria to praxis. Accordingly, we first have a (usually highly abstract) philosophical or ethical "theory," which in itself, as inherently nonapplied, says nothing directly about any practical questions, and then we "apply" it to such questions, seeking to find out what we should think about them in the light of that theory (and, more concretely, how we should morally act after having made our decision about how to think). Philosophical (ethical) theory, or "pure" philosophy, is thus applied to certain concrete problem situations of human life, which almost always contain an irreducibly ethical dimension. This totality of theory and practice, united by the activity of application, is then called applied philosophy. The applier of philosophy must be well informed not only about the philosophical (ethical) theory they wish to apply, but also about the practical problems they are interested in settling by means of that theory.

It seems to me that the following standard construal of applied philosophy well agrees with my loose characterization of the concept:

> [T]here is nothing unique about [the] symbiotic relationship between theory and practice, for most disciplines, from physics to psychology, are termed "applied" when they attempt to use their distinctive body of theory to solve practical problems. It is in this way that "applied philosophy" is already widely understood as the name for philosophical engagement with the many issues of practical life that hinge upon ethical considerations, and are capable of being illuminated by deeper conceptual understanding and by critical analysis of the arguments they involve. (Almond and Hill 1991, 1)

Alternatively, taking the talk about "critical analysis" seriously, we may say that what applied philosophers "apply" is the "philosophical method" they have learned and know how to use (whatever that is), instead of applying any specific philosophical doctrines or theories (Passmore 1988, 682). I do not want to lay too much weight on this distinction, however, since I am not sure whether there is any specifically philosophical methodology (apart from reasonable careful argumentation and analysis) as distinguished from the views and ideas philosophers arrive at by employing their various methods of reflection. Instead, methods seem to be "theory-dependent" or "theory-laden" both in science and in philosophy. For example, the "method" of investigation Kant uses in the *Critique of Pure Reason* (i.e., transcendental reflection) is hardly separable from the overall theoretical conception of human reason discussed in that work; similarly, Charles Peirce's and William James's pragmatic method is at home in the context of their substantial views on the inherent links between conceptualization, belief, and purposive human action. Moreover, philosophical methods are as much objects of philosophical or metaphilosophical dispute as philosophical doctrines or theories (the conclusions arrived at through the use of such methods) themselves. This obviously also applies to the methods and theories within ethics, no matter whether they are consequentialist, deontological, virtue-theoretical, or (in metaethics) conceptual-analytic.

It must be admitted that the process of application in actual cases of applied philosophy may be far more complex than I have described. It has been argued, for example, that applied philosophy should not be conceived as a merely "derivative" activity, that is, as derived from pure or theoretical philosophy, since the application may alter the principles or theories that are applied. Those principles or theories may be reevaluated, specified, challenged, or otherwise considered during the course of application. Therefore, applied philosophy cannot be fruitfully compared to, say, applied mathematics, in which, of course, the mathematical theories themselves, when applied, remain unchanged (see Kopelman 1990). Hence, my critical comments on applied ethics and applied philosophy presupposing a theory-practice structure should be taken only tentatively. We should examine in more detail why (Jamesian) pragmatism, properly understood, is not a form of applied ethics or applied philosophy, even though it might seem to be. In pragmatist philosophy, and especially in pragmatist ethics—particularly from the Jamesian perspective—it is the potential "application" to human life that constitutes the theory, and therefore it makes little sense to speak of any practical applications of (allegedly inherently nonpractical) theories.

DECONSTRUCTING THE THEORY-VERSUS-PRACTICE DICHOTOMY

What I am suggesting, therefore, is that we follow James in deconstructing the very dichotomy between theory and practice that needs to be assumed if one wants to make sense of applied ethics as an application of a moral theory that is, as such, independent of the practical problems it can be applied to. Why, we may ask, do we even need the "pure" versus "applied" dichotomy in philosophy (or especially in ethics)? Does it serve any pragmatic function? If human life or existence as such already is the key problem of philosophical reflection, then we do not, I am inclined to think (and inclined to see James as having thought), need it at all. The "practical" problems of our life and practices are then always already at the center of serious philosophical work. This appears to be a metaphilosophical perspective common to the traditions of, for example, existentialism and pragmatism, which have in different, though perhaps overlapping, ways been preoccupied with the human significance of philosophical positions and arguments.

For pragmatists, theory and practice have always been intrinsically connected. Here pragmatism merely systematizes something already present in ancient Greek conceptions of philosophy, namely, that philosophical problems naturally arise from our natural human life in the natural world we live in. Pragmatism can be seen as a relatively recent attempt to philosophize in ways that are always already relevant to problems of life, just like the ancient philosophical schools of, say, Stoicism, Epicureanism, and skepticism were. Instead of applying some initially "nonapplied" philosophy—philosophical theories or methods, such as ethical theories—to (moral) practice, pragmatists are simply philosophers inevitably operating within human practices. They have not even made any strict theory versus practice distinction in the first place, but are willing to keep all such distinctions always contextualized, that is, relativized to the relevant practices within which they may (in Jamesian terms) have some "cash value." In Deweyan terms, philosophical problems are humanly significant problems, "problems of men," if they are so much as problems worth considering at all. Thus, we can perhaps say that Dewey, with all his social and educational concerns, was an "applied philosopher" (in a pragmatic sense of the term, in which no fundamental distinction between "pure" philosophy and applied philosophy is made). But I think it is better to avoid this vocabulary in describing even Dewey's work—let alone James's.

This is not at all to say that our human problems—the Deweyan problems of men, the kind of "weltanschaulichen" issues that James considered in his writings on religion, or the kind of personally agonizing ethical issues that Wittgensteinian moral thinkers deal with—will necessarily have to be popular or easily understandable. They may still be, so to speak, also "theoretically" difficult problems. Their adequate treatment may require deep theoretical understanding of philosophical and other scholarly traditions, and without such understanding our dealings with them may remain superficial. The idea that anyone could, without proper education, thoroughly understand the "problems of men" they share with their fellow human beings is by no means a part of my Jamesian (or Deweyan) pragmatism. On the contrary, philosophy, for these pragmatists, is a lifelong process of (self-)education.

What the pragmatist questions is the presupposition that we could "first" have a theory, developed quite independently of its applications to any concrete issues, which we could then, "secondly," apply. Even the most abstract ethical theories are based upon, and continuous with, natural human life and its practices structured by different natural needs and practical concerns, embedded in a naturally developing environment. The "application" of philosophy to life is there right from the beginning. To be a philosopher is to be a human being concretely engaged in the "problematic situations" of life. Such situations lead us to philosophical and ethical reflection instead of being mere "test cases" to which theories are applied after such reflections. Pragmatism, then, makes philosophizing practically relevant in human affairs without assuming any artificial theory-application model—and without stopping the vitally important normative debate over the criteria of practical relevance.

However, considerations of the practical relevance of theoretical standpoints often easily move onto a metatheoretical level—even if we wish to follow pragmatism in casting doubt on the theory versus practice dichotomy itself. The danger that our metatheoretical reflections on the relevance of our theoretical reflections to some practical problems (as well as on the entanglement of theory and practice that pragmatism emphasizes) might be even more irrelevant than the theoretical reflections themselves must always, continuously, be faced. The pragmatist philosopher who feels that it is their duty to say something about the "practical," "applied," issues must repeatedly ask the question of whether what they are doing is the right thing to do. Mightn't some "real" social or political action be more advisable for such a thinker than philosophizing, let alone academic "applied philosophy"—not to mention meta-level discussions of what applied philosophy is? The important, though difficult, concern here is to keep our abstractly philosophical and more concretely social or political aspirations (or other "applications") in some balance.

Being prepared to self-critically face the task of exploring humanly relevant yet theoretically challenging and philosophically profound problems, we may "look to a time when philosophy is not 'applied,' but rather grows naturally out of our encounters with the world, a time when we all think philosophically—that is to say, critically—about our individual and species conditions" and ask not simply whether philosophy should be "applied" or not but "why we find this question arising at all" (Warren 1992, 18). It might seem that such a time may be far away and may never come, and that the hope expressed here is vague and insecure. However, such a prospect may turn out to possess some pragmatic cash value, after all. The only way we can "apply" (moral) philosophy here and now is to insist on the fundamental seriousness of the ethical, cautioning against such "applications" that might compromise this seriousness by distorting our understanding of what it is to be ethically committed in the first place. It is right here that we should more explicitly turn to James's pragmatism (and some recent commentators' readings of him), because in my view James's approach to ethics offers us precisely this perspective on ethical seriousness that we may find lacking in too straightforward attempts to "apply" ethical theories to practice. In James's pragmatism, moreover, we find a picture of ethics that rejects the naïve idea that ethical thinkers should, or even could, offer theory-based guidance to people struggling with their practical problems of life.

MONISM VERSUS PLURALISM— AND THE ETHICAL RELEVANCE OF PHILOSOPHY

In addition to exposing the idea of applied philosophy (or applied ethics) to a Jamesian pragmatist critique, I now want to offer a brief Jamesian diagnosis of what actually goes wrong in applied ethics (and applied philosophy more generally). Let me propose such a diagnosis in terms of James's well-known contrast between monism and pluralism (see again James 1975, Lecture IV). What I want to argue is that applied ethics (and applied philosophy generally) is monistic, while James's pragmatism in a considerably richer way incorporates the plurality of ways in which philosophy can be, or can be made, practically relevant. There is also a plurality of ways in which philosophy can be ethically (and socially or politically) relevant without being "applied." In brief, the very idea of "application" assumes a one-directedness that can only be based on a monistic conception of the nature of philosophy.

In order to appreciate these points, let us take a look at James's ethical ideas. Although James wrote little directly on ethics, scholars have increasingly recognized that a central current of his work is ethical. The 1891 essay "The Moral Philosopher and the Moral Life" (James 1979, 141–62) is his only article explicitly dealing with ethics; yet, ethical considerations are built into his pragmatism, especially its leading idea that theories and worldviews should be examined in terms of their practical relevance. Indeed, they are built into the pragmatic method itself (see Pihlström 2009). If one argues that ethics is the core of James's thought, one must recognize that it is found in no single place in his corpus, no book specifically on ethics; it is, rather, to be found everywhere in what he wrote, at least implicitly. In a diary entry in 1870, James asked, "Shall I *frankly* throw the moral business overboard, as one unsuited to my innate aptitudes, or shall I follow it, and it alone, making everything else stuff for it?" (cited in Franzese 2008, 49). Apparently, he did the latter—or hoped to. James was tormented by the problem of ethical nihilism, fearing that the seriousness of our moral perspective and agency might be illusory.

James's key principle, the pragmatic method, was, for James, not only a "method of making our ideas clear," as it primarily was for Peirce, but (arguably) a method of making our ideas *ethically* clear—of tracing out the conceivable ethical implications at the core of our concepts and conceptions, even the most abstractly theoretical ones. Ethics, we may say, is in this sense the center of James's pragmatism. The purpose of his pragmatic method is to "distill" the ethical kernel of (apparently nonethical) issues and ideas, by means of pragmatic reflection that is itself deeply moral.

The profoundly ethical character of pragmatism generally has also been noted in recent secondary literature. For example, Trygve Throntveit treats James's "entire corpus as a lifelong attempt to describe a universe in which freedom, and thus morality, is possible" (2014, 3). Pragmatism as such, he plausibly maintains, was for James "a tool in the quest to imbue human life . . . with moral significance" (ibid., 11). Sergio Franzese argues, in turn, that even in "The Moral Philosopher and the Moral Life" James defends no particular moral theory but critically examines the project of theorizing about morality. James is a "philosophical anthropologist" instead of a moral philosopher narrowly conceived (let alone an applied ethicist). Seeking to correct the misunderstanding that James defends just another ethical theory, Franzese maintains that the 1891 essay is "not the sketch of a system of moral philosophy, but . . . a critical analysis of the conditions of possibility of moral philosophy," an inquiry into "the constitutive attitudes and activity of moral philosophers" (Franzese 2008, 17, 27). James, however, is not only a philosophical anthropologist but engages in what may (following Kant) be called the *metaphysics of morality*. He *seems* to propose a subjectivist theory basing moral obligation in individual interests, but he attacks *any* "totalizing ethical system," because such systems destroy individuals' "real possibilities" (ibid., 26). Totalizing systems would be monistic in the harmful sense criticized pragmatically by James (1975, Lecture IV); no single principle can ground actual moral life in its perspectival variety. It is along these lines that James finds moral philosophy possible "only as a critical science which takes each moral ideal as an hypothesis and each moral choice as an experiment" (Franzese 2008, 40).

Similarly, Sarin Marchetti (2015) suggests, with James, that we should drop the foundationalist system-building of traditional moral philosophy and engage in continuous critical transformative self-reflection focusing on the moral practices we engage in and the moral problems we personally encounter. Thus, not only is there no utilitarian or consequentialist moral theory in James, there is no moral theory at all. Rather, James argues against the very project of constructing such a systematic theory and in favor of something like therapeutic "self-cultivation" (ibid., 22)—thus joining a classical conception of ethical thought that can be traced back to antiquity. The goal of Jamesian philosophy in general is "personal conversion" rather than any theoretical system (ibid., 26); here James can be compared to thinkers like Ralph Waldo Emerson and Ludwig Wittgenstein. All of this, needless to say, is immediately relevant to the prospects of applied ethics, because James, according to these commentators (with whom I largely agree) denies the very idea that there could be such a thing as a moral theory independently of our moral concern of self-reflection and self-cultivation, a theory that could then be perhaps "applied" to such practical projects of cultivation. The pragmatic method itself, I would like to suggest, is (pragmatically) alive only in its applications to "concrete cases," in the service into which we put it when approaching metaphysical and other problems along its lines.

In "The Moral Philosopher," James argues that "there is no such thing possible as an ethical philosophy dogmatically made up in advance" and that "there can be no final truth in ethics . . . until the last man has had his experience and had his say" (1979, 141). This is an expression of what we may call metaethical fallibilism, but it is more: a recognition of the limitations of any theory that would "know better" than individuals. The flaw of a normative ethical theory such as utilitarianism (which James has occasionally been taken to subscribe to), then, is *not* that the consequences of actions are unimportant but that it *is* a moral theory, sacrificing the concrete richness of ethical perspectives to a universal—monistic—principle. Accordingly, a profound *tolerance* of individuals' diverging perspectives, and the urge to actively recognize them, connected with his general pluralism and individualism, plays a key role in James's moral vision.[4]

Even more importantly, one can hardly adequately understand James's ethical perspective without taking seriously his reflections on evil and suffering.[5] James's distinctive "ethics of energy" is a pursuit in which the fight against evil is a key to ethically acceptable human existence. As our fight against evil is continuous, there are no morally indifferent actions at all. Energy, freedom, and spirituality, constituting "the core of the human moral dimension and the fringe of moral action," are integrated (Franzese 2008, 8). This is also where James's interest in religious experience becomes central: the spiritual pursuit of ideals may require both human and divine activity for the "moral salvation" of the world.

Only relatively few scholars have taken the notion of evil in James seriously. In contrast to, say, Josiah Royce's absolute pragmatism, the evil in human experience that James emphasized is not a theoretical metaphysical construct but "lived"—real and concrete. This is clear, for instance, in the brief treatment of evil in Lecture I of *Pragmatism* (cf. Kivistö and Pihlström 2016, ch. 5). Far from being mere imperfection or appearance, the experience of evil "presents us with an access to the reality, ultimate and insuperable, of sorrow," which in turn is necessary for constructing "ideal realities" (Franzese 2008, 21). James's own "philosophical temperament" (to use the vocabulary he introduces in James 1975, Lecture I) was in an important sense tragic and melancholic. The experience of evil is necessary as a condition for the possibility of moral life. Evil is not just ethically but also metaphysically central, "lead[ing] ontology back to anthropology, making human experience the fundamental ontological dimension grounding all ethical demands and efforts toward the construction of a moral order in the world" (Franzese 2008, 21). However, up to now even some of the most perceptive scholars emphasizing the thoroughly ethical nature of James's pragmatism, and his philosophy in general (e.g., Marchetti 2015), have somewhat one-sidedly neglected the central role played by the problem of evil and suffering in James as a kind of frame for the entire development of the pragmatic method.

Now, what exactly does it mean, for James, to evaluate our ideas from an ethical perspective? The pragmatic method remains hopelessly vague if it simply encourages us to look for the practical meaning of, say, metaphysical (and religious/theological) views in their potential ethical impact, unless we have some idea about how to go on investigating that impact. Here, I believe, we should take the further step of interpreting the pragmatic method as a method of taking seriously what James in "The Moral Philosopher and the Moral Life" calls the "cries of the wounded" in relation to the various metaphysical views or theories that could be proposed regarding these matters at issue. It is a method that looks into the possible futures of the world in which we live, focusing on what the different metaphysical views "promise" and on whether they can function as philosophies of hope, especially from the point of view of the "wounded," the sufferers or the victims of evil. This is a profoundly ethical undertaking—but far from any simple-minded applied ethics. Instead of maintaining that our theoretical or metaphysical problems ought to be solved first—or that we could simply get rid of them—in order to turn to ethical problems later, or in order to just apply a practice-independent theory to the practical ethical realm, James is suggesting that we should begin our most theoretical, even metaphysical, inquiries from the ethical examination of the practical relevance of the rival theoretical ideas that have been or can be proposed, and that this ethical examination can take place only if we focus on how "the wounded" would respond to this or that world-picture being true.

This discussion of what I call the ethical grounds of metaphysics (and, more generally, the metaphysics–ethics entanglement) in James's *Pragmatism* (cf. Pihlström 2009, 2013) ought to be placed in a context of a more generally ethically oriented reflection on issues of fundamental human importance, especially evil and death. As both the opening and the closing of *Pragmatism* indicate, James is deeply conscious of the significance of the problem of evil, and he is strongly opposed to any philosophical and theological attempts (e.g., theodicies) to explain evil away or to theoretically justify its existence (see James 1975, Lectures I and VIII; cf. again Kivistö and Pihlström 2016, ch. 5). This is another example of Jamesian pragmatist metaphysics ultimately grounded in ethics. The metaphysical controversy between monism and pluralism, in particular, almost immediately invokes the problem of evil. James offers an ethical argument against monism and in favor of pluralism by pointing out that the former, unlike the latter, leads to an irresolvable theodicy problem. Moreover, the problem of evil is not merely an example by means of which we may illustrate the Jamesian pragmatic method. Much more importantly, it offers a frame for the entire project of James's pragmatism. The problem of evil provides an ethical motivation for exploring, pragmatically, theoretical issues, including metaphysical and theological ones, which ultimately need to be linked with ethics.⁶

James's pragmatism does not contain any theory of ethics, as we saw, and *a fortiori* it does not contain any application of an ethical theory to practice. But James does maintain that philosophical issues, whenever they are pragmatically investigated, can only be adequately explored in an irreducibly ethical context. For James, unlike the more scientifically (and politically) progressivist pragmatist Dewey (and most other pragmatists), ethics is primarily an existential matter inseparably tied up with death, evil, suffering, and our general human finitude, contingency, and vulnerability—and, therefore, with religious and metaphysical concerns about the ultimate nature of reality. In this respect, James is significantly closer to thinkers like Søren Kierkegaard, Ludwig Wittgenstein, and Jean-Paul Sartre (philosophers who would only rarely be associated with the idea of applied ethics) than to his fellow pragmatists like Dewey (or even Peirce). Ethics in general, and evil in particular—as a frame of ethics, as urging us into adopting the moral perspective, as "hurting us into morality," to borrow a phrase from Avishai Margalit (2002)—is a compelling issue for the "sick soul" rather than the "healthy-minded" (cf. James 1985). In other words, to adopt a truly ethical attitude to the cries of the wounded is to embrace a fundamentally melancholic view of the world.

We still need to determine in more detail how exactly the ethical becomes involved in, or even a criterion for, the theoretical and the metaphysical. This does not happen with reference to any specific moral theory, that is, not by requiring metaphysics to serve some specific ethical good, as defined in some such theory, whether utilitarian, deontological, or virtue ethical. On the contrary, James's pluralism must be extended to cover the plurality of humanly possible approaches to ethical reflection—in contrast to the monistic model assumed in applied ethics. There is no single correct moral theory but a plurality of voices we need to carefully listen to whenever we seek to reflect on what we ought to do and how we ought to think. This pluralism is closely related to James's resolute antireductionism—his emphasis on the irreducible significance of individual perspectives, whether religious, metaphysical, political, or moral.

While James has often been simplistically taken to be a utilitarian, or at least a consequentialist, in ethics, more careful examinations of his moral thought, such as Franzese's (2008) and Marchetti's (2015), show how misleading this is. "The Moral Philosopher and the Moral Life," as we saw, is skeptical toward the very possibility of moral theory, insofar as moral theories are understood as systems of principles governing morally right conduct, or true or false sets of beliefs about what the good life consists in (systems that would then be practically applied, as it were). Ethical systems are "totalizing" in a way antireductionist pragmatism emphasizing individual perspectives cannot allow. No single moral principle—or its application—can capture the richness and irreducibility of moral life.

James's above-quoted point about there being 'no such thing possible as an ethical philosophy dogmatically made up in advance," "no final truth in ethics . . . until the last man has had his experience and had his say" (James 1979, 141), provides a context for the phrase, "cries of the wounded":

> On the whole, then, we must conclude that no philosophy of ethics is possible in the old-fashioned absolute sense of the term. Everywhere the ethical philosopher must wait on facts. . . . In point of fact, there are no absolute evils, and there are no non-moral goods; and the *highest* ethical life . . . consists at all times in the breaking of rules which have grown too narrow for the actual case. There is but one unconditional commandment, which is that we should seek incessantly, with fear and trembling, so to vote and to act as to bring about the very largest total universe of good which we can see. Abstract rules indeed can help; but they help the less in proportion as our intuitions are more piercing, and our vocation is the stronger for the moral life. For every real dilemma is in literal strictness a unique situation; and the exact combination of ideals realized and ideals disappointed which each decision creates is always a universe without a precedent, and for which no adequate previous rule exists. The philosopher, then, *qua* philosopher, is no better able to determine the best universe in the concrete emergency than other men. He sees, indeed, somewhat better than most men what the question always is—not a question of this good or that good simply taken, but of the two total universes with which these goods respectively belong. He knows that he must vote always for the richer universe, for the good which seems most organizable, most fit to enter to complex combinations, most apt to be a member of a more inclusive whole. But which particular universe this is he cannot know for certain in advance; he only

knows that *if he makes a bad mistake the cries of the wounded will soon inform him of the fact.* . . . His books upon ethics, therefore, so far as they truly touch the moral life, must more and more ally themselves with a literature which is confessedly tentative and suggestive rather than dogmatic. (ibid., section IV; emphasis added)

While certain elements here again sound like a commitment to applied ethics, such as the emphasis on particularity, uniqueness, and situationality, the basic message seems to be that there is no way of formulating general theories that could then be applied to concrete situations. Moreover, the call for a "largest total universe of good" in passages like this should not be misunderstood as an embracement of utilitarianism. Nor, however, should James's criticism of moral theories such as utilitarianism be misunderstood as claiming that the consequences of our actions should not be taken into account in the moral evaluation of action. Of course they should. The problem with utilitarianism is not that it emphasizes consequences; the problem with deontology is not that it emphasizes principles and obligations (or, in Kantian terms, the moral law). The problem with both is that they seek to reduce morality into some strict system, that is, that they *are* moral theories in the first place. Correspondingly, the problem with any contribution to applied ethics that directly applies such theories to some concrete problems is that they start from such moral theories assumed to be applicable.

A more promising way of approaching moral problems pragmatically can, James seems to think, be found in the employment of the pragmatic method—but then those problems will actually turn out to be inseparable from metaphysical and existential issues concerning human existence in a world in which it is a constant challenge for us to feel "at home," and therefore whenever we deal with James's moral thought we really cannot sharply distinguish it from his more metaphysical and religious concerns, all of which he proposed to explore pragmatically.[7]

JAMESIAN PRAGMATISM AND WITTGENSTEINIAN MORAL PHILOSOPHY: SOME PARALLELS

A deconstruction of any theory versus practice dichotomy very similar to James's deconstruction of such dichotomies takes place in Wittgensteinian moral philosophy (represented by, e.g., Rush Rhees, Peter Winch, Raimond

Gaita, D. Z. Phillips, and many others), which can be usefully interpreted in comparison to Jamesian pragmatism. These Wittgenstein-inspired thinkers reject, as James does, all reductive theories of ethics—that is, any theories that reduce moral values or moral behavior to something allegedly more fundamental (for example, physical, biological, psychological, or social). They reject all standard subjectivist or skeptical conceptions of value, even though they are not prepared to embrace any objectivist theory according to which values (or moral facts) "exist" in some objectively structured, independent realm of the (natural or supernatural) world, either. Their approach can perhaps be interpreted not merely as a view close to pragmatism but also as quasi-Kantian reflection on the necessary conditions for the possibility of occupying a moral perspective: our being able to hold any genuinely ethical views on anything—or, presumably, any views whatsoever—or to make any genuinely moral choices in our lives—or, again, any choices, since all of our choices have an ethical dimension—necessarily requires that certain ethical views are held by us, personally, as genuinely correct, that is, not as mere opinions, subjective attitudes, or beliefs relative to a person or a community.

While Wittgenstein himself can be argued to have been committed to a fact/value dichotomy, at least in the *Tractatus*, the Wittgensteinian move in contemporary moral philosophy is to maintain that "moral viewpoints determine what is and what is not to count as a relevant fact in reaching a moral decision" (Phillips 1992, 8). The facts to be considered in the evaluation of any given ethically relevant situation (that is, any human situation) are, then, partly constituted by the moral viewpoint we have adopted and by the language we speak (as an expression of that standpoint). Philosophy cannot yield proofs, as it can only clarify the structure of our concepts and thus elucidate our moral perspective (see Johnston 1999, 43; Phillips 1992, 103); yet, conceptual clarification and analysis cannot be identified with, nor do they entail, individual persons' own conclusions about what is right and wrong (Johnston 1999, 169). Wittgensteinian ethical thought, precisely like Jamesian pragmatism, highlights the idea that personally relevant moral conclusions cannot be dictated by general (reductive) ethical theories. Therefore, there is no way of simply applying such theories to concrete moral cases.

Nevertheless, the various theories that have been presented in the history of moral philosophy may constitute a part of the background that plays its role in defining the ethically problematic situations we find ourselves in. Jamesian pragmatism need not be as thoroughly antitheoretical as at least some Wittgensteinian currents in moral philosophy seem to be. It seems to me that pragmatism offers an excellent mediator between (1) the view that morality is based on, or can be justified with reference to, some kind of absolute or transcendent foundation, on the one side, and (2) the equally problematic idea that morality is merely a matter of arbitrary preferences, on the other. Whenever we truly engage in our practices of moral reflection and deliberation (unlike the imagined applications of moral theories to such practices), our ethical judgments, unlike mere arbitrary preferences or opinions, do claim "absolute" correctness, but their correctness cannot be determined from any imagined God's-eye view. Instead, the claim to correctness is made from within our actual practices themselves, from the agent's point of view, that is, from the point of view of a serious and personal concern with how one should live and how one should think about the question how to live. The claim to correctness, however absolute, is a human claim, not a transcendent one. Here, in particular, the pragmatist and Wittgensteinian trends in moral philosophy, with little explicit interaction, are closely linked. The very idea of moral rightness is rooted in our (habits of) acting in the world in a seriously concerned way, not in any specific moral realm of values disconnected from our worldly existence.

The idea of applied ethics presupposes the idea of ethics as a special discipline with a special subject-matter, attacked by the entire tradition of Wittgensteinian moral philosophy. In contrast to such a misconception of the nature of the ethical, Jamesian pragmatists, as suggested above, should also firmly reject the distinction between moral theories and their practical applications that appears to be presupposed by the very idea of applied ethics.[8] It is hard to find any significance in the idea of "applying" philosophy in general, if one holds that philosophical questions and positions, insofar as they are genuinely philosophical at all, are always already in touch with human affairs, with our continuous attempt to investigate our place in the world's scheme of things.

Beyond the resistance to any neat theory versus practice dichotomy, Jamesian pragmatism and the Wittgensteinian line of ethical thought converge in the even more fundamental question of what it means to be a human being. Again, such questions or our answers to them should not be construed in terms of any model of applying a theory to practice. The contributions of these two perspectives to contemporary moral philosophy can be brought to the fore more clearly if we recognize that they are, in the end, attempts to engage in something like philosophical anthropology rather than "applied philosophy," attempts to inquire into the "human condition" that makes morality inescapable for us (cf. Pihlström 2016). Such an attempt is made, for example, in Raimond Gaita's (2004) penetrating analysis of how an ethically significant distinction is made, in our ordinary ethical discourse, between human beings and animals—between the preciousness of human life, which has an "inner mystery," and mere animal life, which may be valuable but not in the same sense in which human life is valuable. As usual, this Wittgensteinian analysis focuses on what we typically say, on how we actually use ethical language; a similar approach is adopted by Rush Rhees (1999), the originator of the entire tradition. Furthermore, Peter Winch (1972, 3) is firm in his rejection of certain philosophers' appeal to human nature on the grounds that "ideas of what human nature consists in are themselves expressions of moral ideas." Winch's Wittgensteinian philosophical anthropology does not treat human nature as fixed or given but reminds us that "what we can and what we cannot make sense of determines what we can ascribe to human nature," not vice versa (ibid., 84).

In particular, it would be worthwhile to examine the theodicy versus antitheodicy debate in the philosophy of religion—and "moral antitheodicism" in particular—in this context of comparing Jamesian pragmatism with Wittgensteinian moral philosophy (see again Kivistö and Pihlström 2016). As we briefly saw, the problem of evil and suffering constitutes, for James, a frame of moral philosophy and of morally serious philosophy generally, and in this sense the Jamesian approach resembles the Wittgensteinian one (especially, it seems to me, Phillips's). Neither James nor Phillips or other Wittgensteinians would approve of any theodicy that would excuse God (or the world) for allowing evil and suffering to take place. Both would insist on the need to take seriously the full reality of evil and suffering in any morally appropriate attempt to acknowledge the experiences of another human being, especially experiences of suffering. In this context, however, we cannot further engage in such a comparative inquiry. Let me simply note that it is the same fundamental ethical seriousness, I think, that prevents the Jamesian-cum-Wittgensteinian moral thinker from subscribing to either theodicies in the philosophy of religion or the theory-and-its-applications model in applied ethics. Both are confusions of moral thought that we should give up, through pragmatist ethical inquiry or, perhaps, Wittgensteinian grammatical "therapy."

Moreover, it might be suggested that they are related confusions: applied ethics, by seeking moral problem solving via applications, is (even when fully secular) in a way quasi-theodicist in the sense of maintaining that we may move from our moral problems to engineering-like "happy end" solutions. The antitheodicist maintains, on the contrary, that morality is what makes our lives problematic to us. It is because of morality that we are—our should be—melancholic "sick souls" in James's sense (1985). It is a complete misunderstanding of our moral predicament to suggest that applied ethical problem solving could lead us out of such problems of life—problems whose depth James always acknowledged.

CONCLUSION

Jamesian pragmatism (and especially the pragmatic pluralism James opposed to monistic and totalizing temptations of both moral and metaphysical thinking) should, then, be regarded as diametrically opposed to applied ethics and applied philosophy in the sense in which these have been understood in this chapter (i.e., the "received view" sense, overlooking the more nuanced and both conceptually and historically richer developments that have taken place under the rubrics of applied ethics and applied philosophy recently). It ought to be seen as a much more sophisticated way of defending the practical relevance of philosophy, analogous to the ways in which certain Wittgenstein-inspired thinkers (only very briefly cited here) have regarded philosophy as personally and morally relevant all the way from the beginning.

In particular, it is worth re-emphasizing that James's pragmatism does not apply philosophical theorization to the problem of evil and suffering but views the latter problem (in an antitheodicist way) as a frame for moral philosophy itself, and for philosophy more generally. Far from applying theories to the concrete problems of living with and responding to evil and suffering, Jamesian pragmatism lets those practices crucially inform any theorization worthy of human engagement. This demonstrates that pragmatism, or pragmatically inspired philosophy more generally, can be strikingly relevant to human life, individual and social, without being "applied" ethics or "applied" philosophy in the sense criticized here. Its relevance is not reducible to any such model of application.

NOTES

1. For a useful brief statement of pragmatism in ethics, see Eldridge. Discussions of pragmatist ethics typically draw on Dewey as well as figures like Jane Addams, but James's ethical thought has increasingly been discussed among commentators (see, e.g., Franzese 2008; Throntveit; Marchetti).

2. For a more comprehensive pragmatist criticism of the idea of applied philosophy, see Pihlström (2005, ch. 5). The views of this section are to some extent indebted to that early work of mine.

3. The need to "apply" philosophy to such concerns has presumably generally been felt to become stronger as traditional analytic philosophy has lost some of its school-like integrity, although we may recall that Rupert C. Lodge, for one, insisted on the relevance of philosophy to education, business, government, religion, and everyday living already in his virtually forgotten 1951 book *Applied Philosophy*.

4. James's criticism of the "blindness" in human beings, preventing us from recognizing genuine otherness, can be compared to the ethics of acknowledging the other in the work of philosophers like Emmanuel Levinas and Stanley Cavell (cf. Craig; Kivistö & Pihlström, ch. 5). James's essay, "On a Certain Blindness in Human Beings," is available in James's *Talks to Teachers on Psychology; and to Students on Some of Life's Ideals* (Vol. 12 of *The Works of William James*).

5. My discussion in this section is indebted to the more comprehensive treatment of James on evil and suffering in Kivistö and Pihlström, ch. 5, which offers an *antitheodicist* reading of James.

6. This exploration takes place in a world in which theodicies are no longer possible. No theodicist consolation is an option, James argues, for an ethically serious thinker. What we may call Jamesian antitheodicism is therefore a crucial element of his pragmatic method, framed by the problem of evil (cf. Pihlström 2014; Kivistö and Pihlström).

7. In addition to the pragmatic method, we might say that in a sense the Jamesian approach to theoretical and metaphysical concepts and issues is an application of the pragmatist conception of *truth* (cf. James 1975, Lecture VI). Our ideas expressed or expressible by means of such concepts—our metaphysical or other highly theoretical views and commitments—are pragmatically "true" or "false" in so far forth as they put us in touch with ethically significant experiences. The truth of a metaphysical view can be assessed by means of the pragmatic criterion of its ability to open us to the cries of the wounded. It is right here, in a pragmatist ethically colored and structured metaphysics, that truth, in James's memorable phrase, "*happens* to an idea" (ibid., 97). This "happening" is much more radical than an application of a pre-given theoretical idea to some practical subject-matter. (The phrase, feeling "at home" in the universe, comes from James's "The Sentiment of Rationality.")

8. We may also read a neo-Kantian like Christine Korsgaard (44) as arguing that applied ethics is based on misconceived "substantive" moral realism, according to which morality is thought to be about finding a theoretical solution that can be applied in practice: "According to the substantive realist . . . the moral life is the most sublime feat of technical engineering, the application of theoretical knowledge to the solution of human problems." See further Pihlström 2005.

REFERENCES

Almond, Brenda, and Donald Hill, eds. *Applied Philosophy: Morals and Metaphysics in Contemporary Debate*. London and New York: Routledge, 1991.

Craig, Megan. *Levinas and James*. Bloomington: Indiana University Press, 2010.

Dewey, John. *Problems of Men*. New York: Philosophical Library, 1946.

Eldridge, Michael. "Ethics." In *The Bloomsbury Companion to Pragmatism*. Revised edition, edited by Sami Pihlström. London: Bloomsbury, 2015.

Franzese, Sergio. *The Ethics of Energy: William James's Moral Philosophy in Focus*. Frankfurt: Ontos, 2008.

Gaita, Raimond. *Good and Evil: An Absolute Conception*. Revised edition. London: Routledge, 2004.

James, William. *Pragmatism*. Vol. 1 of *The Works of William James*, edited by Fredson Bowers, and Ignas K. Skrupskelis. Introduction by H. S. Thayer. Cambridge, MA: Harvard University Press. [1907] 1975.

———. *The Will to Believe and Other Essays in Popular Philosophy*. Vol. 6 of *The Works of William James*, edited by Frederick H. Burkhardt, Fredson Bowers, and Ignas K. Skrupskelis. Introduction by Edward H. Madden. Cambridge, MA: Harvard University Press. [1897] 1979.

———. *Talks to Teachers on Psychology; and to Students on Some of Life's Ideals*. Vol. 12 of *The Works of William James*, edited by Frederick H. Burkhardt, Fredson Bowers, and Ignas K. Skrupskelis. Introduction by Gerald E. Myers. Cambridge, MA: Harvard University Press. [1899] 1983.

———. *The Varieties of Religious Experience*. Vol. 15 of *The Works of William James*, edited by Frederick H. Burkhardt, Fredson Bowers, and Ignas K. Skrupskelis. Introduction by John E. Smith. Cambridge, MA: Harvard University Press. [1902] 1985.

Johnston, Paul. *The Contradictions of Modern Moral Philosophy*. London: Routledge, 1999.

Kivistö, Sari, and Sami Pihlström. *Kantian Antitheodicy: Philosophical and Literary Varieties*. Basingstoke, UK: Palgrave Macmillan, 2016.

Kopelman, Loretta M. "What Is Applied about 'Applied' Philosophy?" *Journal of Medicine and Philosophy* 15 (1990): 199–218.

Korsgaard, Christine M. *The Sources of Normativity*. Cambridge: Cambridge University Press, 1996.

Lodge, Rupert C. *Applied Philosophy*. London: Routledge and Kegan Paul, 1951.

Marchetti, Sarin. *Ethics and Philosophical Critique in William James*. Basingstoke, UK: Palgrave Macmillan, 2015.

Margalit, Avishai. *The Ethics of Memory*. Cambridge, MA: Harvard University Press, 2002.

Passmore, John. "The Concept of Applied Philosophy." In *Philosophy and Culture*, Vol. 4, edited by Venant Cauchy. Montreal: Montmorency, 1988.

Phillips, D. Z. *Interventions in Ethics*. Albany, New York: SUNY Press, 1992.
———. "Ethics, Faith, and 'What Can Be Said.'" In *Wittgenstein: A Critical Reader*, edited by Hans-Johann Glock. Malden, MA: Blackwell, 2001.
Pihlström, Sami. *Pragmatic Moral Realism: A Transcendental Defense*. Amsterdam: Rodopi, 2005.
———. *Pragmatist Metaphysics: An Essay on the Ethical Grounds of Ontology*. London: Continuum, 2009.
———. *Pragmatic Pluralism and the Problem of God*. New York: Fordham University Press, 2013.
———. *Taking Evil Seriously*. Basingstoke, UK: Palgrave Macmillan, 2014.
———, ed. *The Bloomsbury Companion to Pragmatism*. Revised edition. London: Bloomsbury, 2015.
———. *Death and Finitude: Toward a Pragmatic Transcendental Anthropology of Human Mortality*. Lanham, MD: Lexington Books, 2016.
Rhees, Rush. *Moral Questions*. Edited by D. Z. Phillips. Houndmills, UK: Macmillan, 1999.
Throntveit, Trygve. *William James and the Quest for an Ethical Republic*. Basingstoke, UK: Palgrave Macmillan, 2014.
Warren, Bill. "Back to Basics: Problems and Prospects for Applied Philosophy." *Journal of Applied Philosophy* 9: 13–19, 1992.
Winch, Peter. *Ethics and Action*. London: Routledge and Kegan Paul, 1972.

CHAPTER 7

UNDERSTANDING EXPERIENCE WITH WILLIAM JAMES

JOHN RYDER

Though in some versions of contemporary pragmatism, for example those that rely heavily on Richard Rorty, a theory of experience is taken to be superfluous, others regard an understanding of experience to be central to a clear handle on thought, cognition, emotions, aesthetics, politics, and human action generally. This essay belongs in the latter camp. It turns out that an adequate conception of experience, one ensconced in the pragmatic naturalist tradition, which is to say the tradition of pragmatism stemming from Charles Sanders Peirce and William James and of the related naturalism of John Dewey and the Columbia school, builds on several resources.[1] One of them is recent work in cognitive science, specifically the empirical and conceptual support for the idea that mind is embodied, indeed extended in an individual's body and environmental locations. Another is the idea that, contra the traditional empiricists, experience is transactional, specifically a transaction between the self or experiencing individual and the environment in which that individual finds herself. In this case the term "environment" is meant to refer not simply to the physical environment but also to one's cultural context, history, intentions, purposes, and principles, indeed to every dimension of a situation that can impact the character of experience as an ongoing process and of "an" experience in Dewey's sense of the term, which is to say experience that is a culmination or fulfillment, a concept that Dewey develops in detail in *Art as Experience*.

These general ideas rest to a considerable degree on features of experience and cognition that James was among the first to notice and develop.

Among these features are James's views of the bodily basis of emotions and cognition, the constitutively relational character of the subjects and objects of experience and the world, and both the experience and ontological parity of relations. Our interest here is to some extent to clarify these and other respects in which James's thought underlies a satisfactory theory of experience. More importantly for current purposes, our interest is in developing aspects of a conception of experience by building on James rather than merely interpreting him. That is not to diminish the importance of interpretation, if only for the obvious reason that one cannot build on a set of ideas if one does not have a reasonably reliable interpretation of them. The point is simply that this is not an effort in exegesis but an attempt to articulate an adequate understanding of experience, or at least a sketch of one, in light of James's noteworthy contributions.

Further by way of introduction, it may be sensible to offer some support for the significance of a theory or understanding of experience, particularly because there may be readers who suspect, as Rorty did, that an effort to develop a theory of experience expresses a conception of philosophy left over from more traditional approaches to the discipline previous to the emergence of pragmatism. On such a view, a pragmatist theory of experience is something of an oxymoron in that pragmatism, by having abandoned traditional attempts to describe the world in lieu of a more action- and future-oriented approach to understanding our world and ourselves, no longer has need of such metaphysically tainted enterprises as the development of a theory of experience. Let us just say that this view of the matter is mistaken, not in the sense of being an inaccurate description of the case but because it is stultifying in its own pragmatist sense of the end of philosophic thought as action- and future-oriented. An interest such as ours in developing a proper understanding of experience is couched in, among other purposes, a desire to understand as fully and adequately as possible what it is to be a live person. Because to be a live person is among other things to engage our world, and for the moment we can leave open any detail of the nature of that engagement, an understanding of the process we designate as experience is a way of coming to grips for ourselves with the character of such engagement. What, we may ask, would be the alternative if indeed we wish to understand a live individual's engagement with the world? The answer from those who would reject the value of developing a theory of experience might be that the fault is in the generality, not in attempting to understand the engagement. On this view, one might say that of course we engage our world and worlds, but we do so in every specific case in specific ways, so that if we want to understand that engagement we need to approach it not at the level of theoretical generality but at the level of the specific engagements that occur. On this view, general theory adds nothing of value to our understanding of cases.

This last point is, one might imagine, precisely that with which we disagree. Of course, it is true that the engagement of individuals with our world and worlds happens in specific and not general circumstances, and of course it is true that to understand any specific case it is necessary to come to terms with the details of that case. The mistake is to think that generality does not contribute to understanding in specific cases, or that theory does not inform detailed inquiry. To see that this is not a useful way to approach the philosophic issue of experience it may be helpful to consider the matter with respect to other topics. Just as biological ecosystems are always individual systems, to pick one sort of example to illustrate the point, we would be misguided to think that an understanding of a given ecosystem is not aided by an understanding of how ecosystems are structured and operate more generally. If we know at a general level that and how the chemical nature of the water in a pond impacts the rate at which amphibians reproduce, for example, then when we consider the details of an individual pond we know better than we would otherwise what to look for and we understand better what we see. Theory, in other words, informs specific inquiry.

We are entitled to say the same when we consider illustrations of a quite different sort. Suppose, for example, that we are interested in understanding the narrative structure of Joyce's *Ulysses*. In this case there are many specific things we need to know, including the Homeric tale that serves as a kind of substructure, aspects of Dublin life at the turn of the twentieth century, trends of the time in Irish literature, Joyce's own understanding of an artist's purposes, along with many other relevant, specific points. In addition, however, our effort would be considerably advantaged if we could bring to bear on the enterprise an understanding of general narrative theory. If we know how in general a narrative arc might work, we would be better able both to recognize it in *Ulysses* and appreciate the extent to which the book diverges from, in fact revolutionizes, traditional characteristics in this regard. Similarly, with an understanding at the theoretical level of how voice and point of view operate in a narrative, and how meaning is to some extent couched therein, we can read *Ulysses*, or any novel, with greater clarity and sophistication. Such theoretical understanding can in fact condition our general reaction to a text. For example, in *The Murder of Roger Ackroyd*, we may feel puzzled and even betrayed at the end when we discover who the murderer is, though our reaction is likely to be considerably more richly textured if we understand that in doing what she did, Agatha Christie was purposely subverting a critical convention of detective literature.[2] This is in fact one of the reasons the work is regarded as highly as it is. As with respect to an ecosystem, the knowledge of the general informs understanding of the particular. We can appreciate quite a bit about *Ulysses* and any novel without narrative theory, but we can understand quite a bit more with it.

The situation is just the same with respect to experience. A general theory of experience helps us to know what to look for in any given case, or at least serves as a guide. For example, if we understand experience to be an interaction between the experiencing individual and the broader environment, rather than, say, as simply a passive reception of sense data, then our conception of any particular experience will be different than it would be otherwise. Or to give another example, if at the theoretical level we take the bodily aspect of experience to involve much more than sense organs and brain processes alone, then our appreciation of how we bodily engage our world in a given case will be different than it would otherwise be. General theory impacts specific analysis, a point that is no less true for a philosophical topic like experience than it is in biology or philology. And to add a note about the pragmatist nature of all this, the point is not that the right theory better describes this or that specific object of inquiry, whether in biology, philology, or philosophy, but that a theoretical conception is a significant tool in the attempt to understand whatever it is that we wish to explore in these ways, and in that respect general theory is no less relevant than any other conceptual tool we may bring to bear. This is the reason there is nothing oxymoronic about a pragmatist theory, of experience or of anything else.

This speaks to the value of theory. With respect to a theory of experience we may add that such a theory would, to give a necessarily superficial description, offer a conception of the generic aspects of experience. It would address, for example, among other related issues, the ways and extent to which experience is passive and active, or assimilative and manipulative; it would address those traits of human life that we know are aspects of our experience, but still require clarification—cognition, for example; it would identify general dimensions of experience, should there in fact be any, such as the aesthetic and cognitive; and, it would account for the character of experience in relation to conceptions of mind and consciousness. In the end, such a theory will be adequate, as is the case for other philosophical theories, insofar as it is coherent, plausible, and useful.

James understood all this, and in part his genius is to have offered us enlightening discussions and analyses at both the particular and the general levels. Moreover, the details of his understanding at both levels provide the basis for a sure-footed development of a theory of experience that incorporates much of what we have learned since James's time, from philosophers such as Dewey, Maurice Merleau-Ponty, and Justus Buchler to contemporary analyses of relevant issues in cognitive studies. Let us turn now in some detail to James and a theory of experience.

I

We may best begin with the concept of embodiment. In one of his most influential essays, "Does Consciousness Exist?" James made the fundamentally important point that consciousness, and by implication mind, is not an object but a function (James 1976).[3] Moreover, he went on to say that ontologically there is no sharp distinction between the self and an object of the self's attention or engagement. Actually, he was speaking in terms of the cognitive function of consciousness, so he said more precisely that the subject, and its knowledge function, is, to use his language, "pure experience" functioning one way, and an object of knowledge is "pure experience" functioning in a different way. We will take issue with the language of "pure experience" below, but James's point is clear, and it is one that we can generalize beyond his immediate concern with the cognitive function to other aspects of experience, mind, and consciousness as well. Contra traditional rationalism, empiricism, Kantianism, and Hegelianism, which, with the exceptions of Marxian materialism, Kierkegaard, and Transcendentalism, pretty much covers all modern European and American philosophy to James's time, there is according to James no sense to be given to a sharp, ontological distinction between consciousness and its objects, which is to say between self and the world, a point with which there is sufficient reason to agree.[4]

James had earlier gone somewhat further in arguing for the embodiment of mental functions. In his *Principles of Psychology* in the 1880s, to give a prominent illustration of the point, he made abundantly clear that in many important respects mind and consciousness, and more specific mental functions such as emotions, are bodily phenomena, and that no adequate understanding of psychology is possible without taking into account an individual's body and its physical functions (James 1981). James was of course no reductionist in this respect, in that he did not hold that psychological or mental activity is thoroughly physical and can be described and explained in purely physical or bodily terms. Rather he held, and developed the view, that the body is a necessary feature of psychological or mental activity. Whether he was entirely consistent in this view is another question. Richard Shusterman, for example, points out that in the end, James wanted to reserve a place for volition that was not in any way a consequence of bodily features, but rather as a purely ideal function that could influence the physical (2008). Despite such inconsistencies, however, James was one of the first philosophers to attend seriously to the bodily aspect of mind, and he was not without influence. Among those whom he influenced was John Dewey, who credits James in general and the *Principles of Psychology* specifically with being instrumental in moving him from his early Hegelian idealism to a fuller sense of the self and of experience as necessarily embodied.

More recently, and by way of influence, one might mention Mark Johnson and Lyubov Bugaeva. Johnson relies on James in *The Meaning of the Body* when he points out that "the idea that thinking is embodied is not the relatively obvious claim that in order to think, one needs a body and a brain. Instead it entails that the nature of our embodiment shapes both what and how we think" (Johnson 2007, 94). Bugaeva, for her part, relies on James's approach to embodiment when she makes a case through a study of viewers' interaction with film for his often-criticized idea from the *Principles of Psychology* that emotions are bodily reactions to the environment, in this case that arise through the interaction of viewer and film. As Bugaeva puts it, "Immersion of a viewer into cinematographic reality leads to the birth of emotions caused by the interaction of the subject with the environment in the virtual reality of the movie" (2013, 95). And in a different article Bugaeva discusses James's influence on Eisenstein in the context of an analysis of the enactive aspect of cinema, which very briefly encompasses the ways in which the viewer actively contributes to the cinematic experience, in which respect this understanding of cinema accords with the transactional conception of experience with which we have been working through James (Bugaeva 2016).

As early as the *Principles*, it is clear that James understood mind and its many functions as embodied in what remains today a contemporary sense of the term. In James, Dewey, Shusterman, Johnson, and Bugaeva's hands the embodiment of mind is not a physicalist reduction of mental functions to physical process, in the sense that mental functions could be described in purely physical terms, nor is it an attempt to make mind or consciousness equivalent to the brain, a popular contemporary enterprise for which there is neither sense nor evidence, in the sense that, for one thing, brains do not undertake or undergo the many traits of experience, and for another, the attributes we may ascribe to experience, for example exciting, boring, moving, enlightening, and so forth, cannot be ascribed to brains. For James, as for Dewey and the other contemporary pragmatists mentioned, the idea is not that mind is physical but that live humans are "minded," we might say. Lived human bodies, to use a locution with something of the sound of Merleau-Ponty, are of such a complexity and sophistication that they enable all the functions that we designate as mental—cognition, emotion, language, imagination, and all the rest. We will not properly understand mind if we regard it as something other than embodied mind, and we will not understand live human bodies as something other than minded bodies. This insight, one that continues to be explored and developed today, has its roots in James's psychology and in his later explorations of radical empiricism.

It is in the context of the latter that James began to speak of "pure experience," and a word is in order about that. We should begin with the caveat that it is not entirely clear to me what James meant by "pure experience." I will proceed, tentatively, on the assumption that he meant to convey two important points: (1) we need a single term to indicate an ontological continuity between what we designate matter and what we designate mind; and (2) experience is a central feature of human being, and by virtue of the ontological continuity of the experiencing person with her environment, of nature in general. One could be tempted to use the term "stuff," or something like it, to designate the ontological continuity, but that would have too physicalist a ring to it in the sense that it might be mistakenly interpreted as describing mind or consciousness as a material thing, and in any case, such a term as "stuff" would not help with the emphasis James wanted to place on experience as an item of general philosophic significance. Consequently, to meet the two purposes just mentioned, he chose the term "pure experience."

There are advantages and disadvantages to the concept of "pure experience" as James wields it, and it is worthwhile to attend somewhat to both. There are two disadvantages that should be spelled out. The first is with the idea that experience, and much of anything else for that matter, can in any meaningful or useful way be described as "pure." This would depend of course on what precisely we mean by "pure." If we mean "pure" in something like the sense in which we mean it when we refer to a particular piece of jewelry as "pure gold," then it is not clear that there is much sense to this at all. When we refer to an object as "pure gold," we mean to say that the gold is not mixed with any other metal. It is not an alloy. This sort of use of the term "pure experience" would of course have to be metaphorical because experience is not a material object and so cannot in a literal sense be a mixture of anything, but for the same reason it cannot in a literal sense be pure either. So, if to say of experience that it is "pure" is to speak metaphorically, what if anything can the metaphor convey? Experience cannot be "unmixed" in either a literal or metaphorical sense, so that does not work. Perhaps it means something like "unmediated," for which there is some evidence because in later years, and in Dewey's hands, we also see the term "immediate experience" used. Dewey used the term in a different sense from James's meaning, though, because Dewey wanted to emphasize an immediacy in experience, for example in *Art as Experience* (2008, 123, 125). For Dewey "immediate" in this sense depicts a character of a person's experience of this or that, whereas for James "pure" depicts an ontological trait or condition. If in either case, however, James or Dewey meant to posit by the term "pure" or "immediate" something unrelated in the sense of being absolute rather than conditioned, which is to say relational, then both would be using their respective terms in indefensible ways.

There is no reason to attribute to either James or Dewey the idea that experience is or even can be unrelated in the sense of being nonrelational. The primary reason is that both philosophers—in James's case in his radical empiricism generally, and in Dewey's case in his concept of a "situation"—were adamant that nature, and experience as an element of nature, is through and through relational. Thus, we have no reason to think that either of them wants to regard experience as unrelated or absolute in any way, which implies that we cannot interpret "pure" in James's case as suggesting that in some respect experience is unrelated. It appears rather that when James talks about "pure experience" he means to indicate that features of nature, or of the world, if one prefers, can take on very different traits depending on their relational contexts. His point about consciousness being a function and not an object is made in precisely these terms, that is, that consciousness is pure experience functioning one way, and an object of consciousness, say an object of knowledge, is pure experience functioning another way. The relational contexts engender different, sometimes very different, traits for any given entity, or in James's language, in any given bit of pure experience.

James in "Does Consciousness Exist?" goes on to use paint as an example, though I prefer to use musical tones to make the same point. Imagine that we play a series of chords grounded in the key of C major, and once the ear is conditioned to the relations that constitute that key, we generate a short progression that stops with a B natural tone. The result is that the B natural tone conveys a strong sense of tension and anticipation, sometimes strong enough that it creates a decided feeling of anxiety in us as we wait for the resolution of the tension in the sounding of a C natural tone or major chord. The tension can be so strong in us that it is said, perhaps as myth more than biography, that Verdi's housekeeper used to get him out of bed in the morning by doing this, but without completing the progression with the home note. Verdi, so the story goes, found the tension unbearable and would have to get up, go to the piano, and resolve the progression to relieve the tension. But to make the point we need to develop the example. Suppose that after having created the tension with the B natural and resolving it with the C natural, we then draw the listener out of the key of C major and begin to play a progression in the key of B major. If we do this for only several seconds, the listener will be acclimated to the key of B major, and if we then proceed to the culmination of the chordal progression, the note that generates the tension will be an A sharp. Now, however, the tone that resolves the tension will be B natural, which is to say the very same tone that created the tension when in the key of C major. This is an example of how a particular entity, in this case the tone that we refer to as B natural, has entirely different, in fact opposite, traits depending on the set of relations in which it prevails. In the key of C major it creates tension, while in the key of B major the very same tone resolves tension. Its constitutive relations are defining contexts for an entity, and an entity can and will have some differing traits in differing relational contexts, simultaneously.

This, as I understand it, is what James means when he talks about "pure experience." This meaning is clear, and it is defensible, as the musical illustration indicates and as we will argue in a bit more detail below. It is, nevertheless, a rather unfortunate term for James to have used because the term also lends itself to a highly idealistic interpretation, which is the second disadvantage referred to above. The use of the term "experience" in this way suggests that the general character of reality, that which precedes subject and object we might say, is subjective. James probably did flirt with subjective idealism of this or some sort, which is indicated by his openness, and even eagerness, to embrace a theological take on the world. Talking about experience this way lends support to the attribution to him of either an overarching subjective idealism, or at least an inconsistency in the heart of his thinking, in that his insistence on the embodiment of consciousness would seem to belie an idealism. Nevertheless, a subjectivist cast, especially when accompanied by his inclination to use American idioms such as the "cash value" of an idea, led Lenin and others to criticize him as philosophically out of step, and in fact as an embodiment of idealist bourgeois philosophy (see Ryder 2015, 168–80). Russell and others from that side of the philosophical world of the time criticized James for what they took to be a sloppy, perhaps facile, and certainly overly subjective, epistemology, for example, his insistence that an idea is true to the extent that it works for us (Russell 1966).

These larger philosophic debates are to be found in embryonic form in James's treatment of experience, even in his use of the term "pure" as applied to experience. We suggested above, though, that there are also advantages to his use of the term. We can now turn to those, and in the process of articulating the good reasons James had to approach the character of experience as he did, we will be able to see how we can respond to critics like Lenin and Russell and those of their descendants who continue to be suspicious of James on similar grounds.

II

To see the advantages of James's approach to experience we need to look a bit closer at how he understands the ideas he brings to bear in its explication. To do this we need to consider not only the idea of pure experience, but also James's more general idea of radical empiricism. It will be most useful, however, if we introduce a term that he does not use, but one that is, I would argue, necessary for us to understand James on experience and to be able to build on his ideas. That term is "constitutive relations."

In the explication above of James's meaning of "pure" experience we said that one of the reasons he had for using it is to be able to say that an entity can function in more than one way. In his case he was concerned to show that consciousness and its object(s) are differing functions of the same thing, the difference being determined by the sets of relations in which they find themselves, or, as we prefer to say, in which they prevail. The example of the traits of the B natural tone differing from one key to another was meant to show that the relational contexts in which an entity finds itself are constitutive of the entity. That a B natural tone has in one context, the key of C major, the trait of tension and in another, the key of B major, the trait of resolution indicates that its traits are in that respect constituted by the relations. The relations are, in other words, constitutive.

James wants to make a comparable point. In fact, he needs the idea of the constitutive character of relations to account for how something, for example a perceived object, can at the same time be objective, or in the room, and subjective, or "in the mind." The room and its objects, as objects of thought, function relationally, just as they do as objects available to us as objects of perception. James uses the term "pure experience" to designate, as we have said above, this general feature of the world. He goes on in "Does Consciousness Exist?" to describe pure experience as the "instant field of the present," which I would argue is an unfortunate turn of phrase. The relational constitution of objects, subjects, and anything at all is not confined to the present, or to what may be available to us in the present as possibilities. That relations are constitutive of their terms, an idea that we may now refer to as "ordinality" because the relations that constitute entities can be understood as orders of relations, is a much more general concept, and that is the reason that we do not want to confine ourselves to a "field of the present," or for that matter to the term "experience" at all, to denote it. James was right, we can say, to point to the ontological continuity of consciousness and its objects, and subject and object, but he was not helpful in referring to the continuity as any kind of experience. People, their environments, and the transaction between them that is experience, are relationally constituted, but the relational context is not experiential, or not necessarily experiential.

James develops the general idea of constitutive relations, though without using the term and indeed well *avant le lettre*, in several of the chapters that constitute *Essays in Radical Empiricism*. The first pages of "The Thing and Its Relations," for example, are an extended argument for the constitutive character of relations (1976, 45–59). And in "A World of Pure Experience" he again makes the point that the objective reference of our ideas has the same general character as the self that has the ideas, which is that both are constituted by sets of relations as a result of which they have the traits that they have (1976, 21–44). James understood, much to his credit, that a satisfactory conception of experience rests to a considerable extent on an understanding of relations. It is this general insight, and many of the details that follow, that makes James's work so valuable for us today, with respect to our approach to experience, to relations, and indeed to many other related issues, knowledge and truth among them.

One of the defining features of radical empiricism, then, is that entities are relationally constituted. Another is that relations are directly experienced, and yet another is that all terms and relations are as real as any other, all points he develops in "A World of Pure Experience." The experience of relations, and the ontological parity among them, which is a contemporary way to indicate James's point that all relations are equally real, is necessary for James to maintain the idea that there is a continuity in experience. He also needs these points to sustain his idea that in cognition there are not intermediaries between the knower and the known, but rather the knower and the known are in direct contact with one another. This distinguishes James's view from the Kantianism then prevalent, especially on the Continent. And to stretch the point a bit more, as James himself does in the same essay, once we understand that knowledge is a relation between the knower and the known that has its place fully within the continuous interaction of the individual with her environment, which is to say within experience, then we can expect knowledge to have a function or functions within experience, and for those functions to be identifiable in practical rather than primarily formal ways. It turns out, in other words, that James's pragmatist understanding of knowledge as a matter of lived consequences and truth as functionally relevant in moving our experience along, as what "works," as James said, have their conceptual roots in his theory of experience. In this respect, we can see again why James has been so important for the subsequent development of the pragmatist approach to experience, knowledge, and philosophical anthropology in Dewey, Buchler, and their contemporary descendants, and why specifically his emphasis on experience was key to his philosophical commitments.

III

We may devote the rest of the chapter to a development of the conception of experience that extends James's several insights. To remind ourselves where we are, the idea is to develop a theory of experience that draws on the following of James's central concepts: (1) the ordinal, constitutive relationality of the entities of nature, including the self and experience; (2) the ontological continuity of the elements in experience; (3) experience as the ongoing, multiply-faceted interaction of the self with one's environment; (4) relations as experienced; (5) the ontological parity of all relations and the entities they constitute; and (6) the practical, in the sense of experiential, character and place of cognition, knowledge, and truth. These concepts, taken together and filled out as the conceptual development requires, allow us to design a coherent, plausible, and valuable theory of experience, one that enables a better understanding of less general forms of experience, for example religious experience, to use an illustration especially appropriate for James, and more generally, what it is to be an experiencing individual, which is to say a live person.

For the sake of ease of expression, let us agree to refer to our conception of experience simply as experience, and if we want to contrast our view with another we will give the other its common name or designation, for example an empiricist or a Kantian conception of experience. We should also acknowledge that experience as we understand it has its roots, certainly in James, which is the point of this chapter, but also in Dewey, Buchler, and indeed in the pragmatic naturalist tradition as it has developed since the late nineteenth century, primarily though not exclusively in the United States. With that said, we would do well to begin by contrasting our view with various features of traditional conceptions of experience.

First, it has been common traditionally to regard the world as experienced and the world independent of experience as cut off from one another. One such traditional conception is that experience should be understood in terms of sense data, which comes to us in perception, and experience is what we then do with those sense data. Another way the philosophical tradition has split the two worlds is in the Kantian approach, wherein the world in itself is whatever it is, but the world of experience is the consequence of operations the self makes on what it perceives. The primary difference between this and the "sense data approach" is that in the latter, empiricists tended to think that experience did in fact give us access to the world from which the sense data arose, whereby the Kantians are forced to grant that by virtue of the way the process works we can only know anything about the world as experienced, not as it is independent of the mind's transcendental constitution of experience. A third version of the "sharp break" view is the idea that as subjects we are in some sense "in here," while the world we experience is "out there." This assumption is still current in the often-used expression that epistemology is the study of "knowledge of the external world," which is to say the world "out there."

Experience as we understand it has none of these characteristics because there is no sharp break, ontologically or epistemologically, in the transaction that is experience. First, we begin with continuity rather than discontinuity because we make use of James's idea that there is no ontological distinction between the self that is experiencing and the object experienced, in the sense that we do not talk in terms of mental entities that must somehow come into contact with physical entities. Second, because experience is a transaction, and because the relations that constitute the transaction, like all relations, are constitutive of all the "entities" in experience, the process is not passive in any general sense. When we talk about our world or environment as being experienced, we mean that we are in certain kinds of constitutive engagement with it, not that we are passively receiving anything from it, sense data, or anything else. Third, because the experiential transaction extends in experience the person into her environment, there is literally no sense to the distinction between "in here" and "out there," or to the idea that the self is engaged with an "external world." The self is embedded in the material and cultural environments that are among the relations that constitute her, in which picture the environment is as much in the self as the self is in the environment, so there is no identifiable "in here" and "out there." Experience simply does not work that way.

Traditionally, philosophers and others have approached experience by emphasizing one or the other of two common poles: undergoing and doing. This dichotomy has been expressed in many ways: passive and active, objectivity and creativity, primary and secondary, immediate and mediate, assimilative and manipulative, pure and refined. There is no necessity to choose one term or the other in these pairs, but for some reason or reasons philosophers have tempted to emphasize one term in each pair and de-emphasize the other. A point worth noting in this regard is that each pair maps onto the distinction between undergoing and doing, in the sense that the first term of each pair suggests undergoing while the second term suggests doing. Our point, then, is that for whatever reasons, philosophers have wanted to come down on one side or the other of this distinction.

In our approach to experience there is no need to choose, in part because it seems rather obvious that in its complexity and richness experience is a matter of both undergoing and doing. First, we can see now why it was important to distance ourselves from some of the terminology James, and Dewey as well, have used in talking about experience. In James's case, it is possible to talk about "pure" experience in the sense of simple prevalence or providingness, both of which are terms Buchler uses to indicate that something simply "is," but because experience is never simply pure in the sense of unrelated, there is little point in talking that way (Buchler 1974; 1978). In Dewey's case, when he says that experience can be immediate, he means not that there is no mediation but, rather, that it is possible for us to have direct experience. About that he is certainly right, though we would avoid potential confusion by avoiding the term "immediate" experience altogether, and say "direct" experience, if that is what we mean. Dewey in fact must have had to deal with this sort of objection in his own day, because in *Art as Experience* he comments that it is "only a twisted and aborted logic" that insists that because something is mediated it cannot therefore be immediately experienced. At the risk of engaging in "twisted and aborted logic," it seems to me best to avoid the term "immediate" when referring to experience (Dewey 2008, 125).

But the problems with terms like "pure" and "immediate" are not the most important issues here. The most important point is that experience indeed has all of these features, and it is only a truncated theory of experience that would insist on emphasizing objectivity over creativity, or the assimilative over the manipulative, or the active over the passive. Here we draw on James's point that we experience not elements of the world, but those elements in relation. That very process is both assimilative and manipulative, and it is characterized by both objectivity and creativity. It turns out, to make the point directly, that the terms of the pairs mentioned above are not contraries but correlatives. The transaction that is experience engages us with aspects of our worlds that we do not create, and at the same time the constitutive engagement of the process is necessarily creative. Experience is at its heart and by necessity both objective and creative, and the same applies to the other pairs to the extent that we can provide all the terms with plausible and useful meanings. There is no experience at all without assimilation and manipulation, without the immediate and the mediate, without passivity and activity, without the primary and secondary, and without the pure and refined. Where the terms require revision in our understanding, as in the case of "immediate experience," as with "primary" and "pure" experience as well, those revisions should and can be accomplished in such a way as to retain the initial sense and import of the terms while allowing them to sit comfortably with their correlative. We are not forced in our theory of experience to make conceptually debilitating choices between artificial dichotomous options. Experience, we may say colloquially, is all of the above.

To be clear, we have indicated several features of a general theory of experience, not a full theory. There is quite a bit to be said about experience, and the same Jamesian foundations that brought us this far also serve to help push the analysis further. There are three points we might make at this juncture to suggest where else this goes:

First, there are features of experience that are so pervasive and generally applicable that they form the very fabric of experience, and we refer to them as the dimensions of experience. There are in fact three such dimensions:

the cognitive, the aesthetic, and the political. We can say very little about them at this point, but the idea is that any and all experience, whatever other traits it may have, can be expected to embody the dimension of knowledge (the cognitive), art (the aesthetic), and power (the political). It is worth noting that, traditionally, discussions of experience have taken place within the context of considerations of knowledge. The traditional question throughout the history of philosophy has concerned the role of experience in knowledge. One reason for this pervasive association of experience with knowledge is that there really is such a close relation, though the traditions have misunderstood it. To put the situation right, it is better to ask the question differently, which is to say that instead of asking what the place of experience is in knowledge, it is more fruitful and interesting to ask what the place of knowledge is in experience. Experience is the broader category, something that, it seems to me, James understood. He put the point in terms of pure experience as the overarching ontological context in which cognition arises, but with the appropriate revisions described above, we want to take up roughly the same point. Cognition is central to experience, and in that respect, it is one of the three dimensions of experience.

That we may posit an aesthetic dimension of experience is something that one may take directly from Dewey, and that is what we have done. Dewey, as we know, drew directly on James for his understanding of the transactional character of experience. Among the many important respects in which he built on James is the idea, developed in detail in *Art as Experience*, that all experience embodies certain features of the aesthetic, specifically the traits of unity, harmony, and dissonance. The aesthetic in these and other senses is, as Dewey argued, pervasive in experience, and as a result we posit it as a dimension of experience.

The third dimension is power, or the political. The basic idea here, and in this we engage the more pragmatist side of James's understanding of elements of experience such as knowledge and truth as importantly consequential, is that in the fabric of experience is the never-ending encounter with and need to resolve problems in the engagement with our environments. That problem solving is so central to experience gives the transactional relation that is experience a dimension of power, hence the political dimension of experience. In the end, this dimension of experience can be explicated through the concepts of the individual, community, and interests. This in turn suggests that the fact that there is a political dimension of experience can illuminate the very general aspects of experience that involve power, which is to say problem solving in general, as well as more specific forms of the expressions or manifestations of power that we necessarily engage by virtue of being individuals in communities, which is to say various forms of social and political power in the more standard sense of the term.

It is worth adding here that while developing the idea of and rationale for positing the three dimensions of experience, one must explore how each engages the other two. It has long been the case, for example, that philosophers and others have referred to the element of beauty in theories and mathematical constructs. It is not unusual to hear even today physicists, among others, say that the elegance or beauty of a theory may be as important a reason for its endorsement as anything else. That we have this inclination points to the place of both the cognitive and the aesthetic in experience, and to the relation between them. One may make similar observations about the relation of knowledge and power, as well as of art and power.

Second, if at the more general level of the dimensions of experience we can posit knowledge, art, and power, we also recognize that any account of experience will have to make a clear place for features of experience that though not as generally pervasive as the dimensions of experience, are nevertheless central features of experience. These are what I prefer to call constituents of experience, and they are most importantly language, emotions, and imagination. The point is that though not all experience has to be linguistic or emotional, or even imaginative, the fact is that language, emotion, and imagination play such an important role in conditioning our experience, in providing its character, and in forging its meaning in any given case, that the general theory has to place them centrally even if not most generally in experience. The centrality of these constituents of experience is clear enough on reflection upon our own experience, and additional rationale appears in the fact that the phenomena of language, emotion, and imagination, especially language and emotion, have routinely been features in discussions of experience, including importantly in James. Though they are not as ubiquitous as knowledge, art, and power, our lives would not be human without language, emotion, and imagination, so it is incumbent on us to understand how they figure in the larger experiential transaction of the self with one's environment.

Third, any theory of experience must be able to appreciate the role played in our lives by what we may refer to as forms of experience. Among the many possible examples of forms of experience are social experience, romantic experience, historical experience, personal experience, military experience, international experience, sexual experience, athletic experience, ethical experience, and play. Philosophic literature is replete with accounts of various forms of experience, perhaps most famously James himself on religious experience. These are the forms our experience takes, and taken together they represent what is probably the richest mine of material for understanding experience and human life generally. No general theory can do justice to any of the many forms of experience, but no general theory can be adequate without recognizing their place and significance.

The final section of the chapter has been largely in the form of an IOU, which waits to be cashed out. For the present, the important point is that the entire edifice rests very much on James's shoulders. His understanding of the transactional character of experience and the embodiment of the self in the environment, of the centrality of relations, as well as their constitutive character and their ontological parity, and the continuity and pragmatic character of the elements of experience, forms the scaffolding on which the theory rests. He would no doubt not agree with some or much of it, though it would certainly be a pleasure to hear what he thought. In any case, the debt is ours, and there is no question that we are far the richer for the careful and creative attention James paid to experience.

NOTES

1. For examples of James's influence on Dewey, see Campbell.
2. Thanks to Lyubov Bugaeva for bringing this reference to my attention.
3. If specific pages are not indicated, references to James are to whole essays or books.
4. Nietzsche could also be mentioned as an alternative to the European traditions, but I leave him out because he is roughly a contemporary of James.

REFERENCES

Buchler, Justus. *The Main of Light: On the Concept of Poetry.* New York: Oxford University Press, 1974.
———. "Probing the Idea of Nature." *Process Studies* 8, no. 3 (1978): 157–68.
Bugaeva, Lyubov. "The Emotional Body and Visual Experience." *Pragmatism Today* 4, no. 1 (2013): 94–98.
———. "Bogdanov and Eisenstein on Emotions: The Affectional Theory of Expressiveness, and Emotional Script." In *Culture as Organization in Early Soviet Thought: Bogdanov, Eisenstein, and the Proletkult,* edited by Pia Tikka. Helsinki: Aalto University, 2016. crucible.org.aalto.fi/spherical.

Campbell, James. "Dewey's Debt to James." In *Oxford Handbook of Dewey*, edited by Steven Fesmire. New York: Oxford University Press, Forthcoming.

Dewey, John. *Art as Experience*. Vol. 10 of *The Later Works of John Dewey, 1925–1953*, edited by Jo Ann Boydston. Carbondale: Southern Illinois University Press, 2008.

James, William. *Essays in Radical Empiricism*. Vol. 3 of *The Works of William James*, edited by Fredson Bowers and Ignas K. Skrupskelis. Introduction by John J. McDermott. Cambridge, MA: Harvard University Press. [1912] 1976.

———. *The Principles of Psychology*. Vols. 8–10 of *The Works of William James*, edited by Frederick H. Burkhardt, Fredson Bowers, and Ignas K. Skrupskelis. Introductions by Rand B. Evans and Gerald E. Myers. Cambridge, MA: Harvard University Press. [1890] 1981.

Johnson, Mark. *The Meaning of the Body*. Chicago: University of Chicago Press, 2007.

Russell, Bertrand. "William James's Conception of Truth." In *Philosophical Essays*. London: Allen and Unwin, 1966.

Ryder, John. "Naturalisme Pragmatiste et Marxisme." In *Le Pragmatisme comme Philosophie Sociale et Politique*, edited by Roberto Frega. Lormont, France: Le Bord de l'eau, 2015.

Shusterman, Richard. *Body Consciousness: A Philosophy of Mindfulness and Somaesthetics*. Cambridge: Cambridge University Press, 2008.

CHAPTER 8

JAMES AND THE MINIMAL SELF

YUMIKO INUKAI

Is there something that we may call a self? It is clear *to me* that *I* am a thinker of *these* thoughts or an experiencer of *these* experiences at this moment insofar as I am conscious. The fact that these conscious thoughts are accessible only *to me* seems to give me a strong feeling of the existence *within*, even when I do not deliberately reflect on the restricted accessibility. It seems therefore ludicrous to doubt the existence of my-*self*; my *self* is, indeed, immediately felt in the conscious act of doubting. So, Descartes concludes, "this proposition, *I am, I exist*, is necessarily true" whenever any forms of thoughts arise in the mind (1984, 17).[1] James, as a psychologist determined to be faithful only to empirically observable and verifiable facts, also claims, "The universal conscious fact is not 'feelings and thoughts exist,' but 'I think' and 'I feel.' No psychology, at any rate, can question the *existence* of personal selves" (1981, 221). There is something about conscious thoughts and experiences that points to the existence of what we call a self.

In recent years, some philosophers have begun to pay more attention to the relationship between phenomenal consciousness and subjectivity again in their investigation of the self. Galen Strawson, for example, argues that since the vivid sense of a self as a subject of experience is what leads us to ask questions about the existence of a self, we need first to look at experience in which such a vivid sense of a self is present and answer first "the *phenomenological* question 'What sort of thing is figured in self-experience?'" (2000, 40). Dan Zahavi also states, "it is nowadays almost commonplace to argue that the experiential or first-personal dimension of consciousness must be taken seriously since an important and non-negligible feature of consciousness is the way in which it is experienced by the subject" (2002, 7). Instead of settling the question regarding the existence and the nature of the self first, as Descartes does, some contemporary philosophers attempt to illuminate the structure of experience in which a sense of the self as a subject of experience arises in the first place, as Husserl and Sartre do. In other words, some contend that the phenomenological investigation of phenomenal, first-personal features of consciousness must precede the ontological investigation of what the self *is*. This approach has proven to be quite fruitful: it has yielded a basic, yet critical, notion of the self—"the minimal self."[2] The minimal self is an immediate subject of experience that remains even when "all of the essential features of self are stripped away" (Gallagher 2000, 15): it is a self at the most fundamental level, which is intimately connected with the character of first-personal perspective of conscious states.

There is another, recently developed, popular account of the self, which is a more robust notion than the minimal self—the self as a narrative construction.[3] In this view, the self is constituted by narratives constructed over time. It captures our ordinary conception of "who I am," which often includes, among other elements, our particular personalities, beliefs, values, and future plans, structured to constitute a life story of "my*self*." Interestingly, however, the notion of the narrative self and that of the minimal self are often not seen as conflicting with each other; rather, they are complementary. The narrative self view describes how we concretely see ourselves and explains how we understand ourselves, whereas the minimal self view points to a ubiquitous sense of the self as a subject of experience. Although the narrative construction of the self includes various particular dimensions of first-personal phenomena, it is the minimal sense of the self that specifically articulates their fundamental, first-personal character that essentially allows the narrative construction.[4] Zahavi, therefore, strongly argues that the two must be integrated to capture the complexity of the self (2009, 567).

That is exactly what James does. James's account of the self, which incorporates the wide range of phenomena and aspects included in the minimal-self view as well as the narrative-self view, has not been unnoticed.[5] Shaun Gallagher gives James credit for being the first to offer such an account: "Ever since William James categorized different senses of the self . . . [,] philosophers and psychologists have refined and expanded the possible variations of this concept" (2000, 14). However, James's contribution should be recognized beyond the fact of having drawn attention to different aspects of the self. His detailed analyses of consciousness and the self contain numerous insightful characterizations of them, which can still provide great resources for us to draw on. To borrow Zahavi's words, it is "counterproductive to ignore the rich and refined accounts of" the self that James offers.[6]

My purpose here is twofold: first to show the similarities between some methodological moves made and general ideas developed by proponents of the minimal self and the narrative self and those in James, and second, to draw attention to some of James's descriptions and points that can still shed some phenomenological light on crucial aspects of the self. In this chapter, I first introduce the general notions of the minimal self and the narrative self, outlining their key characteristics. Next, I discuss some of James's analyses of the stream of consciousness and the self to underscore the similarities between James's findings and the notions of the minimal and narrative self. In so doing, I hope to show James's analyses of the self still provide insightful resources for our investigation of the self. Why? Because he is right!

THE MINIMAL SELF AND THE NARRATIVE SELF

It is widely acknowledged that conscious experiences have a subjective, phenomenal character, which is often captured by the description—"*what it is like*" to undergo them. This characterization of experiences, "what it is like," refers to a *how* of experiences rather than a *what*: it is a phenomenal quality of *how* a taste of coffee or a feeling of frustration is experienced. It characterizes a *first-personal* character of conscious experiences; in other words, it points to a first-person perspective, which is associated with a "self." Thomas Metzinger writes: "For human beings, during the ongoing process of conscious experience characterizing their waking and dreaming life, *a self is present*. Human beings consciously experience themselves as *being someone*" (2003, 5). He connects "being someone" with "the phenomenology of perspectivalness," that is, "a focus of experience, a *point* of view" (ibid., 157). The sense of "a self being present" or "being someone" is a *minimal* sense of self, "an intuition that there is a basic, immediate, or primitive 'something' that we are willing to call a self" (Gallagher 2000, 15). *That* is the minimal self. Pinpointing experiential properties that give rise to "what-it-is-likeness" is not easy because it is a ubiquitous character of conscious experiences that is an integral aspect of them. Zahavi, however, provides an astute analysis of such properties. So, let us look at Zahavi's formulations to obtain a general notion of the minimal self. Now, it is important to keep in mind that the characterizations of relevant properties are conceptually distinguished formulations of an immediate, primitive phenomenal character of experience, which gives rise to the sense of the self. So, they should not be understood to correspond to different elements of consciousness: they are different descriptions of the same experiential character that is described as "what-it-is-likeness."

Zahavi argues first that the quality of "what-it-is-likeness" refers to an experiential quality that is over and above the qualities of intentional objects such as coffee or a cherry. He calls it "the first-personal givenness." To explain the first-personal givenness of experience, Zahavi makes a key distinction among phenomenal characters of experience between "what the object is like for the subject" and "what the experience of the object is like for the subject," both of which could possibly be answers for the question of "what it is like" to taste coffee (2005, 121). Properties of an object experienced, such as the bitterness of coffee, constitute phenomenal characters of the experience of coffee. However, there is another experiential property present in experience; it is first-personally presented or given *to me*. Elucidating this quality, Zahavi offers a case of an epistemic asymmetry involved in two people perceiving the same object:

> Whereas John and Mary can both perceive the exact same cherry, each of them [has] his or her own distinct perception of it and can share these just as little as Mary can share John's bodily pain. . . . It is here customary to speak of an epistemic asymmetry and say that Mary has no access to the *first personal givenness* of John's experience. (2005, 122)

Both John and Mary may perceive exactly the same phenomenal redness of the cherry, which is a property of an object, but the experience of each one has the quality of the first-personal givenness, which is a property of the experiencing of the object. These properties are conceptually distinguished but cannot be separated in experience: they are two aspects of experience, through which the minimal self is disclosed to whom an object is appearing.[7]

Experiences, in which physical objects like coffee and cherry and mental states like frustration and joy are presented, have a common feature that also reveals another phenomenal feature of experience: "mineness." When an experience is given in the first-personal mode, it is experienced as *owned*, or *mine*.[8] This *mineness* does not refer to a feature or element of experience recognized by a reflective act; rather, it is "a subtle background presence" that invariably permeates experience. The mineness of experience in question is an integral experiential feature of immediate conscious states constituted by their first-personal givenness. In other words, to say that a bitter taste of coffee is experienced immediately and pre-reflectively as given *to me* is to say that it is *my* experience. This immediate sense of mineness constitutes a sense of the self, which is considered as a *minimal* one because it does not involve any other, more substantial, phenomena but is constituted only by this immediate sense or "feel." It is important to remember that a constant phenomenal feel of various experiences *being owned by me* does not necessarily indicate the existence of a separate "something" that owns them together. Zahavi writes: "the self is not something that stands opposed to the stream of consciousness, but is, rather, immersed in conscious life; it is an integral part of its structure" (2005, 125).

The first-personal givenness and mineness being integral, experiential features of conscious experiences brings in another character of the minimal self: individuality. Even if there are two perceptions whose intentional contents are the same, say, the supermoon of December in the sky, they are inherently individuated because of the first-personal givenness. The roundness, whiteness, brightness, and size of the supermoon may be presented exactly the same in my perception and your perception of the moon, but they are absolutely differentiated and separated from each other because your perception is presented in a mode of the first-personal givenness only for you, and not at all for me (Zahavi 2005, 127). Perceptions never arise anonymously. Thus, the minimal self associated with the first-personal givenness revealed in each perception is necessarily individuated. A critical issue can be raised at this point. Each minimal self identified by the first-personal givenness in various experiences must be numerically different from any other even within the same stream of consciousness. Although the first-personal givenness is an invariable experiential feature of conscious experiences throughout and may give rise to the same experiential feel, its invariableness cannot establish the diachronic identity of minimal selves that are present in experiences because conscious experiences are all in constant flux. Just as each minimal self revealed in my perception and your perception are numerically different, minimal selves felt in momentary experiences must be numerically different.[9]

Zahavi recognizes this problem of diachronic identity; he writes, "When does my self-awareness contain a reference to such an overarching identity? I think a plausible answer would be that the self-givenness of a single experience is a necessary, but not a sufficient, condition for this type of self-awareness to occur" (2005, 131). He explains that although the minimal self identified by the first-person givenness of a single experience is strictly singular, the first-person givenness is an invariable dimension of changing experiences and thus remains the same. So, he claims, "if I have first-personal access to the past experience, it is automatically given as *my* past experience" (ibid., 132). Multiple experiences are bridged and the diachronic identity of the minimal self is revealed by this remembering act of synthesis that is grounded in the invariably pervasive dimension of the first-personal givenness of experiences. The first-personal givenness, therefore, provides a fundamental structure of individuation and identity of the minimal self. This is where Zahavi introduces a narrative conception of the self to supplement it, as it were. He claims that a more concrete, robust kind of individuality and identity of the self "manifests itself in my personal history, in my moral and intellectual convictions and decisions. It is through such acts that I define myself. . . . I remain the same as long as I adhere to my convictions; when they change, *I* change" (ibid., 129). Particular acts, convictions, and decisions constitute my personal story, because they are *mine*, that is, they share the same mode of the first-givenness, and my story defines who I am, not just as a minimal self at this moment, but as a continuing, particular self. Who I am as a particular self changes and develops over the course of *my* life, or *my* story, as convictions, beliefs, hopes, plans, and values change and develop. However, insofar as they are still *my* convictions, *my* beliefs, and *my* hopes, they constitute *my* story, who *I* am, the same continuing particular *me*.

Let us move to the notion of the narrative self and look at it briefly. The general idea of various narrative approaches to the self is that stories told about me by myself as well by others constitute and shape who I am; in other words, the self is a product of narratives. Daniel Dennett famously writes,

> . . . our tales are spun, but for the most part we don't spin them; they spin us. Our human consciousness, and our narrative selfhood, is their product, not their source. . . . These strings or streams of narrative issue forth *as if* from a single source . . . ; their effect on any audience is to encourage them to (try to) posit a unified agent whose words they are, about whom they are: in short to posit a *center of narrative gravity*. (1991, 418)

Narratives are structured to be an intelligible story in which actions are situated and related with past and future intentions and goals, traits, abilities, interests, values, and so on. What are included and how they are related in a narrative sequence are just not a matter of discovery, but rather that of choice, decision, and thus organization. The self, which is constituted by such narratives, is therefore a construction. Further, such a construction is not done solely by oneself but also by others: it involves social and cultural factors as well.

To recapitulate, the key characteristics of the two popular notions of the self—the minimal self and the narrative self—in the contemporary debate of the self are the following. The minimal self is identified by the experiential characters of (1) "what-it-is-likeness," (2) first-personal givenness, and (3) mineness or ownership, and it is (4) individuated, and (5) formally identical. The narrative self is a particular self (6) constructed and constituted by various factors within the social context and (7) to which a concrete diachronic identity is attributed. In the next section, I will show that all of these features can be found in James's accounts of the stream of consciousness and the self. For James, these two models of the self are two aspects of the self that explain the relations among its constituents and capture its complexity.

JAMES'S ANALYSES OF THE SELF

In the chapter entitled "The Stream of Thought" in *The Principles of Psychology*, James provides a detailed analysis of consciousness, in which some crucial phenomenological features of our conscious experience are discussed. He then moves on to investigate the sense and conception of the self with those features in hand in the following chapter. James's approach to the investigation of the self is exemplified by the way in which these two chapters are connected: the phenomenological analysis of consciousness not only paves the way for an investigation of the self based on introspective observation but also shows that the self is grounded in the structure of consciousness itself. Just like Strawson and Zahavi, James takes it that the phenomenological investigation of essential features of consciousness can answer the question of what the self is.

According to James, one of the five characters of consciousness is that "every thought tends to be part of a personal consciousness" (James 1981, 220).[10] The five characters are immediate features of how "*thought goes on,*" which is the fundamental fact that psychology as "the Science of Mental Life" is entitled to postulate at the beginning (ibid., 15).[11] James claims that being *personal* is an immediate feature of every conscious thought, and he seems to identify this aspect of consciousness with the consciousness of the self, that is, the minimal self discussed above. He writes that " 'personal consciousness' is one of the terms in question. Its meaning we know so long as no one asks us to define it, but to give an accurate account of it is the most difficult philosophic task. This task we must confront in the next chapter," which is called "The Consciousness of Self" (ibid., 220). James mentions this only in passing, but its implication is significant. If being "personal" is an immediate character of consciousness and points to a self of some sort, a self must be present in some way in consciousness at the most fundamental level. This echoes Metzinger's claim that a self is present in the ongoing process of conscious experience. Every conscious thought or experience occurs with a sense of a particular self.

James initially describes the point thus:

> In this room—this lecture-room, say—there are a multitude of thoughts, yours and mine, some of which cohere mutually, and some not. They are as little each-for-itself and reciprocally independent as they are all-belonging-together. They are neither: no one of them is separate, but each belongs with certain others and with none beside. My thought belongs with my other thoughts, and your thought with your other thoughts. Whether anywhere in the room there be a mere thought, which is nobody's thought, we have no means of ascertaining, for we have no experience of its like. The only states of consciousness that we naturally deal with are found in personal consciousness, minds, selves, concrete particular I's and you's. (1981, 220–21)

Thoughts are not individually free-floating in the air, but they belong together with some other thoughts. But James's emphasis is not just the fact of some particular thoughts belonging together; rather, some thoughts belong together because they are *my* thoughts, some others belong together because they are *your* thoughts, and there are no thoughts that are nobody's. Every thought is someone's. James's reason for not being able to determine whether or not there are nobody's thoughts is quite telling. If I cannot verify the existence of nobody's thoughts because I don't have experience of them, how could I be certain about the existence of *your* thoughts when I have no access to them either? James himself acknowledges "absolute insulation" between my personal consciousness and yours: "No thought even comes into direct *sight* of a thought in another personal consciousness than its own" (James

1981, 221). The only thought that I have access to is *my* thought, so I have direct experience of "its like." If James still thinks I have experience of what your thought is like, but not what nobody's thought is like, he must be speaking of experience of what is shared between mine and yours but not between mine and nobody's. I believe that the character shared by mine and yours that James is describing is exactly what Zahavi calls "first-personal givenness." Nobody's thought, or "a mere thought," lacks the character of the first-personal givenness precisely because there is nobody for whom it is given, whereas your thought has that character because it is first-personally given *to you*. Although I don't have direct access to your thought, I have experience of "its like," at least. Therefore, the character of being "personal" consciousness shared by my consciousness and your consciousness, but not by nobody's, is the first-personal givenness, by which the minimal self is identified.

Indeed, James goes on to claim: "It seems as if the elementary psychic fact were not *thought* or *this thought* or *that thought*, but *my thought*, every thought being *owned*" (1981, 221). The difference between my thought and your thought is not a difference between *this* thought and *that* thought; one is first-personally presented to, or owned by, *me*, whereas the other is first-personally presented to, or owned by, *you*. It is under the "form of personal selfhood" that "thoughts appear" (ibid.): that is, thoughts appear as *mine*. James identifies the character of the mineness with the fundamental form of consciousness.

In analyzing immediate features of experience itself, James also makes a distinction between characters of contents of experience (in James's terms, "the things of which [thoughts] are aware") and those of experience itself ("the thoughts themselves") (1981, 233), which corresponds to Zahavi's distinction between "what the object is like for the subject" and "what the experience of the object is like for the subject.' James introduces the distinction specifically to explain the character of continuity of experience as a subjective fact although objects that are presented in it may be discontinuous and discrete.[12] But the distinction can also be applied to the two aspects of thought in question, the *personal* form of thought and appearing thoughts: the former is a property of experience of thoughts—*how* thoughts are experienced—while the latter is objects presented in experience—*what* contents of thoughts are experienced. This distinction might suggest that there are two parts to a thought of an object, for example, the moon: the content of thought (i.e., the moon) and the thought itself as a separate monitoring consciousness. But this is a mistake. James argues that the object is something to which a particular name is given like "moon," "sun," and "star," and it constitutes the content of experience. However, experience contains more than such objects: relations among objects, emotions, feelings of various kinds such as tendencies and direction, and so forth, which James calls "transitive parts" and "fringes."[13] All of these parts are not to be taken as discrete elements of experience. It is not amiss to say that it is James's most unwavering view that, at the experiential level, experience is fundamentally unitary, and yet its structure and essential characteristics can be disclosed by a careful introspective study, which yields various conceptual distinctions. Therefore, recognizing the distinction between objects presented in thoughts and the feature of thoughts themselves under which they appear, James is not implying the existence of a separate something that thinks of the objects and owns those thoughts. The "form of personal selfhood" and the mineness of thought point to a phenomenal feel that essentially accompanies an appearing thought, as if it were "halo or penumbra that surrounds and escorts it,—or rather that is fused into one with it and has become bone of its bone and flesh of its flesh" (1981, 246).

Interestingly, James goes further than contemporary proponents of the minimal self to provide a concrete description of the phenomenal feel identified with the aspect of the personal selfhood and the mineness of conscious thoughts. He calls it "warmth and intimacy." In order to explain the phenomenon where we rarely fail to reconnect our conscious experiences before and after an interruption brought about by deep sleep, James describes the key difference—the presence or absence of "warmth and intimacy"—between the acts of remembering and conceiving and explains how it functions to bring distant conscious experiences together with a present one. He uses an example of two people falling asleep and waking up simultaneously:

> When Paul and Peter wake up in the same bed, and recognize that they have been asleep, each one of them mentally reaches back and makes connection with but *one* of the two streams of thought which were broken by the sleeping hours. . . . Peter's present instantly finds out Peter's past, and never by mistake kits itself on to that of Paul. Paul's thought in turn is as little liable to go astray. The past thought of Peter is appropriated by the present Peter alone. He may have a *knowledge*, and a correct one too, of what Paul's last drowsy states of mind were as he sank into sleep, but it is an entirely different sort of knowledge

from that which he has of his own last states. He *remembers* his own states, whilst he only *conceives* Paul's. Remembrance is like direct feeling; its object is suffused with a warmth and intimacy to which no object of mere conception ever attains. This quality of warmth and intimacy and immediacy is what Peter's *present* thought also possesses for itself. So sure as this present is me, is mine, it says, so sure is anything else that comes with the same warmth and intimacy and immediacy, me and mine. (1981, 232)

Suppose that right before Paul and Peter fell asleep, Peter was thinking about a neighbor's barking dog, whereas Paul was thinking about the same neighbor's crying baby; further, Peter knows exactly what Paul was thinking at the last moment before he fell asleep. When Peter wakes up, according to James, he has no trouble connecting his present waking state to the past thought of the barking dog, even when both the dog and the crying baby are present in Peter's current waking state. This is because there is an important difference in a phenomenal feel between the thought of the dog and the thought of the baby: the former thought is "suffused with a warmth and intimacy," whereas, for Peter, the latter is not. It is important to notice that James is not describing a reflective process where Peter determines which one was his thought by looking for a thought with warmth and intimacy. The thought of the dog is "instantly" given to Peter as *his* past thought, as it is not a mere thought appearing without any *feel* to it but a thought with the feel of the *mineness*, which the description "warmth and intimacy and immediacy" captures. The thought of the dog was first-personally given to Peter the night before so that it appeared with the mineness, that is, the phenomenal feel of warmth and intimacy, while the thought of the baby was given to him only from the *second*-person perspective.

According to James, therefore, a bridge is automatically made between past thoughts and a present thought on the basis of the phenomenal feel of warmth and intimacy, that is, the *mineness* of thoughts. Recall this is what Zahavi also claims in response to the question of the diachronic identity of the minimal self. Just like Zahavi, who maintains that the first-personal givenness is an invariable dimension of the stream of experiences, James also recognizes from the beginning that the aspect of being *personal* is a fundamental feature of consciousness. For James, too, being *personal* is a formal aspect of consciousness that makes thoughts *mine*, which grounds the togetherness of multiple thoughts both at a time and over time. This leads to absolute individuation of the stream of personal consciousness:

> Each of these minds keeps its own thoughts to itself. There is no giving or bartering between them. . . . Absolute insulation, irreducible pluralism is the law. . . . Neither contemporaneity, nor proximity in space, nor similarity of quality and content are able to fuse thoughts together which are sundered by this barrier of belonging to different personal minds. The breaches between such thoughts are the most absolute breaches in nature. (1981, 221)

Individuation of each consciousness is effected by its essential *mineness*. However, according to the second point of the five fundamental characters of consciousness that James describes in the chapter of "The Stream of Thought," thought is always changing within each personal consciousness; hence, there is nothing numerically identical among changing thoughts. If thoughts are in constant flux, then each mineness in each of the changing thoughts cannot be numerically identical with any other mineness. But James sometimes identifies a whole stream as "*myself, I, or me*" (1981, 232). How could a stream of changing thoughts be considered as *myself*? James has a reply.

In the chapter entitled "The Consciousness of Self," James begins a more focused investigation of the self. He connects the phenomenal feel of warmth and intimacy with a sense of the self within the present portion of consciousness. The present self is an aspect of thought itself to which the character of warmth and intimacy clings (which James also calls "the Thought" and "the judging thought" later). Earlier, in the chapter on the stream of thought, James only describes a fundamental experiential aspect of consciousness as a character of being *personal* and thoughts as essentially being *my* thought. As illustrated by the example of Paul and Peter, he then associates the feel of warmth and intimacy with the *mineness*. Now, James finally connects the *personal* aspect of consciousness with the *self* more explicitly. The present self for James is what the minimal self is for its proponents like Zahavi. Since the present self is an aspect of a momentary thought appearing in the present potion of consciousness, it must also be momentary just like the minimal self. James actually admits that the diachronic identity of the self understood as an aspect of thought therefore cannot be found as a fact in the stream of consciousness. However, James claims, "it would exist as a *feeling* all the same; the consciousness of it by the thought would be there" (1981, 316). This means that the diachronic identity of the present self would also be an experiential property of thought. How does such a feeling appear?

There are two characteristics of a stream of thought on which a primitive feeling of the identity of a self is based: resemblance and continuity.[14] We have already seen in what resemblance consists and what it does in the illustration of warmth and intimacy in the example of Peter and Paul. A sense of diachronic identity between the present self and past selves is grounded in the phenomenal feel of warmth and intimacy shared among them: the present self at the current moment, as it were, takes in those past parts of experience with which it feels the same warmth and intimacy, automatically deeming them as *mine* and making a group of the past *Me's* that were present selves at those past moments. James writes:

> The animal warmth, etc., is their herd-mark, the brand from which they can never more escape. It runs through them all like a thread through a chaplet and makes them into a whole, which we treat as a unit, no matter how much in other ways the parts may differ *inter se*. (1981, 317)

Another criterion by which the identity relation is established is *continuity*. A character of temporal continuity of experience also brings the sense of identity: it is grounded in an immediate experience of the continuity between a just-past present self and the present self. It is the idea of the specious present that lies behind this claim.[15] According to James, our present awareness is not like a knife-edge; rather it has a certain extensiveness and duration, in which a just-past, a present, and a just-coming-future are all phenomenally present; in other words, we experience the immediate past along with the present. So, although a present self of two seconds ago is obviously a past self, it nonetheless is phenomenally available at the periphery of a present awareness in which the present self is felt. Accordingly, a continuity between the self of two seconds ago and the present self is immediately experienced in the specious present. On the other hand, when such a direct experience of continuity is absent, as in the case of the self of five weeks ago and the present self, the resemblance of phenomenal feelings (i.e., warmth and intimacy) grounds a sense of identity between them. Unlike Locke who appeals only to memory to forge an identity connection between the distant self and the present self, James, like Hume, takes the characteristic of resemblance as the basis for the connection.

The two experiential features, the feeling of warmth and intimacy and the experiencing of direct continuity, together ground a definite sense of the diachronic identity of the self. On the basis of these characters, James further explains the generation of a more concrete sense of ownership attributed to the present self than the primitive aspect of the mineness of consciousness, thereby explaining the unity of the self. He writes:

> . . . in our own account . . . the herdsman is there, in the shape of something not among the things collected, but superior to them all, namely the real, present onlooking, remembering, "judging thought" or identifying "section" of the stream. This is what collects,—"owns" some of the past facts which it surveys, and disowns the rest,—and so makes a unity that is actualized and anchored and does not merely float in the blue air of possibility. And the reality of such pulses of thought, with their function of knowing, it will be remembered that we did not seek to deduce or explain, but simply assumed them as the ultimate kind of fact that psychologist must admit to exit. (1981, 338)

The unity of multiple past selves is anchored in a currently occurring "judging thought" that serves as a knower of them manifested in the stream of consciousness. James assigns the function of knowing to an aspect of thought itself; a "judging thought" designates such an aspect that grasps and appropriates certain parts of the stream as belonging to itself. The present self whose existence is characterized as the phenomenal feeling of warmth and intimacy is now identified as the "judging thought," which performs an appropriative act of binding past selves with itself to yield a unified whole of the self. Just as the identity of the present self is felt with distant past selves by way of resemblance and with an immediate past self by way of continuity, the appropriative act of the judging thought also operates in those two manners.

First, the judging thought, or the present self, surveys past portions of the stream as presented in the current awareness. Among those presentations, it finds some of them possessing a similar phenomenal feel of warmth and intimacy to its own, on the basis of which it takes them to be *me* and thereby unifies together and anchor them to itself. *Second*, in the specious present, an immediate past self (which was a present self in the immediate past) is directly presented to the present self at the current moment. The direct access of the present self to the immediate past self in the specious present enables the present self to immediately feel its continuity from the immediate past self, on the basis of which the present self takes it to belong to itself. These two types of appropriative act of the present self occur at the same time: as the stream flows, the appropriative act based on immediate continuity ensues from moment to moment, while remote past selves are occasionally presented in the current pulse of the stream and appropriated there. In this way, the unity of the self is experienced and realized in the present self's act of appropriation.

The sense of continuing ownership is also sensed and preserved in the appropriative act of the present self even though the present self at the current moment is not, strictly speaking, numerically identical with other selves. It is like a long succession of individual present selves coming into possession of a group of previous thoughts by transmitting the ownership from one to the next, as each present self dies away and is replaced by a new one:

> Each pulse of cognitive consciousness, each Thought, dies away and is replaced by another. The other, among the things it knows, knows its own predecessor, and finding it 'warm,' . . . greets it, saying; "Thou art mine, and part of the same self with me." Each later Thought, knowing and including thus the Thoughts which went before, is the final receptacle—and appropriating them is the final owner—of all that they contain and own. Each Thought is thus born an owner, and dies owned, transmitting whatever it realized as its Self to its own proprietor. (James 1981, 322)

The owner is the present self at each moment, appropriating a previous present self that was an owner at the last moment, together with what the latter claimed to be its own. James contends that the existence of such experiential features are undeniable psychological facts: the descriptions of appropriating and transmitting the ownership fit in what we immediately feel in our stream of experience itself. The mineness, the identity, the individuality, the unity, and the ownership "are thus accounted for as phenomenal and temporal facts exclusively, and with no need of reference to any more simple or substantial agent than the present Thought or 'section' of the stream" (James 1981, 326–27). Hence, James famously says, the "*thought is itself the thinker*" (379).

The process of appropriation produces the primitive sense of the diachronic identity of the present self, and the unity of the self realized by it encompasses everything that is suffused with warmth and intimacy and thereby presented as *mine*. James's analysis is compelling. He shows that there is no need to postulate a substantive subject in the form of either a soul or a transcendental ego to account for the identity and unity of the self. James also thinks that it generates a particular, "widest sense" of the self, which James calls "the Empirical Self" (1981, 279), for he says, "the consciousness of Self involves a stream of thought, each part of which as 'I' can . . . emphasize and care paramountly for certain ones among them as '*me*,' and *appropriate to these* the rest" (ibid., 378). Among all the things in the stream that are deemed to be part of *me*, certain ones that I "care paramountly" about are considered to be "*constituents* of the me in a larger sense. . . . This me is an empirical aggregate of things objectively known" (379). Admittedly, James's Empirical Self is not the same as the narrative self understood generally; the Empirical Self may include more than narratives of a single character, and James's explanation of what gets to be included in the construction of the Empirical Self does not appeal specifically to a story-telling tendency of humans. However, its construction is also largely interest-based. As one of the five characters of thought is that "it is always interested more in one part of its object than in another, and welcomes and rejects, or chooses, all the while it thinks" (273), the empirical, concrete self is created out of various elements that are chosen because they are found interesting, significant, and important in some way. Whatever are welcome become parts of *me*, defining who I am and determining how I act in the presence of others.

What sorts of things are chosen to be appropriated into a unified Empirical Self? According to James, they are categorized into three types—material, social, and spiritual—and corresponding to these three, he distinguishes three aspects of the Empirical Self into the material self, the social self, and the spiritual self. Briefly, the material self consists not only of our own bodies, but also of our clothes, family, home, property, works, and the like. The material dimension of the self extends to all things that are felt to be uniquely ours so as to produce personal, emotional feelings in us; for example, the loss of our family member often makes us feel that part of us also died. The same is true of our productions, especially those into which we have spent much time and effort. We actually identify with them to such a degree that when they are lost, we would feel "personally annihilated" and have "a sense of the shrinkage of our personality, a partial conversion of ourselves to nothingness" (James 1981, 281). The social self, on the other hand, consists mainly of the images of ourselves in the minds of those whose opinions we care about. Basically, the social self is constituted by our relations to others: depending on with whom we are, we play a different role, which creates a corresponding image in the other's mind, a rebellious daughter, a loyal friend, and an enthusiastic teacher, for instance. All of them, collectively, constitute the social dimension of the self, which may exist either in "a discordant splitting" or in "a perfectly harmonious division of labor" (282). Each of them has its own socially or culturally specified standards and requirements that dictate our behavior, and particular images that others have can also determine how we act even in the future. Whether there is consistency or inconsistency with those diverse images, we care about them, and identify ourselves with them; thus, any damages to them are taken as damages to ourselves, and, moreover, any changes to them are changes to ourselves. Finally, the spiritual self consists in mental capacities to think, doubt, assent, reject, remember, feel, will, desire, and so forth, taken concretely as they are manifested in experience. This is a more internal and enduring aspect of the self than the material and social aspects. James writes:

> [A] certain portion of the stream abstracted from the rest . . . is felt by all men as a sort of innermost center within the circle, of sanctuary within the citadel, constituted by the subjective life as a whole. Compared with this element of the stream, the other parts, even of the subjective life, seem transient external possessions, of which each in turn can be disowned, whilst that which disowns them remains. (1981, 284–85)

Even if the material, social, and spiritual selves are on the same footing as they are all empirically manifested in experience, the spiritual self appears to be a "self of all the other selves" (ibid., 285).

James further explains that constituents of all the three aspects of the Empirical Self are both instinctively and deliberately chosen. For example, much of the material dimension of the self seems to be instinctively driven: our bodies and whatever satisfy their basic needs are objects of our strong self-centered interests because self-preservation is a basic instinctive impulse of humans, according to James. Other objects also could become of interest to us derivatively, which enlarges the sphere of the material dimension of the self (1981, 304–08). On the other hand, most parts of the social self are deliberately selected. James writes:

> The millionaire's work would run counter to the saint's; the *bon-vivant* and the philanthropist would trip each other up; the philosopher and the lady-killer could not well keep house in the same tenement of clay. Such different characters may conceivably at the outset of life be alike *possible* to a man. But to make any one of them actual, the rest must more or less be suppressed. So the seeker of his truest, strongest, deepest self must review the list carefully, and pick out the one on which to stake his salvation. All other selves thereupon become unreal, but the fortunes of this self are real. . . . This is as strong an example as there is of that selective industry of the mind on which I insisted some pages back [273ff]. Our thought, incessantly deciding, among many things of a kind, which ones for it shall be realities, here chooses one of many possible selves or characters, and forthwith reckons it no shame to fail in any of those not adopted expressly as its own. (1981, 295–96)

Depending on our personalities, interests, moral beliefs, and values, some parts of the social self are intentionally given up, suppressed, maintained, and even pursued. The same could be said about some parts of the material self and the spiritual self: the ability to reason and judge but not the disposition to experience intense anger may not be chosen to be part of *my* spiritual self because I am a calm, rational person; and my bicycle, but not my car, may be appropriated to my material self because I am extremely concerned with the environment. The Empirical Self is, therefore, constructed based on impulses, practical and intellectual interests and values, beliefs, personalities, and social and cultural inputs.

The self develops and undergoes changes as experience accrues through the interaction with other people and objects existent in the world, and yet it feels existing *here and now* as well as over time, actively engaging with objects of experience and occupying a particular point of view from which experience is lived through. The self is not a simple, unchanging entity like the Cartesian substantial self; it is a complex, dynamic, unified system, which is experienced as *real* as it can get, unlike the Humean fictitious identical self. Zahavi forcefully asks, "why not rather insist that the self is real if it has experiential reality and that the validity of our account of the self is to be measured by its ability to be faithful to experience, by its ability to capture and articulate (invariant) experiential structures?" (2005, 128). James would give an absolute YES. So, what *is* the self then? It is nothing separate from, or standing over, the stream of thought. The Me is constituted by things concretely experienced, whether they are material possessions, social roles and images, or mental acts and abilities; the I is a perspective, an aspect of a present potion of thought, suffused with "warmth and intimacy." The self is, after all, the stream of thought itself for James, which does not make the self unreal or a fiction; it has strong and definite empirical presence and reality. "[*T*]*hought is itself the thinker*," nothing more, nothing less (James 1981, 379).

James's account of the self is quite radical because ultimately it rejects the idea of the self as some*thing* that has various capacities and qualities including thoughts and feelings. It might seem counterintuitive to say that the self is just an aspect of thought. For this matter, the so-called Cartesian view of the self, which takes the self to be a substance or an entity to which conscious states belong, may better capture our intuitive conception of the self. However, I believe that James is right in insisting that positing a substantial being behind various conscious states would be "a complete superfluity, so far as accounting for the actually verified facts of conscious experience goes" (1981, 329). James's accounts of the phenomenal feels and characters of conscious experience well capture our sense of the self without invoking the existence of anything other than what is available in the stream of experience. Given especially that Descartes himself admits that we are not immediately aware of a substantial mind, or self, itself, but only of different mental acts (1984, 124), it would merely be an unintelligible, unnecessary postulate.

Clearly, empiricists' accounts of the self, such as those offered by Locke and Hume, who have the Cartesian view in mind as their opponent, have some affinities with James's: they all attempt to account for the self solely on empirical grounds. Locke takes the self to be a conscious, intelligent being that is aware of itself as itself, and he argues that its identity depends on the continuity of consciousness forged by memory (1975, 335). Hume, on the other hand, takes the self to be just a collection of distinct, fleeting perceptions, and he explains that the sense of identity attributed to the self is a mere fiction produced by the felt relations among perceptions. James's account contains similar elements to those in Locke's and Hume's: the identity of the self grounded in the continuity of consciousness, the self being a composite of various experiences or perceptions, and the sense of identity produced by experienced relations. However, James makes significant improvements on their views: he has more resources (for example, the notions of specious present, the phenomenal feels associated with the first-personal perspective, and the fundamental continuity of experience, among others) to establish the strictly empiricist account of the self. James also provides an incomparably richer account of the composition of the self than Hume's mere "bundle of perceptions."

CONCLUSION

James's aims in the chapter "The Consciousness of Self" are to lay bare the constituents of what he calls the "Empirical Self," which is concretely and objectively manifested within the stream of experience, and to account for the primitive senses of the identity and unity of the self in terms of immediate, experiential features of experience. These undertakings reflect his keen insights that the self is multilayered and that different types of accounts are needed to capture its complexity appropriately. We find a similar viewpoint in Gallagher, who focuses on both the minimal and narrative notions of the self, and in Zahavi, who explicitly argues the need for a multidimensional account of the self. James's insight doesn't stop here: he vigorously argues that such an account can be generated successfully without going beyond the domain of experience itself—that is, beyond fundamental experiential features of consciousness as well as more concrete, ordinary experiences in which we interact with the world, all of which are available in the stream of consciousness. James not only combines these two experiential levels in his account of the self, but bases his explanation of the construction of the Empirical Me on the fundamental features of experience identified with what he calls the present self and "the pure Ego." These moves are often found in proponents of the minimal self and the later phenomenologists. The similarities are not surprising, because James's projects in *the Principles of Psychology* are professedly observationally based and yet philosophically driven, and contemporary philosophers who advocate the minimal self and the narrative self are interdisciplinarily minded, utilizing findings from the empirical sciences.

The point about James's legacy is not new, either; as Bernard Baars says, "on many of these topics [e.g., attention, habit, concentration, the stream of consciousness, and the distinction of the self as subject and as object] James's thinking is fully up to date, and it is embarrassing but true that much of the time he is still ahead of the scientific curve" (Baars 1997, 16).[16] However, with a few exceptions such as Flanagan and Strawson, explicit recognition of James's significance tends to be rather general, like Baars'. Although Zahavi recognizes that recent philosophical study of the mind has rediscovered some resources in James (Zahavi 2002, 8), he does not in his discussion of the minimal self draw anything directly from James's accounts of consciousness and the self. Granted that Zahavi's inspirations are derived primarily from phenomenologists such as Husserl, Sartre, and the like, and that one of his goals seems to be to draw more attention specifically to the phenomenological tradition as relevant to the contemporary debate about the self, I nonetheless find the lack of reference to James somewhat disconcerting.

I believe that we can still benefit from the *details* of James's analysis of the self: his descriptions of the phenomenal character of experience. For example, the feelings of warmth and intimacy and the continuous feels of identity and ownership associated with current conscious awareness are quite faithful to experience: we feel them immediately and pre-reflectively. His explanations of them are detailed and interesting, which should be taken into consideration even in the contemporary debate, however we may engage with them: to investigate more fully what they entail, to argue against them, or simply to not repeat them. James's descriptive acuity has been recognized, but we should do more justice to his actual findings and ideas.

NOTES

1. Descartes arrives at this initial, indubitable conclusion by way of the method of radical doubt that casts everything into uncertainty with regard to its truth. But there is one thing that is, and has to be, granted for his search for absolute truth to continue: the existence of thought. Every content of thought can be considered to be false, but the existence of "I" cannot, insofar as thought exists. He maintains that the recognition of an "I" in thought is direct and intuitive, and not obtained by syllogism. What this "I" in fact *is* remains to be found. But Descartes only claims at this initial stage that the existence of *something* is revealed in thought itself.

2. Gallagher and Zahavi are often recognized as leading defenders of the minimal self. Strawson's initial analysis of the self also points to something like their notion of the minimal self, which he calls "the minimal subject" (see Strawson 2011, 254). Damasio holds a similar view of the self, which he calls "the core self." He distinguishes consciousness between "core consciousness" and "extended consciousness": the former has one single level of organization whose scope is only a present moment, and the latter has the complex organization in which there are different levels that include memory, reasoning, and language. He then introduces two kinds of self corresponding to those two kinds of consciousness: the core self emerges in core consciousness and the autobiographical self in extended consciousness (Damasio 1999, 16–18).

3. Some of the proponents of the narrative approach to the self include Daniel Dennett, Owen Flanagan, Shaun Gallagher, Alasdair MacIntyre, Antonio Damasio, J. David Velleman, and Marya Schechtman.

4. Damasio and Zahavi argue that the two notions are not only complementary, but the narrative notion of the self is dependent on the existence of the minimal self. Zahavi argues that without events and acts given to a narrator in the mode of the first-personal givenness in the first place, they could not be chosen to be part of *her* narratives, so the minimal self is a condition for the possibility of the narrative self (Zahavi 2005, 114, 129; 2009, 567). Damasio, on the other hand, explains that the autobiographical self emerges from the core self (172–77).

5. Strawson makes multiple references to James in his article, "The Self and the SESMET." Owen Flanagan discusses James's account of the self at length and defends it in *Consciousness Reconsidered* (179–88).

6. Zahavi is not speaking of James's contributions in this statement, but he has in mind phenomenologists like Sartre, Husserl, Heidegger, Merleau-Ponty, and Michel Henry. Recognizing that the recent philosophical study of the mind has rediscovered some resources in Kant and James, he deplores the lack of appropriate attention to the phenomenological tradition (Zahavi 2002, 8). Zahavi may be right about the inadequate treatment of phenomenology in general; however, his point about the reappraisal of James's analyses seems to be an overstatement. I believe that whether it is Husserl or Kant or James, it tends to be the case that their views (and views of historical philosophers) are not necessarily taken seriously in the contemporary philosophical debate, no matter how relevant they may be, and the particular details of James's analysis of the self are not discussed much in the contemporary literature (with some exceptions, such as Strawson and Flanagan).

7. Strawson describes a similar point thus: "experience is experienc*ing*: whatever remains if experience remains, something that is correctly called a subject must remain" (2011).

8. Gallagher also argues that the sense of ownership is one of the two senses (the other being the sense of agency) involved in the sense of the minimal self (15–17).

9. Strawson at this point concedes that there is only a succession of momentary, numerically distinct minimal subjects, which he calls "the pearl view." He summarizes the view thus: "many mental selves exist, one at a time and one after another, like pearls on a string, in the case of something like a human being. According to the Pearl view, each is a distinct existence, an individual physical thing or object, though they may exist for considerably different lengths of time" (1997, 424).

10. The rest of the four characters are: "2) Within each personal consciousness thought is always changing. 3) Within each personal consciousness thought is sensibly continuous. 4) It always appears to deal with objects independent of itself. 5) It is interested in some parts of these objects to the exclusion of others, and welcomes or rejects—*chooses* from among them, in a word—all the while" (James

1981, 220). I am going to discuss (5) in relation to the narrative self, and refer to (2) to motivate the question of the diachronic identity of the self later.

11. James, as a psychologist, professes to take the existence of mental states such as feelings, desires, cognitions, reasonings, and the like to be an undeniable fact, which is available to introspection. His scientific psychology relies in part on introspective observation to collect its material for investigation where thoughts and feelings need be dealt with just as they occur. He indeed begins the chapter, "The Stream of Thought," by stating that "WE now begin our study of the mind from within" (219).

12. Here is what he says: "Things are discrete and discontinuous; they do pass before us in a train or chain, making often explosive appearances and rending each other in twain. But their comings and goings and contrasts no more break the flow of the thought that thinks them than they break the time and the space in which they lie.... The transition between the thought of one object and the thought of another is no more a break in the *thought* than a joint in a bamboo is a break in the wood. It is a part of the *consciousness* as much as the joint is a part of the *bamboo*" (233–34).

13. For the discussion of these points, see James (236–62).

14. Arguing that the sense of the identity of the self arises from experienced relations is a familiar move that we can find in Hume. Hume argues in the section "Of personal identity" in *A Treatise of Human Nature* that the self is "nothing but a bundle or collection of different perceptions" (165), and that it is only the relations of resemblance and causation (which reduces to temporal and spatial contiguity between, and constant conjunction of, two perceptions for Hume) among perceptions that induce us to take ourselves to persist as one and the same beings over time. James is well aware of Humes accounts of the self and personal identity. James openly praised Hume for his empirical approach to the self: "it is to the imperishable glory of Hume . . . to have taken so much of the meaning of personal identity out of the clouds and made of the Self an empirical and verifiable thing" (319).

15. James introduces the notion of "the specious present" only in a later chapter on the perception of time (573–75). He argues that our conception of time is duration, "with a bow and a stern, as it were—a rearward—and a forward-looking end. Only as parts of this *duration-block* that the relation of *succession* of one end to the other is perceived" (574). To hear a melody *as* a melody, for example, we must perceive a succession of more than one note. It is a perception of a sequence of notes, and unless past notes are still present in the mind when we hear a present note, it would not be the hearing of a *melody*; it would merely be the hearing of one note. To perceive a "succession" of things (e.g., notes, words, events, etc.), they must be all experienced in one extended duration as a whole. The question of duration of the specious present is a subject of dispute, but it seems an undeniable fact that the specious present is an important feature of our experience.

16. Zahavi's brief discussion of recognitions that James has received in some contemporary works drew my attention to this strong statement of Baars'.

REFERENCES

Baars, Bernard J. *In the Theater of Consciousness: The Workspace of the Mind.* New York: Oxford University Press, 1997.

Damasio, Antonio. *The Feeling of What Happens: Body and Emotion in the Making of Consciousness.* San Diego: Harcourt, 1999.

Dennett, Daniel. 1991. *Consciousness Explained.* Boston: Back Bay Books.

Descartes, Rene. *The Philosophical Writings of Descartes.* Vol. 2. Translated by John Cottingham, Robert Stoothoff, and Dugald Murdoch. Cambridge: Cambridge University Press, 1984.

Flanagan, Owen. *Consciousness Reconsidered.* Cambridge, MA: MIT Press, 1992.

Gallagher, Shaun. "Philosophical Conception of the Self: Implication for Cognitive Science." *Trends in Cognitive Science* 4, no. 1 (2000): 14–21.

Hume, David. *A Treatise of Human Nature.* Vol. 1. Edited by David Fate Norton and Mary J. Norton. Oxford: Clarendon Press, 2007.

James, William. *The Principles of Psychology.* Vols. 8–10 of The Works of William James, edited by Frederick H. Burkhardt, Fredson Bowers, and Ignas K. Skrupskelis. Introductions by Rand B. Evans and Gerald E. Myers. Cambridge, MA: Harvard University Press, [1890] 1981.

Krueger, Joel. "The Who and the How of Experience." In *Self, No Self?: Perspectives from Analytical, Phenomenological, and Indian Traditions*, edited by Mark Siderits, Evan Thompson, and Dan Zahavi. Oxford: Oxford University Press, 2011.

Locke, John. *An Essay Concerning Human Understanding.* Edited by Peter H. Nidditch. Oxford: Clarendon Press, 1975.

MacIntyre, Alasdair. *After Virtue: A Study in Moral Theory.* London: Duckworth, 1985.

Metzinger, Thomas. *Being No One: The Self-Model Theory of Subjectivity.* Cambridge, MA: MIT Press, 2003.

Schechtman, Marya. *The Constitution of Selves.* Ithaca, NY: Cornell University Press, 1996.

Strawson, Galen. "The Self." *Journal of Consciousness Studies* 4, no. 6 (1997): 405–28.

———. "The Self and the SESMET." In *Models of the Self*, edited by Shaun Gallagher and Jonathan Shear. Thorverton: Imprint Academic, 1999.

———. "The Phenomenology and Ontology of the Self." In *Exploring the Self*, edited by Dan Zahavi. Amsterdam: John Benjamins, 2000.

———. "The Minimal Subject." In *Oxford Handbook of the Self*, edited by Shaun Gallagher. Oxford: Oxford University Press, 2011.

Velleman, J. David. "The Self as Narrator." In *Autonomy and Challenges to Liberalism: New Essays*, edited by John Christman and Joel Anderson. Cambridge: Cambridge University Press, 2015.

Zahavi, Dan. "First-Person Thoughts and Embodied Awareness: Some Reflections on the Relation between Recent Analytical Philosophy and Phenomenology." *Phenomenology and the Cognitive Sciences* 1, no. 1 (2002): 7–26.

———. *Subjectivity and Selfhood: Investigating the First-Person Perspective*. Cambridge, MA: MIT Press, 2005.

———. "Is the Self a Social Construct?" *Inquiry* 52, no 6 (2009): 551–73.

PART 3

PRACTICE: LIVING WITH JAMES

CHAPTER 9

WILLIAM JAMES AND THE WOODS

DOUGLAS R. ANDERSON

> The good of going into the mountains is that life is reconsidered; it is far from the slavery of your own modes of living, and you have opportunity of viewing the town at such a distance as may afford you a just view, nor can you have any such mistaken apprehensions as might be expected from the place you occupy and the round customs you run at home.
>
> —Ralph Waldo Emerson, *Journals and Miscellaneous Notebooks*

William James, like fellow pragmatist Charles Peirce, was not trained as a professional philosopher. Yet from his youth he was inclined to live philosophically. In many ways, his philosophical engagement took the form his father had described to him in a letter: "The requisite, then, of a man being a philosopher, is not to think, however comprehensively or profoundly, but *to become a living man* by the actual putting away of selfishness from his heart" (Perry 1935a, 147; emphasis in original). What I have to say in the chapter at hand will not be understood as philosophy proper by many in the contemporary profession. This is because the last century of focus on the mechanics of linguistic analysis and logical forms has largely ignored or forgotten the Greek origins of philosophical thought—the quest to find good ways of living.[1] William James never lost sight of this quest. Writing to Pauline Goldmark in 1907, James remarked: "We know not what we shall become; and that is what makes life so interesting" (Perry 1935b, 297). I find it philosophically interesting to explore the impact of James's time in the woods of New England on what he became as philosopher and person. To do so, I rely heavily on James's own correspondence—on the telling of his own story.

Since the work of Julius Bixler and Ralph Barton Perry there has been a running debate on whether James lived with a divided soul.[2] More recently, Richard Gale has taken up the task of dividing the life of James.[3] My answer to the question whether James lived with a divided soul is a pragmatic one: yes, and no. He was not a one-dimensional man. Yes, his self was plural and always growing; but no, because the various dimensions of his soul lived in complementary relations to each other. Speaking of one possible point of division, James's student Dickinson Miller pointed out that James "thought there was no sharp line to be drawn between 'healthy' and 'unhealthy' minds, that all have something of both" (James 1920b, 15). Writing from his rural home in Chocorua, New Hampshire, in 1893, James noted that "a divided soul is very bad" (1920a, 359). And a few years later, writing from his Adirondack Lodge, he said, "I am a badly mixed critter, and I experience a certain organic need for simplification and solitude that is quite imperious" (1920b, 22). James seemed to live always with the potential for internal division and yet managed to avoid its actualization; he never fully succumbed to an emotional breakdown, nor do his letters and writings reveal the sort of intellectual schism suggested by Bixler and Gale. James's very awareness of his "bad mixture" indicates the tensions he felt, but not a separation of "selves." For him, as for Augustine, philosophy played a central role in maintaining an inner balance.

In *Walden*, Henry Thoreau noted that he lived a "border existence" somewhere between the wild and the civilized, between the city and the forest. Thoreau challenged civilization when it became unreflective and stagnant, but he never rejected civilization wholesale; he was intent rather on keeping it alive and creative. As he wrote in his essay "Walking": "The civilized nations—Greece, Rome, England—have been sustained by the primitive forests which anciently rotted where they stand. They survive as long as the soil is not exhausted" (1982, 614). I think that William James also sought to live such a border existence. Dickinson Miller's brother visited one of James's classes and remarked that "He looks more like a sportsman than a professor" (James 1920b, 13). He was both. James sought a balance in his own "badly mixed critter:" woods and city, healthy and unhealthy, tough and tender, wild and tame, contemplative and argumentative. He sought to live at the borders where these dimensions could flourish and enable each other in generating new ideas and in creating an interesting life. James's time in the woods was an integral part of this border existence and bore with it important suggestions for living philosophically.

James flourished in his urban and cosmopolitan life. But it was also, for him, an unsettling life—busy, public, and impatient. As his son Henry noted, "In his own house it seemed as if he was always at work; all the more, perhaps, because it was obvious that he possessed no instinct for arranging his days and protecting himself from interruptions" (James 1920b, 7). Moreover, Henry added, "He allowed his conscience to be constantly burdened with a sense of obligation to all sorts of people" (ibid., 9). Family, teaching, writing, organizing all kept James in tension: "Life here in University," he wrote to Francis Pillon, "consists altogether of *interruptions*" (1920a, 204). Moreover, like Diogenes of Sinope, despite the fact that he had excellent social skills, James had little patience for outmoded social conventions; they held little use for a philosophical life. As Henry pointed out concerning his father: "Nothing galled him like *having to be* sociable" (James 1920b, 9). Thus, the extremes of his professional urban existence often called for a source of balance: "Every little while James's sleep would 'go to pieces,' and he would go off to Newport, the Adirondacks, or elsewhere, for a few days" (ibid., 10).

James thus sought to balance his own mixture. James attended to both the physical and soulful benefits. To his brother Henry he wrote during a stay in Chocorua: "[T]he physical luxury of the simplification is something that money can't buy" (1920b, 200). Clearly, the woods were, for James, one mode of escape from social constraints. They offered a reprieve from the things that took him away from reflection and threw his life out of balance. "I am," he wrote later in life, "a poor New Hampshire rustic, in bad health, and long to get back, after four summers' absence, to my own cottage and children, and never come away again for lectures or degrees or anything" (ibid., 165).

But more than escape occurred in the woods. The reprieve was accompanied by empowerment. "I need," James wrote to Charles Renouvier regarding Keene Valley, "to lead a purely animal life for at least two months to carry me through the teaching year" (1920a, 232). The woods yielded the possibility of health: "a little simplification and solidification and sanctification and purification" (1920b, 21). James found himself,

> just filled to satiety with the simpering conventions and vacuous excitements of so-called civilization; hungering for their opposite, the smell of the spruce, the feel of the moss, the sound of

the cataract, the bath in its waters, the divine outlook from the cliff or hill-top over the unbroken forest. (1920b, 21)

In the woods James was well aware that he was a border character, neither entirely wild nor entirely tame: "I aspire downwards, and really *am* nothing, *not becoming* a savage as I would be, and failing to be the civilizee that I really ought to be content with being" (1920a, 147). And he added to his addressee, Mrs. Henry Whitman, and to us, "I wish that *you* also aspired to the wilderness. There are some nooks and summits in the Adirondack region where one can really 'recline' to one's divine composure, and, as long as one stays up there, seem for a while to enjoy one's birthright of freedom and relief from every fever and falsity" (ibid., 147). Escape but also empowerment—to be free of fever and falsity is to come into the presence of health and truth. And here begins James's philosophical instruction. The city and cosmopolitan philosophy is insufficient on its own—it requires a tempering through life in the woods. Public performances become perfunctory; they require a calming and individualizing inwardness and aloneness that provide the possibility of fresh ideas free from the weight of inherited cultural habits and expectations. In nature James's ideas were free to run wild, and as his student Ralph Barton Perry points out, such freedom was at the heart of James's thinking: "The power of his mind lay largely in its extreme mobility, its darting, exploratory impulsiveness" (Perry 1935a, 206).

I think William James's philosophical life offers us a significant reminder of the importance of contemplation, meditation, and the practice of "musement" that allow our ideas to work freely. It is an importance that, I think, has been thoroughly abandoned in the contemporary profession. James did not reject the role of logic nor relinquish the need to explain and to understand; he simply did not see these as sufficient to constitute a philosophical life. The mechanical manipulations of language (narrowly construed) and logical forms of the last century have obscured the original Greek impulse to philosophize—to discover ways of living well. James always kept this impulse at the heart of his own philosophical vision.

In 1920, in *Reconstruction in Philosophy*, John Dewey offered, I think, some remarkably bad advice to a new generation of thinkers. He suggested we should jettison contemplation and "solitary communion" in favor of an experimentalism that would mimic the work of the sciences. For Dewey, "natural science, experimentation, control and progress have been"—and remain—"inextricably bound up together" (Dewey 1998, 103). Dewey of course sought to derail the work of Descartes and its influence on the philosophy of his day. But Dewey threw the baby out with the bath water—meditation need not take the form of a priori construction of geometrical worlds. That was simply the direction Descartes's thought took. The history of ideas discloses many other results—non-totalizing results—found in meditative practices. James did not share Dewey's desire for "control" and, though he was a friend of science and experimentalism, James did not believe that amelioration and wisdom could be achieved cheaply and easily through coarse technological change. For him, science needed to recover its sense of genuine wonder not through control and domination but by returning to experiences of receptivity—experiences that for him were "catalyzed" by direct encounters with nature. James never gave up on contemplation and solitary communion. Rather, he lived at the border where contemplation, including meditation and poesis, and experimentation engage in a loose-fitting dialectic. In short, as did his friend Charles Peirce, James suggested that scientists should be more receptive to a wide range of evidence in creating and developing hypotheses. He gave voice to this in the concluding paragraph of *A Pluralistic Universe*:

> I have now finished these poor lectures, and as you look back on them, they doubtless seem rambling and inconclusive enough. My only hope is that they may possibly have proved suggestive; and if indeed they have been suggestive of one point of method, I am almost willing to let all other suggestions go. That point is that *it is high time for the basis of the discussion in these questions to be broadened and thickened up*. It is for that that I have brought in Fechner and Bergson, and descriptive psychology and religious experiences, and have ventured even to hint at psychical research and other wild beasts of the philosophical desert. (James 1977, 149; emphasis in original)

The woods, through aloneness, beauty, and depth of feeling, provided James a counterweight to his professional and public philosophical life. In the woods, he found a personal, living philosophy that then animated his professional work. James did *not* view philosophy as did some of his contemporaries—and as did most professional philosophers of the twentieth century—as a kind of argumentative combat, as a litiginous *agon*. Following the Greeks, he thought of it as a conversation among friends about questions of existential import. This is why, I think, he so liked Thomas Davidson and his summer school Glenmore in Keene Valley, New York, in the Adirondack

Mountains. At Glenmore, students and teachers lived communally for weeks at a time. The mode of learning was open exchange—conversation, walking, time alone, and more conversation. As Dickinson Miller described James, "he was really not argumentative, not inclined to dialectic and pertinacious debate of any sort" (James 1920b, 12). This was of course in stark contrast to the likes of Bertrand Russell and those who were beginning to frame the analytic bent of the twentieth-century profession. Not having to win arguments or debates meant, for James, that one also did not have to build a cultish following—a trail of students who repeat in various ways the words of a "master." This of course was Socrates's concern for the young men who simply memorized the words of Gorgias. James sought students who would think for themselves, and it is no surprise that many of his students took their philosophies in quite different directions. As his son pointed out, "He never tried to win disciples, to compel allegiance to his own doctrines, or to found a school" (James 1920a, 30). James set his students on their own roads so that they might become friends for genuine philosophical conversation. Consider the diverse careers of students such as Dickinson Miller, Gertrude Stein, W.E.B. Du Bois, and W. E. Hocking, to name but a few.

Underwriting this possibility of friendly conversation was James's individualist belief that we must come to our senses and face ourselves before we can become useful and interesting philosophical interlocutors. In the public and professional setting, we can situate our "positions" in a public forum. But it is only in our inwardness that we can find the soul that animates those positions. As James wrote to his friend Thomas Ward: "We long for sympathy, for a purely *personal* communication, first with the soul of the world, and then with the soul of our fellows" (1920a, 31). James saw early on that professionalized philosophy inverted the situation—either by making one's professed beliefs define one's self or by simply disconnecting one's professional from one's personal living. This latter, it seems to me, is what we have established as the norm for our academic lives. Our politics, our moralities, our aesthetic judgments say one thing in the academy, and when we go home, we live by our unreflective cultural habits. The result is that philosophy has become innocuous and culturally invisible. Philosophy has come to make little difference in the lives of American citizens. Our current practices of giving narrowly focused lectures and writing in exclusive journals could hardly be further removed from the Greek origins of Western philosophy. In contrast, James saw philosophy and personal living in a Hellenistic way, as joined at birth. James sought to find the space for the emergence of one's philosophical being. Thus, when he used the word "trivial" to describe

George Holmes Howison's pluralism, he meant it. In his apology to Howison, he said, "The word came out of one who is unfit to be a philosopher [of the professionalized sort] because at bottom he hates philosophy, especially at the beginning of a vacation, with the fragrance of the spruces and sweet ferns all soaking him through with the conviction that it is better to *be* than to define your being" (1920b, 22–23). For James, philosophy was, in the end, still a pursuit of wisdom and of fruitful ways of living.

As James noted in *Some Problems of Philosophy*, a person without a philosophical inclination is a tedious companion. But living philosophically is not innate for human animals. We seem to prefer to operate by habit, blind association, tradition, and dogma more than by reflection and a willingness to be self-aversive. It is an irony that humans like to think of themselves as exceptional for their reasoning capacities but then ignore, marginalize, imprison, or kill those who reflectively criticize or seek to challenge conventional mores. To become a friend who can engage in philosophy, one must first come to oneself—one must be able to confront one's own thoughts and one's own demons. Winning an "argument" in a professional journal or at a meeting of the American Philosophical Society was not James's idea of philosophical engagement. Genuine philosophical engagement requires a high level of mutual trust—a willingness to be honest with oneself and to leave pretensions behind. For James, visits to the woods afforded opportunity for this kind of internal reflection and self-encounter. "Philosophical discussion proper," he said, "only succeeds between intimates who have learned how to converse by months of weary trials and failure. The philosopher is a lone beast dwelling in his individual burrow" (1920b, 164).

The woods provide this lone beast some space for self and world exploration—for contemplative and meditative thought, and for communion with oneself. In short, adventuring in the woods places the weight of one's philosophical powers on perception, receptivity, and self-awareness. Recall that James, like Charles Peirce, had a nonstandard account of perception. Perception begins with the Emersonian art of receptivity; and it involves an ability to see the whole of nature—the inward and the outward—such that one can perceive feelings as well as rocks, and meanings as well as things themselves. Perception is the animal avenue to the thickness of experience, not yet dissected or analyzed by the work of concepts. It provides a knowing in relative immediacy that is later cashed out but never fully recovered in philosophical writing and conversation. For James, one's living philosophy is an ongoing struggle to give voice to that with which one is already acquainted.

In natural settings, James was released from social bonds that interfered with his art of perceiving. Moreover, the austerities and the beauties of the environments and the force of his feelings lured his contemplative and receptive traits. He attended to his moods, to the mountains, and to the startling visions these catalyzed within him. "It is queer," he wrote to his wife Alice, "how you *feel* things sometimes all at once, which you fail to grasp by thinking" (1999, 530). In the woods, James focused on this "feeling" way of knowing things. Many know the story of James's comprehensive vision of Hegel's logic while under the influence of nitrous oxide, but it is worth repeating: "Truth lies open to the view in depth beneath depth of almost blinding evidence. The mind sees all the logical relations of being with apparent subtlety and instantaneity to which its normal consciousness offers no parallel" (1898). Fewer folks know that in Chocorua James also experimented with peyote hoping for the visions of form and color it was supposed to bring. Unfortunately, the experiment simply made him ill for three days. In a similar vein, in a letter to his parents about his ocean voyage to Brazil in 1865, James wrote:

> No one has a right to write about the "nature of evil" or to have any opinion about evil, who has not been to sea. The awful slough of despond into which you are there plunged furnishes too profound an experience not to be a fruitful one. I cannot yet say what the fruit is in my case but I am sure some day of an accession of wisdom from it. (Perry 1935a, 217)

These indicate some of the more extreme avenues James pursued for the perceptual awareness that would provide him with a philosophical yield. He sought direct acquaintance with what he called the "thickness" of experience; it was this thickness that, he believed, gave life and character to one's philosophical outlook.

James's emphasis on perception and feeling as aboriginal moments in a philosophical life led him to incorporate the poetic and the religious features of life into his philosophical outlook. These two features did not endear him to professional philosophers of the last century. The aversion to religion, felt experience, poesis, and meditation still lingers in the profession today. In the current profession, one may philosophize about poetry or religion, but one should not allow poetry and religiosity to ground and pervade one's philosophy. On this score, James was, like his father, a renegade and a heretic. Moreover, through his emphasis on perception and receptivity, James came to see the poetic and the religious dimensions of human experience as deeply intertwined. In his chapter on religion in *Pragmatism* and in *The Varieties of Religious Experience*, for example, James turned to Walt Whitman and his poetry to flesh out the nature of some features of religious life. And, though I will not argue the details here, one finds James's own experiences in the woods and his self-encounters—poetic and religious—appearing throughout his professional writings. They appear in *Essays in Radical Empiricism*, which he articulated at Davidson's summer school at Glenmore. They can also be found in *A Pluralistic Universe*, *The Varieties of Religious Experience*, *Talks to Teachers*, and in his posthumous metaphysical work in *Some Problems of Philosophy*.

As I bring these thoughts to a close, I will allow James to speak a bit more on his own behalf. I think he, better than his commentators, can provide a clearer sense of how his "animal" life in the woods came to give life to his public philosophy. In a letter to his wife in July of 1898, James wrote of a night spent at Panther Gorge in the Adirondack mountains above Keene Valley:

> The temperature was perfect either inside or outside the cabin, the moon rose and hung above the scene before midnight, leaving only a few of the larger stars visible, and I got into a state of spiritual alertness of the most vital description. . . . I spent a good deal of it in the woods, where the streaming moonlight lit up things in a magical checkered play, and it seemed as if the Gods of all the nature-mythologies were holding an indescribable meeting in my breast with the moral Gods of the inner life. The two kinds of Gods have nothing in common—the Edinburgh lectures [which came to be the *Varieties of Religious Experience*] made quite a hitch ahead. The intense significance of some sort, of the whole scene, if one could only *tell* the significance; the intense inhuman remoteness of its inner life, and yet the intense *appeal* of it, its everlasting freshness and its immemorial antiquity and decay.
>
> It was one of the happiest lonesome nights of my existence, and I understood now what a poet is. He is a person who can feel the immense complexity of influences that I felt, and make some partial tracks in them for verbal statement. In

point of fact, I can't find a single word for all that significance, and don't know what it was significant of, so there it remains, a mere boulder of *impression*. Doubtless in more ways than one, though, things in the Edinburgh lectures will be traceable to it. (1920b, 76–77)

There are several things we might unpack here. James does not say that everyone must turn to nature to engender these sorts of insightful experiences. But he makes it clear that, for him, time in the woods creates a setting for meditative work and for the sort of receptivity that catalyzes his intellectual work. Second, in professional philosophy circles James is often damned with faint praise in being identified as a "good writer."[4] If we look closely, we find he was a good writer because he was a poetic writer—he tried to articulate "some partial tracks" in feelings of "the immense complexity of influences." And in his case, solitude in the forests of the Adirondacks catalyzed his poetic abilities. Finally, we need to note here that James, as a radical empiricist, was a down-to-earth reporter of experience; he was not a glassy-eyed romantic. For him, these kinds of experiences in nature are quite common to the general run of the human animal even if they elude or are intentionally ignored by contemporary professional philosophers. As James wrote to Henry Rankin prior to delivering his Gifford lectures: "In these lectures the ground I am taking is this: The mother sea and fountain-head of all religions lie in the mystical experiences of the individual, taking the word 'mystical' in a very wide sense" (1920b, 149). And, though James never claimed to be a practicing mystic, he did not exclude himself from mystical influences, again, "in the widest sense." He wrote to J. H. Leuba in 1904 of "my mystical *germ*. It is a very common germ. It creates the rank and file of believers" (1920b, 211). As I see it, for James, mysticism in this wide sense is precisely the ground of insight in natural experiences of receptivity and perception. To be in the woods is precisely one way to put oneself in position for the possibility of mystical experiences.

This religiosity or mysticism that, for James, underwrites our philosophies is often enabled or catalyzed by time spent in natural settings.[5] For James, such settings were quite often North American forests; for others, it has been deserts or oceans or mountains. The woods afforded him the perceptual access to his own soul and its relations—an access that was often frustrated or simply overrun in his professional and cosmopolitan world. James lived in greater Boston, taught at what was then the most prestigious philosophy department in the United States, and handled cosmopolitan life with an ease derived from a lifetime of experience. But there were aspects of this life he found wanting—aspects that he seemed to believe could well be addressed through some contemplative time in the woods. In Cambridge and during his cosmopolitan travels James found his life's work as an intellectual. Some of the dimensions of this professional life were not congenial for James: the constant movement, the busy-ness, and the deadlines. Engaged living in the woods, James argued, brought him back to his senses—a sense of calm, a sense of balance, a sense of purity. In Thoreau's way of putting it, the woods brought James back to himself and to a mode of self-recovery and individual creation. He routinely cleansed his body in the cold streams and ponds, and refreshed his mind on the trails and small peaks of the Laurentian chain. In the woods, James became a Cynic cosmopolitan akin to Diogenes—one who lives in and *with* the cosmos, one whose primal affinities are with nature itself and not the conventions of a specific culture. To Rankin, he added:

> I attach the mystical or religious consciousness to the possession of an extended subliminal self, with a thin partition through which messages make irruption. We are thus made convincingly aware of life larger and more powerful than our usual consciousness, with which the latter is nevertheless continuous. The impressions and impulsions and emotions and excitements which we thence receive help us to live, they found invincible assurance of a world beyond sense, they melt our hearts and communicate significance and value to everything and make us happy. . . . Something, not our immediate self, does act on our life. (1920b, 149–50)

Keene Valley and Chocorua were places that elevated James to moments of perception and poetry—and consequently to a life of philosophy. But it would be a mistake to think that all of these experiences were of happiness and exhilaration. A wide variety of nature experiences affect our ways of life and, for James, there is equal depth in the darker and the more haunting moments. I have already noted his response to his voyage to Brazil. There were like experiences closer to home. At the close of summer in 1881, James wrote to his wife from Keene Valley: "I have been rather sad and lonesome the past few days. One by one, most of the people have dropped away, the weather has been glorious, and in the sort of Sabbath stillness and loveliness of the valley, the mountains have sunk into my soul with their beauty as at no previous time this summer" (1997, 177). And, upon opening his cottage in Chocorua in 1896, he wrote to his brother Henry:

> The little place is the most curious mixture of sadness with delight. The sadness of *things*—things every one of which was done either by our hands or by our planning, old furniture renovated, there isn't an object in the house that isn't associated with past life, old summers, dead people, people who will never come again . . . and the way it catches you round the heart when you first come and open the house from its long winter sleep is most extraordinary. (1920b, 137)

As for Emerson, meaning and significance are to be found, for James, not only in exotic or extraordinary settings but also at home. But to be at home often requires a move to a natural setting where the usuals of life are thrown out of gear, where our ability to attend, to receive, and to see are enhanced. Only to the extent that we are attentive and receptive can we begin to grasp and give articulation to the insights that underwrite our worlds and our lives. The extraordinary is normal and natural, and can be found pervasively in the ordinary. William James found the extraordinary in the ordinariness of his time in the woods. For him, Chocorua and Keene Valley repeatedly brought the art of receptivity home to him—and his adeptness at this art both inspired and informed his living philosophy.

NOTES

1. In the twentieth century there was some public philosophy in the United States, but much of it was written by thinkers outside the profession. John Dewey was a notable exception. More recently, there has been some revival of "engaged" philosophy as in the work of Richard Rorty, Judith Butler, and more recently, John Kaag (see his *American Philosophy: A Love Story*). However, despite these changes, much of the profession remains entrenched and isolated.

2. See Bixler.

3. See Gale.

4. In 1916, Rebecca West published her now well-worn description of the James brothers: "the two charming little boys in tight trousers and brass-buttoned jackets, one of whom grew up to write fiction as though it were philosophy and the other to write philosophy as though it were fiction." Since that time it has become commonplace in the philosophical rumor world to treat James as a kind

of "fiction" writer without much philosophical agility. Even when James's "engaging literary style" is used to praise James, as in Wayne Pomerlau's entry in the *Internet Encyclopedia of Philosophy*, it is coupled with the idea that James "cobbled together a psychology rich in philosophical implications and a philosophy enriched by psychological expertise." I think that James was more than a cobbler in the sense indicated. It may be worth noting that Bertrand Russell set off a similar trend concerning the misconstrual of what James meant by "truth."

5. For James, the city and the woods established an important contrast in this regard. However, one needn't universalize James's experience. It is true that many people across times and cultures share James's focus on the reorienting and energizing capacities of natural settings. It remains plausible, however, that, for some, city life might act as a catalyst in a similar fashion.

REFERENCES

Bixler, Julius. *Religion in the Philosophy of William James*. Boston: Marshall Jones, 1926.

Dewey, John. *Essays, Miscellany, and Reconstruction in Philosophy Published during 1920*. Vol. 12. John Dewey: The Middle Works: 1899–1924, edited by Jo Ann Boydston. Carbondale: Southern Illinois University Press, 1998.

Emerson, Ralph Waldo. *The Heart of Emerson's Journals*. Edited by Bliss Perry. New York: Dover, 1995.

———. *Journals and Miscellaneous Notebooks, Volume 4*. Edited by A. R. Ferguson. Cambridge: Harvard University Press, 1964.

Gale, Richard. *The Divided Self of William James*. Cambridge: Cambridge University Press, 1999.

James, William. "Consciousness under Nitrous Oxide." *Psychological Review* 6, no. 2 (1898): n.p.

———. Vol. 1 of *The Letters of William James*, edited by Henry James. Boston: Atlantic Monthly Press, 1920a.

———. Vol. 2 of *The Letters of William James*, edited by Henry James. Boston: Atlantic Monthly Press, 1920b.

———. *A Pluralistic Universe*. Vol. 4 of *The Works of William James*, edited by Fredson Bowers and Ignas K. Skrupskelis. Introduction by Richard J. Bernstein. Cambridge, MA: Harvard University Press. [1909] 1977.

———. *The Correspondence of William* James, Vol. 5 (1878–1884), edited by Ignas K. Skrupskelis and Elizabeth M. Berkeley. Charlottesville: University of Virginia Press, 1997.

———. *The Correspondence of William* James, Vol. 7 (1890–1894), edited by Ignas K. Skrupskelis and Elizabeth M. Berkeley. Charlottesville: University of Virginia Press, 1999.

Kaag, John. *American Philosophy: A Love Story*. New York: Farrar, Straus, Giroux, 2016.

Perry, Ralph Barton. *The Thought and Character of William James*, Vol. 1. Cambridge, MA: Harvard University Press, 1935a.

———. *The Thought and Character of William James*, Vol. 2. Cambridge, MA. Harvard University Press. 1935b.

Pomerlau, Wayne. "William James." *Internet Encyclopedia of Philosophy*. www.iep.utm.edu/james-o

Russell, Bertrand. "William James's Conception of Truth." bertrandrussellsocietylibrary.org/br-pe/br-pe-ch5.html

———. "Transatlantic Truth." *The Albany Review* no. 2 (1908), 393–410. [Review of William James, *Pragmatism*]

West, Rebecca. *Henry James: A Critical Biography*. New York: Henry Holt, 1916.

CHAPTER 10

TAKING JAMES TO WORK
Pragmatism for Managers

CLIFFORD S. STAGOLL

INTRODUCTION

Granted management's inherent action-orientation—the focus on "getting things done" in pursuit of tangible goals and in the face of resource and other constraints—the very name "pragmatism" suggests it as appropriate for use in philosophy of management. It is not straightforwardly the case, however, that theoretical resources offered by classical philosophical pragmatism are always or obviously in the service of practical ends, or that managerial pragmatism is evident in all actions meant to achieve tangible business results.

Nonetheless, the importance of outcomes and consequences in Charles S. Peirce's versions of pragmatism and again in William James's individualized, psychologized, and epistemology-focused adaptations, support the notion of a thematic orientation toward action shared by classical pragmatism and management practice.[1] Thus, for example, James states that "my thinking is first and last and always for the sake of my doing," and he conceives of truth principally in terms of consequences: "any idea upon which we can ride, so to speak; any idea that will carry us prosperously from any one part of our experience to any other part, linking things satisfactorily, working securely, simplifying, saving labor; is true for just so much . . . true *instrumentally*" (1984, 309; 1975b, 34).

Writing of pragmatism's application to organization studies, Bidhan Parmar and colleagues contend that "pragmatism encourages scholars to show how theoretical differences make a real difference to practice. This focus on practice shifts the focus on theory building . . . away from insular conversations between academics and towards practice-relevant research" (2016, 207). Identifying pragmatism's potential for re-orienting philosophical research into management is one thing, but realizing it is another. To date, philosophers of management sympathetic to pragmatism have tended to deploy their ideological resources to advance conceptual models of management practices, and propose solutions to workplace issues predefined by philosophers. Organization theory has been studied in terms of a debate between dualism and anti-dualism, for example, and business ethics in terms of alternative conceptions of value (see Elkjaer and Simpson 2011; Rosenthal and Buchholz 2000). Such conceptual accounts of problems abstracted from real-world complications tend more to the needs of academics "concerned with the issue of methodological rigor" and less to practitioners for whom "academic knowledge becomes relevant . . . when it is context-specific, providing concrete recommendations for action or plans of action" (Vo and Kelemen 2014, 242).

This chapter will show how James's version of classical pragmatism might underwrite a philosophy of management that engages *directly* with the demands of management practice and with practitioners. Specifically, his methodological commitment to experience provides means by which managers might better understand the ways that they think about and respond to the complicated circumstances that define their jobs. In contrast to other management theories, it has potential to influence the moral and existential realities of managers, rather than just, say, their means for improving productivity or workplace success. On this account, James's philosophy might not merely inform managerial practices, but also encourage more productive and ongoing exchanges between philosophers and managers.

JAMES'S EXPERIENTIAL PRAGMATISM AND MANAGEMENT

James's attitudes toward the dramatic socioeconomic changes experienced by Americans in the late-nineteenth and early-twentieth centuries make him an unlikely source for ideas helpful to philosophy of management. Living "on the fulcrum between two historical worlds: the gentility of late

Victorian New England and the cosmopolitan currents of modernity," he was keenly aware of the impacts upon individuals and communities of large-scale industrial manufacturing, bigger business organizations, sophisticated financial and goods markets, and the managerialism that enabled them all (Halliwell and Rasmussen 2014, 5). "The resounding ideal of mere empty 'bigness' and 'success' is killing every genuine quality and ideal," he wrote, and so he proclaimed himself "against bigness and greatness in all their forms," including "all big organizations as such" (James 1920, 2: 90). But rather than holding out hope that the new capitalism might be revoked and former values and lifestyles reinstated by way of wholesale revolution, James contends that "it is enough to ask of each of us that he should be faithful to his own opportunities and make the most of his own blessings" (1983, 149).² If one goes about life carefully and thoughtfully and is "willing to live on possibilities that are not certainties," then some improvement of one's lot is possible, even in the face of unmitigated "market-war demands" and "success-worship" (1975a, 124). Philosophy's role is to stand "for the dignity of smaller worldly successes, or of worldly failures"; to enable and encourage people to identify and commit effort to realizing those opportunities still open to them, even if these are few (1988, 107).

Consequently, like Peirce and John Dewey, James wanted to find, in the words of Bente Elkjaer and Barbara Simpson, "practical ways of accounting for human conduct and meaning-making in all of [their] dynamic and social complexity" as aids for developing "practical solutions to the myriad practical problems that arise in lived human experience" (2011, 56–57). By linking knowledge and action in this way, the classical pragmatists departed from a then-prevalent philosophical idealism championed by T. H. Green, F. H. Bradley, Josiah Royce and others, which they saw as too far removed from daily life to have practical merit. Arguments resting on universal teleology or some speculative philosophical concept were unlikely to encourage energetic pursuit of one's opportunities, whereas tangible, real-world possibilities conceived in terms of one's own thoughts and practices stood a better chance of motivating one to act, and clarifying one's purpose for acting. As such, James sets out to engage as directly as possible with real-world circumstances, focusing on "our actual hopes and needs" amidst "the world of concrete personal experiences to which the street belongs," "multitudinous beyond imagination, tangled, muddy, painful and perplexed," and evidencing "the contradictions of real life" (1975b, 137, 17–18).

Throughout his corpus, James highlights "the contrast between the richness of life and the poverty of all possible formulas," maintaining that theorization of lived reality ought to begin with the characteristics of that reality as they are experienced rather than by way of philosophical preconceptualization (1987, 489). Typically, he thinks, "Philosophy is dogmatic, and pretends to settle things by pure reason," substituting conceptual abstractions for "real life" (1979a, 18–19). But to work from conceptual generalities is to miss life's intensely complicated and personal character. "So long as we deal with the cosmic and the general, we deal only with the symbols of reality," James insists, "but *as soon as we deal with private and personal phenomena as such, we deal with realities in the completest sense of the term*" (1985, 393). He concludes that "the only fruitful mode of getting at truth is to appeal to concrete experience," and so his philosophy rests squarely on deciphering lived consciousness, drawing out the implications of its characteristics for the ways that we live, and proposing recommendations for recovering one's energetic engagement with life's possibilities (1979a, 18–19).

James's insistence on the need for philosophical inquiry to begin with the particulars of lived experience is in stark contrast with the usual approach adopted by philosophers of management. With few exceptions, philosophy of management follows the example set by much philosophy of art and philosophy of science, serving as a descriptive, diagnostic, or prescriptive process (or some combination of these) whereby pre-established theoretical resources are applied to generalized attributes of the field under review.[3] The philosopher sits "outside the action," as it were, ignoring, downplaying, or redefining the chaotic contingencies of real-world circumstances by altering the level of conceptual abstraction. Philosophy of management commonly contains broad generalizations about how management is done and what constitutes a "problem" for managers, and proceeds without acknowledgment of the range of roles, industries, cultures, and geographies (let alone personal circumstances) to which its conclusions ought to be applied. The question guiding such a project might be "what ought a manager to do in a situation like this one?" or "how might a person properly understand such a workplace problem?" without acknowledging how unlike one another are particular situations or problems of that general kind.

By comparison, the work done by a manager (or indeed a machine operator, administrator, tradesperson, maintainer, entrepreneur, or truck driver) is not so conceptually malleable: decisions about how to think through and enact one's work are more often decided by the circumstances of the moment. The question is more likely to be, "what must *I* do *now*?" So long as the philosopher deals in abstractions that simplify or set aside the complexity and first-personal character of management work, then in

James's words, he will "fire his volley of new vocables out of his conceptual shotgun, for his profession condemns him to this industry, but he secretly knows the hollowness and irrelevancy" (1985, 360). There will be no spanning the "gap" between the philosopher's quest for rigor and the manager's demand for relevance. A pragmatist approach to management will demand both the ability to generalize and extreme particularization.

James's alternative approach locates all philosophies of practice in the study of conscious life. Rather than first deciding which kinds of action or problem define or typify management in the abstract, Jamesian philosophy of management would begin by investigating how people conceive and think through challenges associated with their work. Then, instead of proposing or applying a philosophical construct to such base conceptions with the aim of determining a prescription for each similar case, the pragmatist would alert managers to tendencies and opportunities in their thought, and equip them with means for thinking more carefully and insightfully about their circumstances. The rigor of Jamesian philosophy of management would derive from addressing the whole panoply of mental activity associated with work, and its relevance from helping managers to think through and cope with their work-related challenges. That it would be distinctively a philosophy of *management* rather than some other field of practice, such as education, is not a matter of the phenomena to which James's theoretical commitments and ideas *could* be applied. After all, it is not the case that a manager's conscious capabilities are fundamentally different from a teacher's. Rather, it pertains to the problematic cases in which managers find it useful to apply them—problems such as poor work habits, the ethics of disciplining employees, mediating personal preferences and corporate policies, ways of discerning formal organization structures from informal ones, and so on.

While such an approach has the advantage of engaging with a manager's capabilities and momentary circumstances, it seems burdened by a significant constraint: If philosophy ought to "deal with private and personal phenomena," as James proposes, what about the kinds of social and publicly observable activity commonly taken to define management? What about the manager's interactions with colleagues, employers, family, and friends?

James's experiential philosophy is inherently individualistic, consistent with his belief that rebellion against "the moral flabbiness born of the . . . squalid cash interpretation put on the word success" ("our national disease," no less) relies on each individual's remaining alive to his or her opportunities (1920, 2: 260). This view chimes with his overarching ontology. James conceives the world as "*a set of eaches, just as it seems*" (1977, 62).

When we use words like "experience," "being," "reality," "environment," and "world," he thinks, we denote merely conceptual groupings of such diverse and multitudinous elements as experiences, individual lives, objects, perspectives, and so on, and not any shared essence. This ontological perspective, combined with James's intense interest in the human condition, focuses him squarely on prospects for fulfillment in the lives of individuals rather than the development of communities. He writes that "surely the individual, the person in the singular number, is the more fundamental phenomenon, and the social institution, of whatever grade, is but secondary and ministerial" (1987, 97). It is individuals (rather than families, communities, work groups, or companies) that identify options, conduct evaluations, make decisions, and then either act upon them or not.

James's emphasis on individuals is significant for philosophy of management, being contrary to a tendency among organization theorists since the 1980s to emphasize the social aspects of businesses. In respect of managers specifically, an approach like James's can be seen as promoting conceptions of an atomic individual standing apart from a collection of other atomic individuals who are cast into the role of followers, encouraging what Peter Edward describes as "a division between managers who use their minds to make reasoned decisions and workers who, preferably largely unthinkingly, are required merely to use their bodies to enact those decisions" (2016, 352). The political overtones of such a view are plain, and contrary to James's own beliefs: power and influence rest—and perhaps should remain—with the boss, and what matters most is what the boss thinks. By contrast, the more prevalent modern view tends to emphasize "the embedded dynamics of leadership" and the extent to which every individual, regardless of role or power, is "continuous with others and with the historically situated social institutions of which they are a part" (Rosenthal and Buchholz 2000, 189, 192). Particular people or roles are more or less powerful, and that power can be used more or less selfishly, but it is not possible to properly understand those people or roles separate from the wider organization (and communities) of which they are part.

Although James acknowledged the importance of relations with others for constituting one's self (e.g., James 1981, 281–82), only in one essay published late in his life, "The Moral Equivalent of War" (1982, 162–73), did he address social relations explicitly. Even some of James's fellow travelers and popularizers have taken him to task for overemphasizing the individual. For example, his pragmatist contemporaries, Peirce and Dewey, criticized him for being overly concerned with individual agency and failing to acknowledge the extent to which it was enabled and constrained by social interrelations (see Menand 2001, 88). More recently, John McDermott has claimed that James's "position on the individual was dramatically one-sided and his innocence of the social matrix by which we became single selves was most unusual for a late nineteenth-century thinker" (1986, 80–81).

In terms of understanding and guiding the *practice* of management, however, James's individualism may prove no handicap. Doubtless it is important for a manager to remain mindful of the extent and subtleties of interpersonal relationships both within the organization and outside it: most management roles have a significant social dimension. As James writes (suggestively, though not very instructively): "[O]ur lives are like islands in the sea or like trees in the forest. The maple and the pine may whisper to each other with their leaves, and Conanicut and Newport hear each other's fog-horns. But the trees also commingle their roots in the darkness underground, and the islands also hang together through the ocean's bottom" (1986, 374). In other words, even apparently isolated individuals interact with and are influenced by those around them, so that, as the pragmatist organizational theorist Mary Parker Follett writes, for James, "we cannot put the individual on one side and society on the other, we must understand the complete interrelation of the two. Each has no value, no existence without the other" (1926, 61–62).

But coupling James's acknowledgment of the significance of social relations with his quest for a philosophically "concrete" conception of first-person experience, his focus on the individual seems well-founded. James can be understood as less concerned with providing a generalized description of interpersonal relations from the perspective of someone observing and organizing them conceptually, and more interested in identifying the ways in which those involved in such relations think about and respond to them, and proposing new ways in which they might do so. In a business setting, James's approach means dropping such questions as "what is the nature of the relationship between managers and their staff (or peers, or other stakeholders)?" in favor of ones like "how might this manager think through her social interactions?"—together, perhaps, with ". . . and how might a theoretical account of the process help her if she is not very good at it?" The former approach abstracts from the particularity of a manager's experiences in the cause of broad applicability. It pursues a conceptualized account of how a set of people in relatively similar jobs interact with other people in or around the workplace, where criteria for determining the similarity of jobs and the particular interactions under review are often left unstated. By contrast, the latter one acknowledges the wide range of factors relevant to how a manager might conceive of and address her specific circumstances, and the possibility that some particular aspect of an interaction might be crucial for deciding how to go about it. It ensures that the social nuances of a job, task, or work group (deeply embedded friendships among team members, say, or the disruptive presence of a truculent naysayer) are acknowledged not just in terms of their being experienced at all, but because of the feelings of worry and doubt (or confidence and determination) that they engender in the manager. As such, James's approach to social relations has the advantage (ideally) of respecting the complicated realities of coping with budget, time, and performance pressures while at the same time dealing with the views, words, expectations, frustrations, friendships, and rewards of working with others.

James's focus on first-person experience is the most distinctive aspect of his philosophy. Perhaps naively given the various roles and meanings assigned to experience in the history of philosophy, James intended it to be philosophically uncontroversial; after all, he explains, "experience in its immediacy seems perfectly fluent. The active sense of living which we all enjoy, before reflection shatters our instinctive world for us, is self-luminous and suggests no paradoxes. Its difficulties are disappointments and uncertainties. They are not intellectual contradictions" (1976, 45). We go through daily life generally unconcerned by theoretical questions regarding the nature of first-personal experience, even though *what* we experience can be deeply troubling. Moreover, as James points out, "the more primitive flux of the sensational life" and the "concrete pulse of experience appear pent in by no such definite limits as our conceptual substitutes for them are confined by" (1977, 127). In making our way in the world, we simply accept that our experiences are limited by our senses and intellect rather than by such logical constraints as determine our explanatory concepts. As Thomas Powell puts it: "[O]ur explanations are accountable to experience and not to the concepts we devise to explain it; and if the concepts fail, then perhaps we have learned an even bigger lesson: that human experience is not the kind of thing that goes into a theory" (2014, 167).

To understand how radically James's approach differs from those that usually underpin philosophies of practice (including philosophy of management) requires an appreciation of his account of experience. Specifically, it demands an understanding of his preoccupation with the complex dynamics of consciousness. James is more interested in describing the rich potential for thinking things afresh granted one's circumstances and capabilities, and less in assessing patterns of thought and action evident amongst a group of people or under some general set of conditions. As such, we will turn next to the critical aspects of James's theory of experience.

Experience for James is best understood as the first-person, introspectively accessible product of encounters between one's self and the world. As "the entire process of phenomena," it is the most basic fact of human existence: one's life just *is* experiential, defined in terms of the world as it is taken, consciously considered, and responded to (1988, 95). As such, it includes not just sense experience (although, as McDermott points out, James emphasized the perceptual "in an effort to condemn as potentially dangerous a conceptual order not rooted in our actual experiencing"), but also moral, aesthetic, and religious experiences, enjoyment and pain, anger and fear, desire and repulsion, effort and ease, deduction and creation, matters of interest and indifference, dependencies and independencies, and so on (McDermott 1976, xxi). Further, on James's account, experience includes memories, needs, desires, and dreams just as much (and in the same ways) as cause-effect relationships, logical constructs, and perceptual observations, and interruptions and abrupt leaps of focus as much as smoothly continuous trains of thought.

Rather than applying pragmatist concepts to pre-ordered phenomena, James studies the often disorderly first-personal reality of those phenomena in pursuit of normative guidance for locating and realizing life's prospects. In following him, Dewey makes the point that philosophers typically have "denied that common experience is capable of developing within itself methods which will secure direction for itself and . . . create inherent standards of judgement and value. . . . To the waste of time and energy, to disillusionment of life that attends every deviation from concrete experience must be added the tragic failure to discover what intelligent search would reveal and mature among the things of ordinary experience" (1929, 38). By ignoring or downplaying the potential for everyday experience to guide future thoughts and actions, most philosophers have missed much that is important about how we make our way in the world. James means to correct such failures. In his pragmatism, the transience of human experience emphasizes what McDermott calls "the profound inferential character of our values, decisions, and disabilities" and James's task is, "in phenomenological terms, . . . to diagnose the experience of the individual as we cast about in the flow of experience, bringing a mind-set but also getting and begetting as the press of the world filtered into our consciousness" (McDermott 1984, 668). James liked to refer to Søren Kierkegaard's reminder that we must "live forward" even though we "understand backward" (James 1975b, 107). All our ideals and most important judgments—including those made in the course of our trades and professions—are prospective rather than retrospective, yet our understanding of what we might reasonably hope for and how best to pursue it relies on lessons, habits, expectations, and evidence drawn from experience to date.

For James, in Powell's words, "all enquiry, whether in science, literature, or metaphysics, is a fundamentally *human* enterprise, a narrative told by humans about how it feels to be human," and "the task of the philosopher-psychologist" is "reporting what happens [in consciousness] as truly and completely as possible" (Powell 2014, 166–67). James's methodological challenge is to reflect the first-personal immediacy of experience without adopting a purely hypothetical approach (with which he charges Descartes), underlying ontological structures (as in Plato and Kant), or final positions and teleological paths (like Hegel). James sees such approaches as flawed not because they originate outside experience (as if that were possible), but by dint of being too general. No such theoretical approach can account for the immediacy, subtlety, and open-endedness of one's own thought, James contends, and the only valid "observational" approach is "the looking into our own minds and reporting what we there discover," paying careful heed to the states and circumstances of one's own consciousness (1981, 185).[4] Consequently, James's justly celebrated *The Principles of Psychology* is "an extended essay on what it is like to be human—based largely on what it was like to be William James," in which he describes in detail an enormous range of "types" or "aspects" of experience (sensation, perception, thought, memory, habit, self-conception, and so on) (Powell 2014, 170). Rather than conceptualizing thought "from the outside," as though experience were simply another object for philosophical study, James locates relevant concepts descriptively within experience, preserving rather than simplifying the complexity of mental phenomena.

Foremost among James's observations is the essentially dynamic character of experience, an attribute that precludes universalizable philosophical guidance for practice. Experience on James's account is, as James Kloppenberg summarizes, "always relational (it never exists in the abstract or in isolation from a world containing both other persons and concrete realities, as did Descartes's rationalist cogito), creative (it never merely registers sense data passively, as did Locke's empiricist tabula rasa), and imbued with historically specific cultural values (it is never 'human' or universal, but always personal and particular)" (1986, 102). Its contents are contingent and ever-changing, depending upon the chance configuration of circumstances. Further, relations between thoughts are always open-ended and multifarious, a conflux of "existence, succession, resemblance, contrast, contradiction, cause and effect, means and end, genus and species, part and whole, substance and property, early and late, large and small, landlord and tenant, master and servant," and much else besides (James 1981, 520). Through experience we come to realize that "possibilities, not finished facts, are the realities with which we have actively to deal" (1979b, 55). As such, however we go about theorizing experience, it "has a way of boiling over and making us correct our present formulas," so that, whether in constructing theories or making commonplace judgments, "we have to live today by what truth we can get today, and be ready tomorrow to call it a falsehood" (1975b, 106, 107).

There can be no more relevant realization for a philosophy of practice. One's decisions and actions will be guided by the concrete, ever-changing particulars of one's experience. Not only might our actions prove erroneous, even if well-founded on what we have learned previously, but our conceptions of even such stable things as organizations, cultures, and institutions might prove unreliable should circumstances change (Chia 2002, 866). Any theory proposing that tomorrow's managerial decisions should rely on the same criteria as today's, without acknowledging the (perhaps preeminent) need for flexibility, is at best a crude device and at worst misleading. A manager new to her role might rely on lessons from business school, unaware that they "work" in only a limited range of ideal instances. A dogmatic boss might cling to the example of one early, career-defining decision. By contrast, a flexible, seasoned manager is likely to have learned that unexpected events can make even the most carefully considered decision seem wrong in retrospect, that decisions considered inconsistent by others can in fact be well-founded in contextual subtleties, that few significant management decisions are straightforward, and that management training typically says little about such realities of professional life as these.

James abandons more traditional ways of framing problems of practice because they risk abstracting from experience to too great a degree. As Gregory Pappas reminds us, conceiving of any problem as a spectator, a theorist operating outside life's push and pull, means losing much of what we take from actually having an experience, including the meaning of the problem (2008, 33–35, 206–07). The point of a Jamesian approach is not to abandon theory, but to reorient it toward the experience it means to describe and aid. For philosophy of management to be relevant for practitioners, it must recover the concreteness and intricate complexities of management decisions and practices and the circumstances that frame them. It must account for the fact that managers are not, by dint of a job title, soulless automatons, but people who must reconcile sometimes contradictory ethical commitments and sometimes conflicting familial and social obligations. It must consider the influence upon them of rapidly changing circumstances, the burden of decisions, the impacts of status and material rewards, and the particularities of job, skill, company, industry, location, training, culture, colleagues, and so on. Business schools would produce more job-ready graduates by providing greater exposure to the complicated realities of managing and to Jamesian ways of thinking them through, and less to theories encouraging a too-orderly, overly systematized view. We turn next to theoretical resources provided by James that might support such a change.

RESOURCES FOR MANAGEMENT PRACTICE IN JAMES'S PRAGMATISM

To this point, we have seen that James's commitment to experience is consonant with a methodological pragmatism capable of surmounting the "gap" between management theorists and practitioners. Rather than predetermining thoughts and actions that typify or define "management," and then conceptualizing them, a Jamesian approach would instead propose ways in which managers might understand and become more sensitive to the resources and patterns of consciousness that guide them in coping with circumstances encountered in their job. James's philosophy enables what John E. Smith describes as "an opening of horizons so that experience no longer meant merely a *content* passively received but many *contexts* in which that content could be taken and its full meaning developed" (1993, 122). By attending carefully to the context and purpose of one's thought and action, the relevant details will tend to be self-disclosing. The academic's insistence on rigor is satisfied through careful study of experience in all its intricate and confusing richness; the practitioner's desire for relevance is met through a set of constructs capable of informing thought and action throughout and beyond professional life.

To leave things there, however, might suggest that James had provided just a theoretical base for a philosophy of management, but none of the tools for realizing it. How might mere awareness of one's patterns of thought help to improve one's abilities as a manager? What does "improvement" of one's capabilities mean? What concrete guidance does James offer managerial decisions? If pragmatism is just "a way of thinking about thinking," as sometimes proposed, what help is it for thinking toward action (Westbrook 2005, ix)? But in fact, James does address the implications of his philosophy of experience for practice, either by describing the connotations of specific patterns of thought, or proposing ways in which these might be conceived and deployed more effectively. Whilst a comprehensive catalogue of these is beyond our scope, some indicative examples will help to alleviate the worry that James's pragmatism is, despite its promising methodology, still too abstract.

Foremost among the characteristics of human thought studied by James and most obviously relevant to management practices is reliance on habit. According to James, much about our thought and action is habitual. "When we look at living creatures from an outward point of view, one of the first things that strikes us is that they are bundles of habits" (1981, 109), products of a tendency to "*make automatic and habitual, as early as possible, as many useful actions as we can*" (1984, 134). But whereas the everyday conception of habits pertains typically to actions of minor import (brushing one's teeth, verbal ticks, or routine sequencing of behaviors, for instance), James recognizes that habits range from the most primitive animal instinct (or "innate tendency") to the most sophisticated aspects of human life (in "acts of reason"). Simple bodily habits of the former kind are merely activations of "ready-made arrangements" in the brain and body, whereas more complex cases (taking up a new language, learning to lead, coping in a crisis, . . .) demand careful, conscious effort and repetitive training in pursuit of habituation that "*diminishes the conscious attention with which our acts are performed*" (1981, 119). Since such effort and practice are products of deliberate attention, we have the capacity to amend our habits, at least before they become "embedded," and James proposes a set of tools for how we might achieve this (1983, 48–53).

To the extent that each individual is defined by consistent thoughts and actions, habit is "an invisible law, as strong as gravitation" which "keeps him within his orbit, arrayed this year as he was the last" (James 1981, 126). Habituated relational connections, whether between ideas or between ideas and consequent actions, require less energy and effort than less familiar ones. Not only is habit a matter of practical convenience, but also, as James writes, "the more of the details of our daily life we can hand over to the effortless custody of automatism, the more our higher powers of mind will be set free for their own proper work" (ibid.). Greater conscious capacity becomes available for dealing with more interesting, perplexing, and unformed situations.

But the advantages that habit confers are accompanied by risks. For example, one's actions can become to an uncertain degree a product of tendencies of which one might remain unaware; it is not always clear which habits are (or will become) beneficial, and which detrimental (James 1983, 53); and, habits can be means for engraining the kind of "conservative inertia" with which James was so deeply concerned (1982, 131). To avoid dissipating one's energy and risking the loss of "potentialities" (or "opportunities") by continuing to enact detrimental or outdated habits requires deliberate, ongoing self-review. As Michael Eldridge and Sami Pihlström write: "[O]ne of our most important habits is the meta-level habit of critically reflecting on, revising, and transforming our habits. Thus, our habits are not simply given to us once and for all; we are responsible for continuously self-critically examining whether they enable us to achieve our purposes (which are themselves in view only through the habitual actions we engage in) or not" (2011, 34).

That an effective manager relies in large part on making and maintaining good habits is obvious. Not only do habits enable a manager to make the most of relatively scarce time and attentive effort, but they enable such reliable and predictable judgements and responses as necessary for staff to conduct their work with confidence, and for a productive organizational culture. Indeed, James suggests: "[I]t is your despised business man, your common man of affairs" whose ability to voluntarily focus attention "is likely to be the most developed; for he has to listen to the concerns of so many uninteresting people, and to transact so much drudging detail" (1983, 67). But the manager needs to watch out for problematic habits, too, whether devoting too much time to short-term tasks (such as clearing e-mails), adopting an overly aggressive physical posture, or favoring risk-laden strategies over conservative ones. In short, every habit carries with it the risk of becoming insensitive or unresponsive to context, and the "antidote" is remaining alert to the presence and appropriateness of one's own habits

James provides a second example of a pattern of human thought with clear implications for management in *A Pluralistic Universe*, where he describes conceptualization in terms of the construction of various symbolic systems representing different aspects of, or perspectives on, the same reality. James's point is that we ought to remain alert to the risks of adopting any singular perspective on reality, and to entertain and encourage others in pursuit of richer, more complete perspectives. An organization can be depicted in such diverse terms as organization charts, flow charts, balance sheets, and annual reports, for instance (Harter 2013, 73). For a manager to cling to some conceptual depiction as *the* one (the most right, complete, accurate, or insightful) to the detriment of insights from others is to risk parochial or poorly informed judgments, and to handicap her engagement with people holding different views. We might imagine a Chief Financial Officer so wedded to the significance of monthly profit and loss figures that the contribution of the production schedule to the organization's financial health is lost from view.

James also proposes specific guides to action. Examples include: his lecture titled "The Gospel of Relaxation," which speaks to overly stressed managers about their environment and means for coping as much as to the students who were its original audience (1983, 117–31); his multifaceted theory of self-development, spanning much of his corpus, which addresses the existential challenges of marrying one's circumstances (including one's work environment) with realization of one's capabilities and opportunities; and a range of practical exercises for altering one's habits by means of concentrated and persistent effort (for example, James admonishes us to "*never suffer an exception to occur until the new habit is securely rooted in your life*" and to "*seize the very first possible opportunity to act on every resolution you make*") (1983, 49, 50).

Whether James's ethics ought to be classified as a primarily prescriptive offering or a merely descriptive one is difficult to decide, but its relevance for busy managers is plain. As Joshua Margolis points out: "[E]thical issues tax people cognitively, and 'cognitive busyness' reduces our capacity to make appropriate judgements, let alone search for and construct creative courses of action. Just when people most need to draw on their fullest capacities, those very situations elicit a lower level of functioning" (1998, 413). In his essay "The Moral Philosopher and the Moral Life," James proposes a wholly naturalistic ethics in which questions about ethical value would be resolved by reference to experience rather than any transcendent source or measure of ethical value. For James, much like David Hume, words like "good," "bad," "right," and "obligation" do not refer to the "absolute natures" of acts, but instead to "objects of feeling and desire" with "no foothold or anchorage in Being, apart from the existence of actually living minds" so that "nothing can be good or right except so far as some consciousness feels it to be good or thinks it to be right" (James 1979b, 150, 147). His account emphasizes the sensitivity of our judgments to subjective assessments of which circumstances are relevant, the often-contradictory nature of our ethical principles and inclinations, and the need to sometimes make ethical judgments in the absence of relevant facts or the presence of confusion.

Whether taken to be descriptive or normative, James's views chime with the often complicated and compromised moral options faced by managers, where "a plurality of conflicting interests must be integrated, and that can only be done by the morally perceptive, creative, individual operating in a specific context in response to specific conflicts" (Rosenthal and Buchholz 1999, 118). Often, the manager's role is to mediate between predetermined corporate rules and other imperatives, or to apply organizational regulations effectively. Not only is such a task sometimes very complicated and the correct approach unclear, but it encourages the manager to substitute corporate rules for her own moral sensitivities. James's observations serve to remind managers that their judgments of right and wrong ought to rely on the full range of previous experience to help decide *which* facts are relevant, *how* they ought to be assessed, and whether or not corporate rules ought to be called into question. As Doug Anderson writes: "[T]he pragmatic attitude does not allow the business practitioner a moral holiday in his or her role as business person. It reveals that we are all engaged in the moral experiment of producing our own world and socio-economic environment; it gives us each a stake in the care of the conditions of human flourishing" (1999, 63). As such, "the agent cannot retreat to the harbour of dogmatic belief but must actively address the situation" (Anderson 1999, 61). To develop the moral capabilities of managers is not a matter just of teaching corporate policies and legal requirements (although of course there is a place for these), but of "find[ing] ways to improve moral perception and awareness on the front-end of judgement; and we must find ways to translate resulting judgements into action. Practitioners need to be equipped with a complementary set of tools for discerning the mere presence of ethical issues and for constructing action amid the panoply of considerations" (Margolis 1998, 420).

Of course, there is no guarantee that the mere availability of philosophical resources such as James's for enhancing managers' capabilities will result in their adoption by practitioners. Some theorists have questioned whether it is possible for any philosophy to usefully inform business practices (e.g., Wallis 2012, 69) and others have suggested that the predominant view among philosophers of how best to develop theoretical knowledge has alienated it conceptually from the mercantile activity of Western economies (Capaldi 2006). Perhaps the two endeavors are simply too disparate for meaningful engagement, management practice being defined by such actions as setting objectives, organizing, motivating, measuring, and developing professional skills under the press of urgent circumstances (Drucker 2011), and philosophy a matter of contemplating abstract ideas at leisure, and teasing out ambiguities in intricate models of the world.

Yet there are good reasons to suppose that productive engagement between philosophy and management practice is both achievable and desirable. Despite evident differences, they share much common ground. As Peter Koslowski observes: "[B]oth deal with human action, its quality of goal attainment and . . . the need for the coordination of human actions. The governing of oneself and the governing of others is the central concern of philosophical ethics and of political philosophy. Managing oneself and managing others is the goal of management" (2010a, 4). On my reading, "governing" and "managing oneself" are sound representations of James's intent in his work on ethics and habit, and his insights there seem capable of informing empathetic interactions with others. Further, "the practice of management cannot be separated from the practice of conceptualizing what needs to be done and from understanding the consequences this will have," as Mihaela Kelemen points out (2011a, 7). For a manager to assess her circumstances, determine an appropriate course of action from a range of alternatives, and then plan, enact, and learn from it necessitates a series of conceptual arrangements and assessments. No other field of theory has yet produced a definitive account of how best to go about this activity. Management styles, tools, and techniques come and go, and modern corporations tend to adopt first one kind of training or "framework" and then another, but management training has not settled on any one, reliable approach.

It might be that philosophy holds an advantage over such provisional, one-dimensional management devices as organizational culture surveys and "the quality movement" (where managerial emphasis is placed on process controls in pursuit of product and corporate success) by dint of its broad scope, diverse methodologies, and historically authoritative standing. The case for incorporating any particular management approach into an organization's training and development program often rests on its being underpinned by analytic, data-driven research that is claimed to "prove" its value (often in terms of profitability alone). Yet such research tends to involve tightly defined and small-scale theses, methodological standardization, and testing under controlled conditions, characteristics quite alien to the messy realities of management (Vo and Kelemen 2014, 250). Managers alert to the complicated realities of their work, and those who have experienced short-lived frameworks or half-hearted training trends, can become cynical about such tools. By contrast, philosophy need not follow "the siren call" of empirical evidence, or address only observable phenomena, but can instead draw out and address the range of theoretical challenges faced by managers and the variety of ways in which they might be conceived and responded to.

We have seen that James's pragmatism provides theoretical means for bridging the gap between philosophers and the practitioners of management. Prospects for its adoption in workplaces would be best served by attending to straightforwardly pragmatic factors. For example, it will be necessary to make clear the relevance and richness of pragmatist resources amidst its particular terminology, argumentative style, historical assumptions, and theoretical preconceptions. So, for example, James's mellifluous and suggestive writing would need to be condensed and modernized, salient points made pithy and approachable for a new audience. In this regard, lessons might be learned from other areas of applied philosophy, and from the numerous forums and technologies being used to expand philosophy's audience (including, but not limited to, works of "popular philosophy").[5] It might be, too, that philosophers would "get a foot in the door" by engaging with management consultancies and training institutions rather than operating entirely from universities.

Moreover, pragmatist philosophers of management will need to remain mindful that they will meet resistance from those corporate leaders wary of thinking that promotes questioning rather than conformance, and sensitivity to context over blanket application of rules. While company leaders often profess appreciation for original thinking amongst their employees, they realize that it makes top-down decisions more difficult to implement and their consequences harder to predict. In short, training managers to attend more carefully to the ways that they think and the nuanced circumstances defining their work can make managing them more difficult, and might even threaten the interests of organizational superiors. The case for pragmatism's adoption by corporations will have to be carefully framed and utterly convincing. Otherwise, the philosophers will be left to chat amongst themselves.

CONCLUSION

The organization theorist Edward Lawler has argued that the "usefulness" of any field of organizational study rests on satisfying two criteria: contributing to the body of knowledge comprising the academic discipline *and* improving practitioners' understanding of organizations, thereby promoting improved practices (1999). Although "the potential American pragmatism holds for informing how scholars and practitioners understand, analyze, and 'improve' forms of organization and management to the benefit of human experience is, with some notable exceptions, unrealized," as Kelemen and Nick Rumens contend, a recent rush of publications seems to suggest that this is changing (Rumens and Kelemen 2013, 4). Two recently published essay collections apply pragmatism to a range of topics in organization and management, while others contain a chapter or two devoted to justifying and encouraging such a project.[6] There has been a long-running and colorful debate about pragmatism's influence on, and relevance to, the management of public resources.[7] Numerous articles and chapters have been published in organization studies discussing management-related topics from a pragmatist perspective.[8] Other publications have covered topics more obviously within the remit of philosophy of management, applying pragmatist resources to such projects as defining management, developing business strategies, justifying the quality movement, conducting human resources management in ethical ways, determining corporate social responsibilities, and constructing corporate leadership models.[9]

Yet there is little evidence that these publications have done much to promote the relevance of philosophy for the conduct of management, or to bring philosophers and managers into a dialogue that might alter how management is taught and practiced. Indeed, they generally fail even to acknowledge any need to reconcile a preoccupation with rigor with a concern for how theory might be applied. It is as though pragmatism's ideological preoccupation with action is deemed sufficient to demonstrate its relevance for management practice, leaving it to managers to locate germane ideas and modes of application. Like philosophers of management from other schools, pragmatists have tended to begin by defining "management problems" or "issues" or "concepts" in abstract terms, cleansed of the situational messiness that characterizes them in practice, and then to deploy conceptual resources to understand or solve them. For pragmatists, as for philosophers of management from other schools, processes of predefinition and conceptualization are sources of abstraction, and even the most perspicacious, resourceful, and elegantly expressed theory cannot undo its methodological biases.

Given the classical pragmatists' preoccupation with locating practices for making the best of an open-ended future, and the extent to which management practices influence the economic, social, environmental, and personal well-being of those living in modern economies, the failure so far to encourage dialogue between philosophers and managers is significant. As

Vo and Kelemen suggest of Dewey, James too would "see organization studies as a vehicle to help people lead better lives" (2014, 242). James's version of pragmatism addresses both methodologically and practically those matters crucial for a philosophy providing "the opportunity to reconceptualize the divide between theory and practice in management studies in a theoretically robust and practically useful way" (Kelemen 2011b).[10] For him, our most meaningful problems are always to do with how we think about and respond to our urgent and particular circumstances, rather than with how we conceptualize *kinds* of issues, and conscious life is largely occupied with the particulars of context, problem, and consequence. Philosophy should concern itself above all with alerting people to the opportunities contained within their circumstances for thinking in fresh and productive ways. As such, James encourages careful attention toward the particularity and dynamism of one's own experience, rather than toward simplifying theoretical constructs. The most specific tools that he provides—those to do with habit, ethics, conceptualization, and so on—are general resources for addressing momentary, specific, unique circumstances. The gap between philosopher and manager is bridged not just by the philosopher's "immersing herself in the details" of a particular management problem, but by providing guidance for the manager's own thinking of the details long after the philosopher has returned to her office.

NOTES

1. John Dewey's pragmatist analyses of early twentieth-century socioeconomic and institutional arrangements reflect this same preoccupation and derive in large part from the work of Peirce and James.

2. This general characterization ought not to detract from James's social progressivism. From the mid-1890s until the end of his life, James participated in public debates about issues as diverse as American imperialism, regulation of big business, care of the mentally ill, lynching, homogenization of university teaching qualifications, medical licensing, and the status of heterodox approaches to science and medicine, among others.

3. There are exceptions. A few philosophers have pursued "fields where philosophy can be of use for management as a resource for improving the performance of the firm" or laid out theoretical resources that they believe might be helpful for managers in better performing their duties (see Koslowski [2010b, 7] for a discussion).

4. James considered in depth the myriad methodological problems posed by introspection, particularly the faithfulness of introspective reports to experience's immediacy. Finally, though, he insisted on the fallible utility of his method, finding

no alternative for accessing experience without prior conceptualization (James 1981, 191). Nonetheless, he remains careful to avoid drawing universal conclusions on the basis of introspective reports alone.

5. Examples include philosophy-themed podcasts and videos, such journals of popular philosophy as *Philosophy Now* and *Philosophy Today*, philosophy blogs, *The School of Life*'s resources. and philosophical columns in newspapers, such as "The Stone" in *The New York Times*. Lessons can be taken also from the ways in which various psychological theories have been adapted in staff selection tools, "cultural inventories," tests of leadership potential, and so on.

6. For the former, see Kelemen and Rumens (2013) and Khalil; for the latter, see Helin et al.

7. See, for example Snider; Hildebrand (2004; 2008); Shields; Whetsell and Shields; Brom and Shields.

8. See, for example, Brandi and Elkjaer; Siegers; Taylor and Bell; Bidet and Chave; Parmar, Phillips, and Freeman.

9. See, respectively, Kelemen and Rumens (2008); Nonaka and Zhu; Lorino; Watson; Margolis and Walsh; Wood and Dibben.

10. Wicks and Freeman see the rapprochement in different terms: "For the pragmatist, the criterion of usefulness applies across two dimensions that the positivist views as sharply distinct: epistemological (is this information credible, well-informed, reliable?) and normative (does this help advance our projects?)" (130).

REFERENCES

Anderson, Douglas R. "Business Ethics and the Pragmatic Attitude." In *A Companion to Business Ethics*, edited by Robert E. Frederick, 56–64. Malden, MA: Blackwell, 1999.

Bidet, Alexandra, and Frédérique Chave. "From Pragmatism to Today's Work Dramas: The Ethicized and Public Dimensions of Work." *European Journal of Pragmatism and American Philosophy* 7, no. 1 (2015): 143–68.

Brandi, Ulrik, and Bente Elkjaer. 2013. "Organizational Learning: Knowing in Organizing." In *American Pragmatism and Organization: Issues and Controversies*, edited by Mihaela Kelemen and Nick Rumens. Farnham, UK: Gower.

Brom, Robert, and Patricia M. Shields. "Classical Pragmatism, the American Experiment, and Public Administration." In *Organization Theory and Management: The Philosophical Approach*, edited by Thomas D. Lynch and Peter L. Cruise. Boca Raton, FL: Taylor and Francis, 2006.

Capaldi, Nicholas. "What Philosophy Can and Cannot Contribute to Business Ethics." *Journal of Private Enterprise* 21, no. 2 (2006): 68–86.

Chia, Robert. "Essay: Time, Duration and Simultaneity: Rethinking Process and Change in Organization Analysis." *Organization Studies* 23, no. 6 (2002): 863–68.

Dewey, John. *Experience and Nature*. London: George Allen and Unwin, 1929.
Drucker, Peter F. *Management*. New York: Routledge, 2011.
Edward, Peter. "Decision-Making: Coping with Madness Beyond Reason." In *Routledge Companion to Philosophy in Organization Studies*, edited by Raza Mir, Hugh Willmott and Michelle Greenwood. London: Routledge, 2016.
Eldridge, Michael, and Sami Pihlström. "Glossary." In *The Continuum Companion to Pragmatism*, edited by Sami Pihlström. London: Continuum, 2011.
Elkjaer, Bente, and Barbara Simpson. "Pragmatism: A lived and living philosophy. What can it offer to contemporary organization theory?" *Philosophy and Organization Theory* 32 (2011): 55–84.
Follett, Mary P. *The New State: Group Organization the Solution of Popular Government*. New York: Longmans Green, 1926.
Halliwell, Martin, and Joel D. S. Rasmussen. "Introduction: William James and the Transatlantic Conversation." In *William James and the Transatlantic Conversation: Pragmatism, Pluralism, and Philosophy of Religion*. Oxford: Oxford University Press, 2014.
Harter, Nathan. "Eric Voegelin's Reading of William James: Towards an Understanding of Leading within the Tensions of a Pluralistic Universe." In *American Pragmatism and Organization: Issues and Controversies*, edited by Mihaela Kelemen and Nick Rumens. Farnham, UK: Gower, 2013.
Helin, Jenny, Tor Hernes, Daniel Hjorth, and Robin Holt, eds. *Oxford Handbook of Process Philosophy and Organization Studies*. Oxford, 2014.
Hildebrand, David L. "Avoiding Wrong Turns: A Philippic Against the Linguistification of Pragmatism." In *Dewey, Pragmatism, and Economic Methodology*, edited by Elias L. Khalil. London: Routledge, 2004.
———. "Public Administration as Pragmatic, Democratic, and Objective." *Public Administration Review* 68, no. 2 (2008): 222–29.
James, William. *Letters of William James*. 2 vols. Boston: Atlantic Monthly Press, 1920.
———. *The Meaning of Truth*. Vol. 2 of *The Works of William James*, edited by Fredson Bowers and Ignas K. Skrupskelis. Introduction by H. S. Thayer. Cambridge, MA: Harvard University Press, [1909] 1975a.
———. *Pragmatism*. Vol. 1 of *The Works of William James*, edited by Fredson Bowers, and Ignas K. Skrupskelis. Introduction by H. S. Thayer. Cambridge, MA: Harvard University Press, [1907] 1975b.
———. *Essays in Radical Empiricism*. Vol. 3 of *The Works of William James*, edited by Fredson Bowers, and Ignas K. Skrupskelis. Introduction by John J. McDermott. Cambridge, MA: Harvard University Press, [1912] 1976.
———. *A Pluralistic Universe*. Vol. 4 of *The Works of William James*, edited by Fredson Bowers and Ignas K. Skrupskelis. Introduction by Richard J. Bernstein. Cambridge, MA: Harvard University Press, [1909] 1977.
———. *Some Problems of Philosophy*. Vol. 7 of *The Works of William James*, edited by Frederick H. Burkhardt, Fredson Bowers, and Ignas K. Skrupskelis. Introduction Peter H. Hare. Cambridge, MA: Harvard University Press, [1910] 1979a.

———. *The Will to Believe and Other Essays in Popular Philosophy*. Vol. 6 of *The Works of William James*, edited by Frederick H. Burkhardt, Fredson Bowers, and Ignas K. Skrupskelis. Introduction by Edward H. Madden. Cambridge, MA: Harvard University Press, [1897] 1979b.

———. *The Principles of Psychology*. Vols. 8–10 of *The Works of William James*, edited by Frederick H. Burkhardt, Fredson Bowers, and Ignas K. Skrupskelis. Introductions by Rand B. Evans and Gerald E. Myers. Cambridge, MA: Harvard University Press, [1890] 1981.

———. *Essays in Religion and Morality*. Vol. 11 of *The Works of William James*, edited by Frederick H. Burkhardt, Fredson Bowers, and Ignas K. Skrupskelis. Introduction by John J. McDermott. Cambridge, MA: Harvard University Press, [1884–1910] 1982.

———. *Talks to Teachers on Psychology; and to Students on Some of Life's Ideals*. Vol. 12 of *The Works of William James*, edited by Frederick H. Burkhardt, Fredson Bowers, and Ignas K. Skrupskelis. Introduction by Gerald E. Myers. Cambridge, MA: Harvard University Press, [1899] 1983.

———. *Psychology: Briefer Course*. Vol. 14 of *The Works of William James*, edited by Frederick H. Burkhardt, Fredson Bowers, and Ignas K. Skrupskelis. Introduction by Michael M. Sokal. Cambridge, MA: Harvard University Press, [1892] 1984.

———. *The Varieties of Religious Experience*. Vol. 15 of *The Works of William James*, edited by Frederick H. Burkhardt, Fredson Bowers, and Ignas K. Skrupskelis. Introduction by John E. Smith. Cambridge, MA: Harvard University Press, [1902] 1985.

———. *Essays in Psychical Research*. Vol. 16 of *The Works of William James*, edited by Frederick H. Burkhardt, Fredson Bowers, and Ignas K. Skrupskelis. Introduction by Robert A. McDermott. Cambridge, MA: Harvard University Press, [1869–1909], 1986.

———. *Essays, Comments, and Reviews*. Vol. 17 of *The Works of William James*, edited by Frederick H. Burkhardt, Fredson Bowers, and Ignas K. Skrupskelis. Introduction by Ignas K. Skrupskelis. Cambridge, MA: Harvard University Press, [1865–1909] 1987.

———. *Manuscript Lectures*. Vol. 19 of *The Works of William James*, edited by Frederick H. Burkhardt, Fredson Bowers, and Ignas K. Skrupskelis. Introduction by Ignas K. Skrupskelis. Cambridge, MA: Harvard University Press, [1872–1907] 1988.

Kelemen, Mihaela. "The Ambiguity of Inquiry in Management Research: An American Pragmatist Perspective." Fourth Nordic Pragmatism Conference, Copenhagen, 2011a.

———. "American Pragmatism." In *Key Concepts in Critical Management Studies* edited by Mark Tadajewski, Pauline Maclaran, Elizabeth Parsons and Martin Parker. London: Sage Publications, 2011b.

Kelemen, Mihaela, and Nick Rumens. *An Introduction to Critical Management Research*. London: Sage Publications, 2008.

———, eds. *American Pragmatism and Organization: Issues and Controversies*. Farnham, UK: Gower, 2013.

Khalil, Elias L., ed. *Dewey, Pragmatism, and Economic Methodology*. London: Routledge, 2004.

Kloppenberg, James T. *Uncertain Victory: Social Democracy and Progressivism in European and American Thought, 1870–1920*. New York: Oxford University Press, 1986.

Koslowski, Peter, ed. *Elements of a Philosophy of Management and Organization*. Berlin: Springer Verlag, 2010a.

———. "The Philosophy of Management." In *Elements of a Philosophy of Management and Organization*, edited by Peter Koslowski. Berlin: Springer Verlag, 2010b.

Lawler, Edward E. III. "Challenging Traditional Research Assumptions." In *Doing Research That Is Useful for Theory and Practice*, edited by Edward E. III Lawler, Allan M. Jr. Mohrman, Susan A. Mohrman, Gerald E. Jr. Ledford, and Thomas G. Cummings. Lanham, MD: Lexington, 1999.

Lorino, Phillipe. "Pragmatism: A Key Source for the Renewal of Organization and Management Studies." Second European Pragmatism Conference, Paris, 2015.

Margolis, Joshua D. "Psychological Pragmatism and the Imperative of Aims: A New Approach to Business Ethics." *Business Ethics Quarterly* 8, no. 3 (1998): 409–30.

Margolis, Joshua D., and James P. Walsh. "Misery Loves Companies: Rethinking Social Initiatives by Business." *Administrative Science Quarterly* 48, no. 2 (2003): 268–305.

McDermott, John J. "Introduction." In *Essays in Radical Empiricism*, edited by Frederick H. Burkhardt, Fredson Bowers, and Ignas K. Skrupskelis, xi–xlviii. Cambridge, MA: Harvard University Press, 1976.

———. "The Promethean Self and Community in the Philosophy of William James." *Rice University Studies* (1980): 87–101.

———. "Classical American Philosophy: A Reflective Bequest to the Twenty-First Century." *Journal of Philosophy* 81, no. 11 (1984): 663–75.

———. *Streams of Experience: Reflections on the History and Philosophy of American Culture*. Amherst: University of Massachusetts Press, 1986.

Menand, Louis. *The Metaphysical Club: A Story of Ideas in America*. New York: Farrar, Straus and Giroux, 2001.

Nonaka, Ikujiro, and Zhichang Zhu. *Pragmatic Strategy, Eastern Wisdom, Global Success*. New York: Cambridge University Press, 2012.

Pappas, Gregory F. *John Dewey's Ethics: Democracy as Experience*. Bloomington, IN: Indiana University Press, 2008.

Parmar, Bidhan L., Robert Phillips, and R. Edward Freeman. "Pragmatism and Organization Studies." In *Routledge Companion to Philosophy in Organization Studies*, edited by Raza Mir, Hugh Willmott, and Michelle Greenwood. London: Routledge, 2016.

Powell, Thomas C. "William James." In *Oxford Handbook of Process Philosophy and Organization Studies*, edited by Jenny Helin, Tor Hernes, Daniel Hjorth, and Robin Holt. Oxford: Oxford University Press, 2014.

Rosenthal, Sandra B., and Rogene A. Buchholz. "Toward New Directions in Business Ethics: Some Pragmatic Pathways." In *A Companion to Business Ethics*, edited by Robert E. Frederick. Malden, MA: Blackwell, 1999.

———. *Rethinking Business Ethics: A Pragmatic Approach*. Edited by R. Edward Freeman. New York: Oxford University Press, 2000.

Rumens, Nick, and Mihaela Kelemen. "American Pragmatism and Organization Studies: Concepts, Themes and Possibilities." In *American Pragmatism and Organization: Issues and Controversies*, edited by Mihaela Kelemen and Nick Rumens. Farnham, UK: Gower, 2013.

Shields, Patricia M. "Rediscovering the Taproot: Is Classical Pragmatism the Route to Renew Public Administration?" *Public Administration Review* 68, no. 2 (2008): 205–21.

Siegers, Rosa. "A Pragmatist Approach to Emotional Intelligence and Managerial Regret." In *American Pragmatism and Organization: Issues and Controversies*, edited by Mihaela Kelemen and Nick Rumens. Farnham, UK: Gower, 2013.

Smith, John E. "Experience, God, and Classical American Philosophy." *American Journal of Theology and Philosophy* 14, no. 2 (1993): 119–45.

Snider, Keith F. "Expertise or Experimenting? Pragmatism and American Public Administration, 1920–1950." *Administration and Society* 32 (2000): 329–53.

Taylor, Scott, and Emma Bell. "Believing in a Pragmatist Business Ethics." In *American Pragmatism and Organization: Issues and Controversies*, edited by Mihaela Kelemen and Nick Rumens. Farnham, UK: Gower, 2013.

Vo, Linh Chi, and Mihaela Kelemen. "John Dewey." In *Oxford Handbook of Process Philosophy and Organization Studies*, edited by Jenny Helin, Tor Hernes, Daniel Hjorth and Robin Holt. Oxford: Oxford University Press, 2014.

Wallis, Steven E. "The Right Tool for the Job: Philosophy's Evolving Role in Advancing Management Theory." *Philosophy of Management* 11, no. 3 (2012): 67–99.

Watson, Tony J. "Critical social science, pragmatism, and the realities of HRM." *The International Journal of Human Resources Management* 21, no. 6 (2010): 915–31.

Westbrook, Robert B. *Democratic Hope: Pragmatism and the Politics of Truth.* Ithaca, NY: Cornell University Press, 2005.

Whetsell, T. A., and Patricia M. Shields. "Reconciling the varieties of pragmatism in public administration." *Administration and Society* 43, no. 4 (2011): 474–83.

Wicks, Andrew C., and R. Edward Freeman. "Organization Studies and the New Pragmatism: Positivism, Anti-Positivism, and the Search for Ethics." *Organization Studies* 9, no. 2 (1998): 123–40.

Wood, Martin, and Mark Dibben. "Leadership as Relational Process." *Process Studies* 44, no. 1 (2015): 24–47.

CHAPTER 11

HABITS IN A WORLD OF CHANGE

JAMES CAMPBELL

This chapter explores the centrality of habits in the work of William James, and considers how his largely descriptive emphases can be applied to our current situations. For James, habits are central to our ways of interpreting and dealing with the world; but, because they are means of stabilizing experience, habits make us less adaptive to novelty. At long last when several of our habitual ways of sorting our experiences—for example, through the blinders of traditional understandings of race, class, and gender—are finally under increasing assault, adapting James's understanding of the nature and power of habits can assist us in our attempts to face the future.

I

In his psychological work, James considers a broad sweep of topics, including the stream of consciousness, the social self, memory, reasoning, and necessary truth. He also discusses the importance of habits: the relationship between nature and nurture, between instinct and learning. "All our life, so far as it has definite form, is but a mass of habits—practical, emotional, and intellectual—systematically organized for our weal or woe, and bearing us irresistibly towards our destiny, whatever the latter may be" (1983, 47).

James is greatly concerned with the physiological basis of habits. "*An acquired habit, from the physiological point of view,*" he writes, "*is nothing but a new pathway of discharge formed in the brain, by which certain incoming currents ever after tend to escape*" (1984, 125). This development of habits is related to the mutability of organic life that makes the human so adaptive. He writes that "*the phenomena of habit in living beings are due to the plasticity of the organic materials of which their bodies are composed.*" Plasticity, in general, means "the possession of a structure weak enough to yield to an influence, but strong enough not to yield all at once" (1981, 110); and nervous tissue is extraordinarily plastic in this sense. The "habitualness" of the habit is caused by modifications of nervous pathways. "The currents, once in, must find a way out," James writes, and "in getting out they leave their traces in the paths which they take" (ibid., 112). New currents must follow the old paths or create new ones; but the tendency is to follow the old, and habits come to replace plasticity.

Individuals inevitably become less plastic as they grow older, a problem that is being powerfully felt in our world of change as the population ages and the pace of innovation quickens. "Most of us grow more and more enslaved to the stock conceptions with which we have once become familiar, and less and less capable of assimilating impressions in any but the old ways," he writes. "Old-fogyism, in short, is the inevitable terminus to which life sweeps us on" (1981, 754). He continues that, at some point, "disinterested curiosity is past, the mental grooves and channels set, the power of assimilation gone." While learning will continue at some level, James believes that it will always carry a "sense of insecurity" when compared "with things learned in the plastic days of instinctive curiosity," about which we will "never lose entirely our sense of being at home" (1981, 1021).

With the physiology clarified, James turns to the practical effects of habits. The primary effect to which he points is greater simplification and accuracy—and a resultant decrease in fatigue—in the performance of repetitive tasks like playing the piano and typing.[1] "If an act require for its execution a chain, A, B, C, D, E, F, G, etc., of successive nervous events," he writes, "then in the first performances of the action the conscious will must choose each of these events from a number of wrong alternatives that tend to present themselves." As time goes on and habit develops, however, "each event calls up its own appropriate successor without any alternative offering itself, and without any reference to the conscious will, until at last the whole chain, A, B, C, D, E, F, G, rattles itself off as soon as A occurs, just as if A and the rest of the chain were fused into a continuous stream." Thus, unlike the person who is learning "to walk, to ride, to swim, skate, fence, write, play, or sing" (1981, 119) and is constantly concentrating on performing each step of the process, the skilled person simply acts. The second important effect for creatures like us is that habit frees up the mind for reverie or thinking. "A strictly voluntary act has to be guided by idea, perception, and volition, throughout its whole course," James notes; but "in an habitual action, mere sensation is a sufficient guide, and the upper regions of brain and mind are set comparatively free." Oftentimes, the mind even "forgets" some of the unimportant information, like the location of the letters on a keyboard, but the fingers do not. "Few men can tell off-hand which sock, shoe, or trousers-leg they put on first," he continues. "Which way does my door swing? . . . I cannot *tell* the answer; yet my *hand* never makes a mistake" (1981, 120). Our habits ride our bicycles for us and drive our cars; and, when we think about many of these mechanical activities, our performance often suffers.

Although it is not his central concern, James clearly understands the connection between individual habits and the broader social habits that we call custom or tradition. In some contexts, the ability to kick a ball accurately is a more valued skill to develop than the ability to throw it. Similarly, not all children find themselves in a situation where a good ear and nimble fingers will draw them into a culture of violin playing. He also considers the ethical or pedagogical importance of individual and social habits. While society can only proceed if there is some level of order, our instincts offer us little help here. Our various needs—for food, clothing, shelter, and so on—will somehow be met; but it is usually the traditional diet, customary dress, and familiar structures of our culture that determine just how. "Habit is thus the enormous fly-wheel of society," he writes, "its most precious conservative agent." It is habit alone, he continues, that "saves the children of fortune from the envious uprisings of the poor" and "prevents the hardest and most repulsive walks of life from being deserted by those brought up to tread therein." If not for habit, James continues, nothing would keep "the fisherman and the deck-hand at sea through the winter," nor "the miner in his darkness," nor the farmer on "his lonely farm through all the months of snow." There is, no doubt, personal tragedy in a process that "dooms us all to fight out the battle of life upon the lines of our nurture or our early choice," however disagreeable it becomes, "because there is no other for which we are fitted, and it is too late to begin again." Still, he writes, it is a good thing for society that "in most of us, by the age of thirty, the character has set like plaster, and will never soften again" (1981, 125–26). Moreover, he continues, these traditions and customs are all habits, contained not just in our nerves, but more broadly in our literature and mythologies, in our spelling, our ways of laying out roadways and dividing the year. Similarly, our customary moralities are communal habits that, for better or worse, combine religious and legal constraints to channel our basic human drives—for companionship, sex, child-rearing, and so on—into a narrow set of pre-selected possibilities. James further denies the often-heard claims that there is an instinct of acquisitiveness that necessarily leads to capitalism or, as we shall see shortly, an instinct of bellicosity that necessarily leads to warfare. For him, our instincts are more plastic, and there are powerful cultural components in their shaping.

Following this analysis, institutions are habitual social responses that tend to promote or stymie social change, and at the same time to foster or prevent the flourishing of individuals. Reliance upon precedent—one kind of social habit—can preserve institutions of gender inequality, while a feminist political program—another kind of social habit—can work in the opposite direction. James's evaluation of institutions, however, was mostly negative. He writes, for example, that, when human wants are formalized into institutions, the institutions themselves tend to hamper "the natural gratification" of the wants. Whether the institution be legal or religious, educational or medical, he believes that too often "such institutions frustrate the spiritual purpose to which they were appointed to minister" (1982, 77). Rather than advancing justice or holiness, learning or health, such institutions tend rather to advance institutional values like conformity and economic stability. "*Every* great institution is perforce a means of corruption—whatever good it may also do," he writes to one correspondent (James 1992–2004, 9:41). To another he writes "the bigger the unit you deal with, the hollower, the more brutal, the more mendacious is the life displayed" (ibid., 8:546). He was a strong individualist who remained ever suspicious of social organizations and group cooperation.

While psychology is not necessarily a moral inquiry, it does examine human behavior, and thus it must intersect at times with morality. Habits are of both good and bad sorts, James notes, although our moral discussions usually emphasize the latter, our habitual vices. People "talk of the smoking-habit and the swearing-habit and the drinking-habit, but not of the abstention-habit or the moderation-habit or the courage-habit" (1983, 47). Maintaining that the larger the portion of our daily activities that we can consign to "the effortless custody of automatism, the more our higher powers of mind will be set free for their own proper work," he stresses that we must recognize the definite temporal limits on human plasticity, either on the learning of languages or "the formation of intellectual and professional habits" (1981, 126). If the young would realize that they are quickly becoming "mere walking bundles of habits," they would watch their conduct much more carefully while still in "the plastic state," he writes. Drunkards become drunkards, and saints saints, "by so many separate acts and hours of work" (ibid., 130–31). Of course, the power of habits to set the mind free for other actions also means that the mind is not concentrating on the full meaning of what is being done. Habits thus can lead to a failure to question what we are doing.

In a pair of ethical essays, "On a Certain Blindness in Human Beings" and "What Makes a Life Significant," James also stresses that habits function to narrow our responses. In the former essay, he begins by developing the psychological principle that we are generally unfeeling to the values "of creatures and people different from ourselves," and that following our customs often makes the situation worse. As "practical beings," we are all "bound to feel intensely" the importance of our own duties and of the situations that require our actions. Still, he continues, "this feeling is in each of us a vital secret"; and we look in vain to others who are too absorbed living out their lives to take much interest in ours. The two primary results of our blindness are "the stupidity and injustice of our opinions, so far as they deal with the significance of alien lives," and "the falsity of our judgments, so far as they presume to decide in an absolute way on the value of other persons' conditions or ideals" (1983, 132; cf. 1982, 98, 101). Additionally, our customary biases lead us to fear those who have abandoned the familiar and common for values of their own devising.

Our partiality results from the fact that we are actors rather than spectators, partisans rather than philosophers. Significance, where we find it, is direct and personal. "Wherever a process of life communicates an eagerness to him who lives it, there the life becomes genuinely significant," James writes. Wherever such receptivity is found, "there is the zest, the tingle, the excitement, of reality; and there *is* 'importance' in the only real and positive sense in which importance ever anywhere can be" (1983, 134–35). Our beliefs are not formal catalogues of "orthodoxies and heresies"; they are tools for us "to live by" (1979b, 52). The corollary to this personal significance is that we can seldom appreciate the lives of others. "Our deadness toward all but one particular kind of joy would thus be the price we inevitably have to pay for being practical creatures." Only in the case of the dreamer or lover—the "philosopher, poet, or romancer" (1983, 133)—is this fundamental practicality mitigated. He maintains that such intellectuals, because of their lives of disengagement from the sharp edges of reality, are weakened in "responsive sensibilities." As a remedy for this situation, James suggests a descent to "a more profound and primitive level": the experience of imprisonment or shipwreck or military life would, he believes, "permanently show the good of life to many an over-educated pessimist." By reconnecting with the lives of "savages and children of nature, to whom we deem ourselves so much superior," we might be able to reanimate our lives because frequently they are "alive where we are often dead" (ibid., 146).

The second part of the "Blindness" essay is a series of illustrations of this psychological principle. One is a comparison of the values of a dog's life to those of a human's. Although the canine and the human are connected "by a tie more intimate than most ties in this world," James writes, each is insensible to the values of the other: "we to the rapture of bones under hedges, or smells of trees and lamp-posts, they to the delights of literature and art." In spite of the fox-terrier's general regard for its owner, for example, much of the latter's conduct remains incomprehensible to the faithful pooch, who will never be able to understand the hours spent every day reading, "paralyzed of motion and vacant of all conscious life." A second illustration is the result of a trip to North Carolina, where he found, in the midst of the "unmitigated squalor" that had been carved out of a place of pristine natural beauty, a local resident who was quite proud of his misguided improvements. James eventually realized that he was missing "the whole inward significance of the situation." For the residents, "the chips, the girdled trees, and the vile split rails spoke of honest sweat, persistent toil and final reward. The cabin was a warrant of safety for self and wife and babes." What to him was only an "ugly picture on the retina" was to the residents "a very paean of duty, struggle, and success." Turning the tables as best he can, he admits that he had been "as blind to the peculiar ideality of their conditions as they certainly would also have been to the ideality of mine, had they had a peep at my strange indoor academic ways of life at Cambridge" (1983, 132–34).

James's pluralistic conclusion is a two-part principle. Negatively, he writes, "it absolutely forbids us to be forward in pronouncing on the meaninglessness of forms of existence other than our own." While each individual "gains a partial superiority of insight from the peculiar position in which he stands," we must remember that "neither the whole of truth, nor the whole of good, is revealed to any single observer." Positively, his principle "commands us to tolerate, respect, and indulge those whom we see harmlessly interested and happy in their own ways, however unintelligible these may be to us." Each of us, James continues, "should be faithful to his own opportunities and make the most of his blessings, without presuming to regulate the rest of the vast field" (1983, 149).

The second essay, "What Makes a Life Significant," continues James's line of thinking. As an example of how we do not understand what makes others "tick," he urges us to consider our inability to grasp the attraction of one person for another. "Every Jack sees in his own particular Jill," he writes, "charms and perfections to the enchantment of which we stolid onlookers are stone-cold." Still, he wonders, who understands the situation better: the smitten Jack or the rest of us who are "victims of a pathological anaesthesia as regards Jill's magical importance?" We may recognize this attraction intellectually or conceptually—we may know about it—but "dead clocks that we are," we cannot really know it from within (1983, 150–51; cf. 1985, 260). Thus, if we cannot fully understand others' lives, we should be less hasty to judge them. Our uninformed inclination to disregard the values of others is "the root of most human injustices and cruelties, and the trait in human character most likely to make the angels weep." We should neither judge others' conduct, nor interfere with how they lead their lives. "The first thing to learn in intercourse with others," James writes, "is non-interference with their own peculiar ways of being happy, provided those ways do not assume to interfere by violence with ours." Others will fail to grasp our "inner secrets," and we theirs, because "beings as essentially practical as we are are necessarily short of sight" (1983, 150–51; cf. 4; 1979b 154–55). Our response to our blindness should be to strive for tolerance; but our habits, and often our social customs, prevent our attainment of this goal.

II

Having outlined this general understanding of James's sense of our complex habitual nature, it is possible to consider his vision of social conflict and moral change. In his writings, we find little discussion of social issues that appear central at present. In particular, questions of race and class engaged him only seldom, and questions of gender even less frequently.[2] His focus was elsewhere, on issues of personal fulfillment: the greatest evil that he saw was the crushing of individuals by social institutions. Of course, institutional problems rooted in gender, race, and class discrimination crushed individuals; but, like all of us on occasion, James at times failed to follow his own advice. As we survey some of his efforts, it is important to keep in mind that our concern in this chapter is less upon what James made of his world than upon how his insights on the nature and power of habit can help us to deal with ours.

Race was an issue about which James wrote little. Slavery was a powerful, if increasingly embattled, American institution when he was born in 1842; but the Civil War, which raged between his nineteenth and twenty-fourth birthday, was widely viewed to be more about preserving the Union than about emancipation, about sectionalism rather than abolition. In any case, he took no part in this great struggle. Looking back with greater insight in 1897, he notes that "our great western republic had from its very origin" been both a "land of freedom, boastfully so called," and one "with human slavery enthroned at the heart of it." The Founders' reluctance to challenge slavery had left Americans with a country that was "a thing of falsehood and horrible self-contradiction . . ." He continues that slavery had become such a pervasive force that it eventually was "dictating terms of unconditional surrender to every other organ of its life," and that "the only alternative for the nation was to fight or die" (1982, 66). Deciphering the meaning of the War for the present and the future, he reminds his audience that, while "no future problem can be like that problem," the Northern victory at Appomattox had not solved all of America's problems. As we move forward, "tasks enough await us" and our "democracy is still upon its trial" (ibid., 73–74).

One of America's future tasks was dealing with its inheritance of institutionalized racism. James offered a pair of statements in 1903 on the rash of lynchings that had occurred over the last decade and gave little indication of abating. He is especially interested in conveying his sense of the horror of this custom, a custom that was not "a transient contagion destined soon to exhaust its virulence." On the contrary, it had become "a profound social disease, spreading now like forest fire, and certain to become permanently endemic in every corner of our country, North and South, unless heroic remedies are swiftly adopted to check it" (1987, 170). Writing as a psychologist in the face of this "epidemic of lynching," he maintains that "the average church-going Civilizee" fails to recognize that our "homicidal potentialities" remain cloaked in the respectability of social custom. In fact, he continues, "Negro lynching claims more and more the character of a public right. It appeals to the punitive instinct, to race antipathy and to the white man's pride, as well as to the homicidal frenzy" (ibid., 171–72). Although he is attempting to uncover the psychology behind these monstrous actions, James has no tolerance for the actions themselves; and, as a response to this epidemic, he calls for harsh legislation that would guarantee that, when lynchings occurred, "the members of the mob" would be "indicted and hanged" (ibid., 175). Regarding the lesser but related issue of racial discrimination, James seems to have been, however sensitive as a psychologist, personally comfortable with all sorts of racial and ethnic aspersions.³ At the same time, most of his criticisms seem counterbalanced in the fashion of the following passage: "Negro-suffrage shows indeed a sorry history, but so, for the matter of that, does white suffrage" (ibid., 193). All in all, he is clear about our powerful fear of the unfamiliar and the danger of compounding this personal fear through harmful social customs.

Turning to issues of class, we see that James had a skewed understanding of the labor question. His comments in these cases are an indication of his acceptance of the bifurcation of society into owners and workers. Moreover, we get some sense of his own class position when he writes that the term "labor-question" covers "all sorts of anarchistic discontents and socialistic projects, and the conservative resistances which they provoke." His own social myopia prevents him from seeing any causal factors and provocations the other way around. He continues in a marginally better fashion that the two "halves" do not understand each other: "one-half of our fellow-countrymen remain entirely blind to the internal significance of the lives of the other half." Without accepting the percentages implied by the term "half," we can see that, for James, each portion of society fails to grasp the "joys and sorrows" of the other; each misses the other's "moral virtue" and "intellectual ideals" (1983, 165–66).

Clearly James does attempt to overcome his blindness and to recognize the claims of the poor. He admits that society has to "pass towards some newer and better equilibrium, and the distribution of wealth has doubtless slowly got to change," because such changes are part of the evolution of social life. Still, he maintains that, should we believe that these economic changes will bring "any *genuine vital difference*, on a large scale, to the lives of our descendants," we had missed his point. "The solid meaning of life" always involves the combination of human struggle with an ideal (1983, 166). Surely James would have said in a clearer moment, however, that many of these workers—and their families—were living in accordance with an ideal that he, as a partisan of his own values, failed to understand. Again, here we see his recognition of the power of habit and custom, even if he seems unable personally to break free.

To summarize what we have seen so far, James emphasizes the value of personal insights. On the one hand, we can point to his important recognition of what he calls "our national disease": "the moral flabbiness born of the exclusive worship of the bitch-Goddess SUCCESS" (1992–2004, 11:267). On the other hand, we recognize that following our insights can make us blind to others' values. We have also seen his consideration of the many harmful effects of custom-enhanced blindness, as in his discussion of lynching. Another factor that we need to consider is James's version of individualism. While he frequently displayed concern and sensitivity regarding those who suffered from the cruelties of life, his felt need to protect individuals from external forces was translatable only in the most extreme cases into a need to unite them in group self-protection to oppose forces that were too strong for isolated individuals to resist. Both James and John Dewey point to the importance of recognizing meaning in all experience; but the latter's emphasis is on helping to solve social problems through cooperative institutional reconstruction. The primary ethical difference between the two is that Dewey, along with other pragmatic social thinkers, emphasizes the social aspect to the downplaying of the individual, whereas James's emphasis is just the reverse. Dewey's problems are thus of a different sort from James's: What future should we try to build for ourselves and for our children? How should the bounty of the earth be managed? How can the members of our society and the peoples of the rest of the world get along with each other? These are social questions that require an ethics of reform. The answers to these new social questions must be developed through group interaction and collective choice, through a method of social criticism that changes people's minds and eventually builds new social customs. Addressing these questions seems to require that we turn away from James and his noncritical openness toward Dewey and the critical reconstruction of our social and natural environment to facilitate the development of fuller lives for individuals. James's position of noninterference with the values of others undermines this type of reconstruction. In his defense of personal values, he opposes institutions as obstacles rather than uses them as means to the fulfillment of individuality. He is unwilling, or unable, to emphasize the need for the reconstruction of our institutions as a means to fuller lives because the institutions themselves, reconstructed or not, are deadening.

The question remains of the value of James's individualistic approach and his pluralistic method of inclusion for advancing his stated goal of maximizing satisfactions. For him, the ethics of fulfillment, at least in his formulation, is in a fundamental way opposed to the ethics of reform. Further, there is no recognition in James that individualism itself could lead to social problems. For him, human atavisms arise in groups, as his discussions of lynching and imperialism indicate. When individuals become part of something external to themselves—lynch mobs as we have just seen, or warring nations as we shall see shortly—their ideality is abandoned. Their individual blindness becomes social blindness. When individuals choose their values in an intelligent and responsible fashion, however, and shape their lives around these vibrant values, social good results.

III

We have seen that James's moral thought largely undercuts the likelihood of social engagement. Still, if we turn to his discussion of imperialism and war as social problems, we find there a more fully engaged thinker. His ideas had developed in the context of the Spanish American War of 1898 and the prior surge of imperialism that had contributed to it. In both cases, dangerous social habits were in place. About this public mood, he writes to a correspondent in January 1896 of "the most extraordinary exhibition of a whole nation going fighting-mad in 24 hours." He calls this episode "the most discouraging relapse into barbarism that I have ever seen"; and he notes that it demonstrates "how near the surface the fighting instinct remains in Mankind, and how little stimulus is required to touch-off the fighting nerve" (1992–2004, 8:117; cf. 114). In early 1898 he writes that "we eat, drink and sleep War." He continues that he is witnessing "collective attacks of genuine madness sweeping over peoples and stampeding them" (ibid. 3:25–26; cf. 8:540). As the country moved toward war, it seems that James himself was briefly caught up in the spirit of the war.[4] Quickly, however, he realized problems.

In early 1899, James writes that, although pluralism demands "democratic respect for the sacredness of individuality," he believes that the "passionate inner meaning" of such notions had been destroyed by "the pretension of our nation to inflict its own inner ideals and institutions *vi et armis* upon Orientals" (1983, 4). Earlier still he had noted that, because of our use of violence, our claim to being "a better nation morally than the rest, safe at home, and without the old savage ambitions, destined to exert great international influence by throwing in our 'moral weight' etc." had been exposed as delusional. "Human Nature is everywhere the same," he continues, "and at the least temptation all the old military passions rise, and sweep everything before them" (1992–2004, 8:373; cf. 1987, 82). Despite its claims to exceptionalism, America had been willing to "puke up its own historic soul in five minutes" (1992–2004, 9:4; cf. 11:375; 1987, 85), and any process of recovery would be lengthy. In the course of the War, the Americans had especially demonstrated a blindness to Filipino values. "We are now openly engaged in crushing out the sacredest thing in this great human world," James writes, "the attempt of a people long enslaved to attain to the possession of itself, to organize its laws and government, to be free to follow its internal destinies according to its own ideals"; and, in the process, "we are cold-bloodedly, wantonly and abominably destroying the soul of a people who never did us an atom of harm in their lives" (1987, 156–57; cf. 160, 179–80). Thus, "the stars and stripes which did truly stand for something ideal, and on the whole mean it, in spite of imperfect ways of fulfillment," has now been exposed as "a lying rag, pure and simple" (1992–2004, 8:523). Although our country had claimed to live by "the faith that a man requires no master to take care of him, and that common people can work out their salvation well enough together if left free to try" (1982, 66), it was clear that that faith did not include other peoples.

In his 1910 essay "The Moral Equivalent of War,"[5] James presents a further claim: that the modern military situation is not amenable to individual control. Through habituation, we have ceded too much military power to those who benefit from its use, and a reconstruction of the whole military complex and its role in our society will be necessary before we can hope to move toward a more viable pacifism. His war essay offers a summary statement of a position that he had been developing since at least the 1890s. In this essay, he discusses war primarily as a social-psychological, rather than as a political, phenomenon. As he had noted a few years earlier, the pacifist movement finds its "permanent enemy" in "the noted bellicosity of human nature." The human being is "simply the most formidable of all beasts of prey, and, indeed, the only one that preys systematically on its own species." Because of what evolution has made us, he continues, "a millennium of peace would not breed the fighting disposition out of our bone and marrow, . . . and [it] will always find impassioned apologists and idealizers." He continues that war functions as "the final bouquet of life's fireworks" (1982, 121–22). Because of our inclinations, it is inadequate simply to blame militarists and munitions makers. They are able to succeed so well only because their actions integrate with the visceral responses of the general public. We have been molded into societies by "the gory nurse" of combat. "Dead men tell no tales, and if there were tribes of other type than this, they have left no survivors," he writes. We have inherited pugnacity as a central trait, and "thousands of years of peace won't breed it out of us" (1982, 164; cf. 1981, 1028–29). As James had noted earlier, "war was the gory cradle of mankind, the grim-featured nurse that alone could train our savage progenitors into some semblance of social virtue, teach them to be faithful one to another, and force them to sink their selfishness in wider tribal ends." We realize that we are "the survivors of one successful massacre after another" (1982, 72).

James notes that our society is profoundly ambivalent about warfare, and we must assume the same of all our presumed enemies. We recognize, on the one hand, that war is the source of unlimited destruction and suffering; on the other hand, we experience in warfare the highest acts of honor and courage. He discusses, as an example, the powerful meaning of the American Civil War, North and South. Few, he believes, would prefer in 1910 to have that war eliminated from our history, since "those ancestors, those efforts, those memories and legends, are the most ideal part of what we now own together, a sacred spiritual possession worth more than all the blood poured out.' At the same time, he continues, "not one man or woman would vote" to take up such a war. "In modern eyes, precious tho' wars may be, they must not be waged solely for the sake of the ideal harvest" (1982, 162).

James indicates, however, that in practice our ambivalence about war is often overcome by the rhetoric of unscrupulous individuals who, using time-worn traditions, wield powerful ideas like "duty" and "destiny" as tools in the service of militarism.[6] One particularly strong idea is "defense," an elevated substitute for the more direct "war." We reject as much as possible, he writes, "the bestial side of military service"; and "pure loot and mastery seem no longer morally avowable motives" (1982, 164). We can only fight legitimately in self-defense, although we can be quite imaginative in our malinterpretations of this concept. "Only when forced upon one," he writes, "only when an enemy's injustice leaves us no alternative, is a war now thought permissible" (ibid., 162). Fortunately for militarists, we have had no shortage of "unjust" enemies—nor, for that matter, do our enemies. Another powerful notion is "patriotism," a value that functions most powerfully when blind and unquestioning.[7] "Patriotism no one thinks discreditable," James writes, and "war is the romance of history." Wrapped in the ambition of victory and unfazed by the possibility of death, "the militarily patriotic and romantic-minded, and especially the professional military class, refuse to admit for a moment that war may be a transitory phenomenon in social evolution" (ibid., 165). A third powerful notion is "hardihood," a value with which James is more in agreement. He at least partly concurs that "militarism is the great preserver of our ideals of hardihood, and human life without hardihood would be contemptible," and that we have a duty to keep "military characters in stock" and thus to prevent the "weaklings and mollycoddles" (ibid., 166), whom Theodore Roosevelt condemns,[8] from taking over society. James continues to characterize the habitual ideas of his opponents when he notes that war, whatever its negative consequences, is the only way to prevent the triumph "of a world of clerks and teachers, of co-education and zoophily, of 'consumers leagues' and 'associated charities,' of industrialism unlimited, and feminism unabashed. . . . Fie upon such a cattleyard of a planet!" (1982, 166; cf. 1985, 291). Still, James rejects any equation of a "peace-economy" with a "pleasure-economy"; and he continues that in the future "we must still subject ourselves collectively to those severities that answer to our real position upon this only partly hospitable globe." He finds in the military virtues "the enduring cement" of society: "intrepidity, contempt of softness, surrender of private interest, obedience to command." James writes further that "the martial virtues, altho' originally gained by the race through war, are absolute and permanent human goods." Those who turn their backs on hardihood open themselves to "dangerous reactions against commonwealths fit only for contempt," and are "liable to invite attack whenever a center of crystallization for military-minded enterprise is formed anywhere in their neighborhood" (1982, 170).

Operating in the midst of this rhetoric, and with an inheritance of "all the innate pugnacity and all the love of glory" of our ancestors, we have given warfare a religious role in our culture as "a sort of sacrament" of purification (1982, 163, 165). James further maintains that humans live for "thrills and excitements"; and "from time immemorial wars have been, especially for non-combatants, the supremely thrilling excitement" (ibid., 122). In this situation, he rightly notes that recognizing the destructiveness, the moral evil, of war will not be enough. Our societal practice needs to be significantly reconstructed, and new customs need to be developed. To do so is possible, he believed, because our social practices are habitual rather that "instinctual." Thus, if with effort we can become more conscious of the habitual nature of these practices, we can change them. "The military feelings are too deeply grounded to abdicate their place among our ideals," he continues, "until better substitutes are offered than the glory and shame that come to nations as well as to individuals from the ups and downs of politics and the vicissitudes of trade." No society can be expected to abandon war until it feels that it has another way to instill the values which militarism now brings. James thus maintains that we must rescue such notions as "defense," "patriotism," and "hardihood" from the militarists—a task that he does not believe will be easy. As he puts it, "the war against war is going to be no holiday excursion or camping party" (ibid., 162).

Because of the problematic makeup of human nature, James fears that our attempts to tame our war selves will allow only "for preventive medicine, not for radical cure." His recommendations revolve around making a new set of social habits: "Put peace-men in power; educate the editors and statesmen to responsibility. . . . Seize every pretext, however small, for arbitration methods, and multiply the precedents; foster rival excitements and invent new outlets for heroic energy" (1982, 122–23). His hope was that over time the occasions of war could be prevented. His larger prescription for advancing "the ultimate reign of peace" and "the gradual advent of some sort of socialistic equilibrium" involves, first, the rejection of "the fatalistic view of the war-function." He writes that war *can* be stopped because "war-making is due to definite motives and subject to prudential checks and reasonable criticisms, just like any other form of enterprise." Further, he notes, war *must* be stopped: "when whole nations are the armies, and the science of destruction vies in intellectual refinement with the sciences of production, I see that war becomes absurd and impossible from its own monstrosity." Eventually, he believes, nations will come to understand this and make "common cause" against war. As he writes, "I look forward to a future when acts of war shall be formally outlawed among civilized peoples" (ibid., 170). Our only "safeguard" is to keep "the passion of military conquest" forever chained and "never to let it get its start" (1987, 154).

In 1902, James wrote of our familiarity with "the mechanical equivalent of heat"; and he suggested that we needed "to discover in the social realm . . . the moral equivalent of war," by which he meant "something heroic that will speak to men as universally as war does, and yet will be as compatible with their spiritual selves as war has proved itself to be incompatible." In what other ways, he wonders, might we be able to achieve "'the strenuous life,' without the need of crushing weaker peoples?" (1985, 292). As a moral equivalent of war, James proposes that we attempt to break our war habit with "a conscription of the whole youthful [male] population to form for a certain number of years a part of the army enlisted against *nature*"—"for" nature, we would now phrase this point—that would work to minimize the injustice of selective suffering and result in other benefits to society. Among these would be the following: "The military ideals of hardihood and discipline would be wrought into the growing fiber of the people; no one would remain blind, as the luxurious classes now are blind, to man's relations to the globe he lives on, and to the permanently solid and hard foundations of his higher life." To bring about these goods, he suggests sending these young men "to coal and iron mines, to freight trains, to fishing fleets in December, to dish-washing, clothes-washing, and window-washing, to road-building and tunnel-making, to foundries and stoke-holes, and to the frames of skyscrapers, would our gilded youths be drafted off, according to their choice, to get the childishness knocked out of them, and to come back into society with healthier sympathies and soberer ideas." After these conscripts had paid "their blood-tax, done their own part in the immemorial human warfare against nature," James believed that "they would tread the earth more proudly, the women would value them more highly, they would be better fathers and teachers of the following generation" (1982, 171–72).

This kind of conscription, he believed, would be able to preserve, even "in the midst of a pacific civilization," the virtues of hardihood that defenders of militarism feared would disappear in peacetime. "We should get toughness without callousness, authority with as little criminal cruelty as possible, and painful work done cheerily because the duty is temporary, and threatens not, as now, to degrade the whole remainder of one's life." By developing a recognition of social place among our youth and a better form of patriotism, and by developing in them a version of the "strenuous honor and disinterestedness" that is found in clergy and physicians, James believes that "the martial type of character can be bred without war" (1982, 172; cf. 1992–2004, 12:8), and that war thus has a moral equivalent. Whether this new social habit would work remains an unanswered question; but James's approach here, as in the other cases considered, is the same. We need to recognize how our lives of openness to possibilities can slip into the thoughtless following of custom and tradition, and how we can allow our fellow humans to be casually converted into our presumed enemies. If we are to address this ongoing problem, we will need to recognize the powerful operations of habits in a world of change.[9]

NOTES

1. For most of us, there is also a resultant cost elsewhere. As James writes: "We overlook misprints, imagining the right letters, though we see the wrong ones" (1983, 96).

2. For a sample of James's scattered comments on gender, see 1987 (246–56, 402–7); 1981 (991, 1055–57); 1982 (152); 1985 (212). Charlene Haddock Seigfried writes that James's "explicit support of the ideology of separate spheres, which restricts women to the privacy of the home and reserves the public sphere for men, mires him in sentimentality rather than in the sympathetic understanding so characteristic of his interactions with others whose way of life differs dramatically from his own." She continues that James "consistently viewed" women "from a masculinist, or ideologically patriarchal angle of vision; that is, one which equates humanness with maleness and believes that women's proper role is to serve men's interests" (111; cf. 111–41). See also Miller (33–53).

3. For an array of these remarks, see James 1985 (69); 1982 (170, 173); 1981 (991, 1144); 1986 (268–69); 1979b (192, 239); 1992–2004 (3:39; 4:474; 6:269; 7:282, 11:263).

4. See James 1975b (269–270); 1992–2004 (8:355, 360).

5. John Dewey writes of the "immense debt" that we owe to James "for the mere title of his essay: 'The Moral Equivalent of War.'" He continues that "the suggestion of an *equivalent* for war calls attention to the medley of impulses which are casually bunched together under the caption of belligerent impulse; and it calls attention to the fact that the elements of the medley may be woven together into many differing types of activity," of which some enable us to deal with these impulses "in much better ways than war has ever done" (79–80; cf. 65).

6. See James 1987 (81, 157, 164); 1979a (42–43).

7. James's long-time friend, Oliver Wendell Holmes, Jr., writes in 1895: "Now, at least, and perhaps as long as man dwells upon the globe, his destiny is battle, and he has to take the chances of war. If it is our business to fight, the book for the army is a war-song, not a hospital-sketch. It is not well for soldiers to think much about wounds. Sooner or later we shall fall; but meantime it is for us to fix our eyes upon the point to be stormed, and to get there if we can. . . . The faith is true and adorable which leads a soldier to throw away his life in obedience to a blindly accepted duty, in a cause which he little understands, in a plan of campaign of which he has no notion, under tactics of which he does not see the use" (487).

8. Consider, for example, the following passage from Roosevelt's pen: "I wish to preach, not the doctrine of ignoble ease, but the doctrine of the strenuous life, the life of toil and effort, of labor and strife. . . . The man must be glad to do a man's work, to dare and endure and to labor; to keep himself, and to keep those dependent upon him. The woman must be the housewife, the helpmeet of the homemaker, the wise and fearless mother of many healthy children. . . . When men fear work or fear righteous war, when women fear motherhood, they tremble on the brink of doom; and well it is that they should vanish from the earth, where they are fit subjects for the scorn of all men and women who are themselves strong and brave and high-minded" (1, 3–4). For James's comments on Roosevelt's worship of war, see 1987 (152–53, 162–66).

9. Many of the themes considered in this essay are explored further in my volume, *Experiencing William James*.

REFERENCES

Campbell, James. *Experiencing William James: Belief in a Pluralistic World.* Charlottesville: University of Virginia Press, 2017.

Dewey, John. *Human Nature and Conduct.* Vol. 14 of *John Dewey: The Middle Works: 1899–1924.* Edited by Jo Ann Boydston. Carbondale: Southern Illinois University Press, 2008.

Holmes, Oliver Wendell, Jr. "The Soldier's Faith" in Vol. 3 of *The Collected Works of Justice Holmes: Complete Published Writings and Selected Judicial Opinions of Oliver Wendell Holmes*. Edited by Sheldon M. Novak. Chicago: University of Chicago Press, [1895] 1995.

James, William. *The Correspondence of William James*. 12 vols. Edited by Ignas K. Skrupskelis and Elizabeth M. Berkeley. Charlottesville: University Press of Virginia, 1992–2004.

———. *Pragmatism*. Vol. 1 of *The Works of William James*, edited by Fredson Bowers and Ignas K. Skrupskelis. Introduction by H. S. Thayer. Cambridge, MA: Harvard University Press, [1907] 1975b.

———. *Some Problems of Philosophy*. Vol. 7 of *The Works of William James*, edited by Frederick H. Burkhardt, Fredson Bowers, and Ignas K. Skrupskelis. Introduction by Peter H. Hare. Cambridge, MA: Harvard University Press, [1910] 1979a.

———. *The Will to Believe and Other Essays in Popular Philosophy*. Vol. 6 of *The Works of William James*, edited by Frederick H. Burkhardt, Fredson Bowers, and Ignas K. Skrupskelis. Introduction by Edward H. Madden. Cambridge, MA: Harvard University Press, [1897] 1979b.

———. *The Principles of Psychology*. Vols. 8–10 of *The Works of William James*, edited by Frederick H. Burkhardt, Fredson Bowers, and Ignas K. Skrupskelis. Introductions by Rand B. Evans and Gerald E. Myers. Cambridge, MA: Harvard University Press, [1890] 1981.

———. *Essays in Religion and Morality*. Vol. 11 of *The Works of William James*, edited by Frederick H. Burkhardt, Fredson Bowers, and Ignas K. Skrupskelis. Introduction by John J. McDermott. Cambridge, MA: Harvard University Press, [1884–1910] 1982.

———. *Talks to Teachers on Psychology; and to Students on Some of Life's Ideals*. Vol. 12 of *The Works of William James*, edited by Frederick H. Burkhardt, Fredson Bowers, and Ignas K. Skrupskelis. Introduction by Gerald E. Myers. Cambridge, MA: Harvard University Press, [1899] 1983.

———. *Psychology: Briefer Course*. Vol. 14 of *The Works of William James*, edited by Frederick H. Burkhardt, Fredson Bowers, and Ignas K. Skrupskelis. Introduction by Michael M. Sokal. Cambridge, MA: Harvard University Press, [1892] 1984.

———. *The Varieties of Religious Experience*. Vol. 15 of *The Works of William James*, edited by Frederick H. Burkhardt, Fredson Bowers, and Ignas K. Skrupskelis. Introduction by John E. Smith. Cambridge, MA: Harvard University Press, [1902] 1985.

———. *Essays in Psychical Research*. Vol. 16 of *The Works of William James*, edited by Frederick H. Burkhardt, Fredson Bowers, and Ignas K. Skrupskelis. Introduction by Robert A. McDermott. Cambridge, MA: Harvard University Press, [1869–1909] 1986.

———. *Essays, Comments, and Reviews*. Vol. 17 of *The Works of William James*, edited by Frederick H. Burkhardt, Fredson Bowers, and Ignas K. Skrupskelis.

Introduction by Ignas K. Skrupskelis. Cambridge, MA: Harvard University Press, [1865–1909] 1987.

Miller, Joshua I. *Democratic Temperament: The Legacy of William James*. Lawrence: University Press of Kansas, 1997.

Roosevelt, Theodore. *The Strenuous Life: Essays and Addresses*. New York: Century, [1900] 1918.

Seigfried, Charlene Haddock. *Pragmatism and Feminism: Reweaving the Social Fabric*. Chicago: University of Chicago Press, 1996.

CONTRIBUTORS

James M. Albrecht is a professor of English and former dean of humanities at Pacific Lutheran University in Tacoma, Washington. He is the author of *Reconstructing Individualism: A Pragmatic Tradition from Emerson to Ellison* (2012).

Douglas R. Anderson is an author and editor of nine books dealing with American philosophy, including *Conversations on Peirce: Reals and Ideals* (with Carl Hausman; 2012), *Bruce Springsteen and Philosophy* (with Randall E. Auxier; 2008), and *The Drama of Possibility: Experience as Philosophy of Culture* (with John J. McDermott; 2007). He has also been editor for the *Journal of Speculative Philosophy*, the *Transactions of the Charles S. Peirce Society*, and the *Library of Living Philosophers*. Presently he is chair and professor of philosophy and religion at the University of North Texas.

James Campbell was educated at Temple University, where he received his BA in 1972, and SUNY/Stony Brook, where he received his MA in 1978 and PhD in 1979. He is an emeritus professor of philosophy at the University of Toledo, Ohio. He was a Fulbright lecturer at the University of Innsbruck from 1990–1991, and at the University of Munich from 2003–2004. He is the author of numerous articles and reviews, as well as five volumes: *The Community Reconstructs: The Meaning of Pragmatic Social Thought* (1992), *Understanding John Dewey: Nature and Cooperative Intelligence* (1995), *Recovering Benjamin Franklin: An Exploration of a Life of Science and Service* (1999), *A Thoughtful Profession: The Early Years of the American Philosophical Association* (2006), and *Experiencing William James: Belief in a Pluralistic World* (2017). He is also editor of *Selected Writings of James Hayden Tufts* (1992), and co-editor of *Experience as Philosophy: On the*

Work of John J. McDermott (with Richard E. Hart; 2006). He is a former president of the American Association of Philosophy Teachers (1996–1998), of the Society for the Advancement of American Philosophy (2008–2010), and the William James Society (2013–2014).

Damian Cox is an associate professor of philosophy at Bond University, Australia. His qualifications include a PhD from the University of Melbourne. He teaches ethics, political philosophy, and philosophy and film, and has taught business ethics, critical thinking, philosophy of science, and cognitive science. He has co-authored three books: *Integrity and the Fragile Self*, *A Politics Most Unusual: Violence, Sovereignty and Democracy in the "War on Terror,"* and *Thinking through Film*. He has published over forty journal articles on a wide variety of topics, including philosophical logic and epistemology, ethics, moral psychology, and the philosophy of film. His work on integrity includes co-authorship of entries on integrity in the *Stanford Encyclopedia of Philosophy* and the *Acumen Handbook of Virtue Ethics*.

Loren Goldman is an assistant professor in the Department of Political Science at the University of Pennsylvania. His articles have appeared in *Political Theory*, *Transactions of the Charles S. Peirce Society*, *Journal of the Philosophy of History*, and *William James Studies*, of which he is book review editor, as well as in various edited volumes. He is currently writing a book on hope in political thought, and has translated and introduced Ernst Bloch's *Avicenna and the Aristotelian Left* for Columbia University Press (2018). He holds degrees from Yale, Oxford, and the University of Chicago, enjoyed postdoctoral fellowships at Rutgers and Berkeley, and was previously a visiting assistant professor at Ohio University.

Yumiko Inukai is an associate professor of philosophy at the University of Massachusetts, Boston. She has written and presented extensively on the relationships between William James's radical empiricism and the work of other figures in the history of philosophy. Her recent publications include "Radical Empiricism: James and Hume on the Reality of Relations" in *The Oxford Handbook of William James* (forthcoming); "The World of the Vulgar and the Ignorant: Hume and Nāgārjuna on the Substantiality and Independence of Objects" (*Res Philosophica*, 2015); and, "Perceptions and Objects: Hume's Radical Empiricism" (*Hume Studies*, 2013).

Nate Jackson is an assistant professor of philosophy at Capital University in Columbus, Ohio, where he teaches broadly within the philosophy curriculum. He has recently published in *The Pluralist* and *European Journal of Pragmatism and American Philosophy*. His current research centers on the implications of John Dewey's political philosophy for understanding disability, as well as other work at the intersection of American philosophy and disability studies.

Michael P. Levine is a professor of philosophy at the University of Western Australia. His qualifications include a PhD from Brown University and an MA from the University of Virginia. He has taught at the University of Pennsylvania, Swarthmore College, the University of Virginia, and in Moscow as a Fulbright fellow. His publications include *Leadership and Ethics* (with Jacqueline Boaks,; 2015), *The "Katrina Effect": On the Nature of Catastrophe* (with William Taylor, et al.; 2015), *Engineering and War: Ethics, Institutions, Alternatives* (with Ethan Blue and Dean Nieusma; 2013), *Prospects for an Ethics of Architecture* (with Bill Taylor; 2011), *Thinking Through Film* (with Damian Cox; 2011), *Politics Most Unusual* (with Damian Cox and Saul Newman; 2009), *Integrity and the Fragile Self* (with Damian Cox and Marguerite La Caze; 2003), and *The Analytic Freud: Philosophy and Psychoanalysis* (1999). In 2014 he was a Senior Fellow at Durham University's Institute of Advanced Study.

Erin McKenna is a professor of philosophy at University of Oregon. Some of her published work in American philosophy includes *American Philosophy: From Wounded Knee to the Present* (with Scott L. Pratt; 2015), *The Task of Utopia: A Pragmatist and Feminist Perspective* (2001), and essays in *Feminist Interpretations of John Dewey* (2001) and *Feminist Interpretations of William James* (2015). Some of her published work on animal issues includes *Livestock: Food, Fiber, and Friends* (2018), *Pets, People, and Pragmatism* (2013) and *Animal Pragmatism: Rethinking Human-Nonhuman Relationships* (with Andrew Light; 2004). She has served as president of the Society for the Advancement of American Philosophy and on several committees of the American Philosophical Association.

Sami Pihlström is a professor of Philosophy of Religion at the Faculty of Theology, University of Helsinki, Finland. He leads the research group focusing on contemporary philosophy of religion within the Academy of Finland Centre of Excellence project, "Reason and Religious Recognition." He has previously served as the Director of the Helsinki Collegium for Advanced Studies (2009–2015). His research focuses on pragmatism, the problem of realism, transcendental philosophy, philosophical anthropology, and philosophical methodology, often integrating "theoretical" (e.g., metaphysics) and "practical" philosophy (ethics) in the philosophy of religion and more widely. He is the author of several books and dozens of articles. His recent books include *Transcendental Guilt: Reflections on Ethical Finitude* (2011), *Pragmatic Pluralism and the Problem of God* (2013), *Taking Evil Seriously* (2014), and *Death and Finitude* (2016), as well as the joint monograph with Sari Kivistö, *Kantian Antitheodicy: Philosophical and Literary Varieties* (Palgrave Macmillan, 2016). His academic activities include past or present positions of trust in the Philosophical Society of Finland, the Charles S. Peirce Society, the Nordic Pragmatism Network, the European Pragmatism Association, the Nordic Society for Philosophy of Religion, and the Institut International de Philosophie.

John Ryder is Provost and a professor of philosophy at the American University of Malta. His philosophical work spans American philosophy, systematic metaphysics, aesthetics, and social and political philosophy. He is the author of *The Things in Heaven and Earth: An Essay in Pragmatic Naturalism* (2013), and *Interpreting America: Russian and Soviet Studies of the History of American Thought* (1999). He is the editor of *American Philosophic Naturalism in the 20th Century* (Prometheus, 1994), and co-editor of the *Blackwell Guide to American Philosophy* (2004), *The Philosophical Writings of Cadwallader Colden* (2002), and five volumes of selected works from the Central European Pragmatist Forum, of which is he co-founder and co-director.

Clifford S. Stagoll is a lecturer in the School of Philosophy and Theology, University of Notre Dame Australia (Fremantle). He received his PhD in philosophy from University of Warwick, where he was a Commonwealth Scholar, and an MA from Texas A&M University, and holds tertiary qualifications in economics and management. He is currently working on a book on William James's ethics of self-creation. In addition to pragmatism and ethics, his research interests include history of philosophy, philosophy of management, and issues in philosophical psychology. He was formerly an Officer of the Royal Australian Air Force and a consultant with The Boston Consulting Group, and has held management positions with Qantas Airways, Arnott's Biscuits, and BHP Billiton.

INDEX

Adams, Henry, 40–41
Adams, Marian "Clover," ix
Adirondack Mountains, 193, 199 200, 201, 205, 206
animal ethics, 59, 68
animal experimentation, 68
animal welfare, xv, xvii, 59–60, 68
animals, 57–71; use in product testing, 69; value of lives, 143
aristocracy, 31, 35, 36, 46
Aristotle, 129

Baum, Don, 18–23 passim
Bentham, Jeremy, 34, 49n3
bigness: James's rejection of, 32, 213
Bixler, Julius, 198
body, human, xv, xix, 149, 153–55; and habits, 223
"Brute and Human Intellect" (James), 63
Bugaeva, Lyubov, 154
Burke, Kenneth, 23
business ethics, 212, 215
business, study of, 37, 38, 39, 42, 43, 45

Cambridge Declaration on Consciousness, The, 67
Cambridge, University of, 41, 51n24
Chautauqua, Lake, 89–90

Chocorua, xx 198, 199, 204, 207, 208
Class, James on, 35, 46, 243, 245, 251
Clinton, Hillary, 7
Cold War, 44
college education: distinguished from university education, 41, 48; meaning, 33; and practical education, 37–38; purpose, 33, 37, 39
colleges, and universities, 39–44
Columbine High School, 10
Congress, U.S., 4, 6, 8
consciousness: animal, 64, 76; and brain, 154; and habits, 237–38; James on, 153–60; lived, 214; patterns of, 222; and personages, 81; phenomenal, xix, 169–70, 218–20; and religion, 207; and self, 173–92
consciousness, stream of. *See* stream of consciousness
Constitution, U.S., Second Amendment to, 6, 7, 9–10, 21
contextualism, 103, 108–10

Darwin, Charles, 60–61, 62, 64; *On the Origin of Species*, 60
democracy: Dewey on, xiii, 25; and higher education, xvi, 31–37, 44; as ideal, 24; James on, 34–37,

democracy *(continued)* 44, 244; liberal, xiii; Mill on, 34; and progress, 113; spirit of, 114; mentioned, 76

Democratic Party, U.S. (Democrats), 7, 9, 10, 22

deontology, 59, 130, 138, 140

depression, James's, xi, 80

Deresiewicz, William, 46

Descartes, René, and self, 169, 170, 186–87, 189n1, 220

Dewey, John: on Darwinian evolution, 60–61; on democracy, 25, 116; on ethics, 128, 130–31; on experience, 156, 161–64, 219, 246; and higher education, 49; and James, xiii–xiv, 154; instrumentalism, 200–1; on progress, 107, 109, 117–18; social theory, 17; mentioned, x, xiii, xvii, 15, 43, 48, 102, 104, 110, 117, 126, 138, 149, 213, 216

disability, xvii–xviii, 73–95; and democratic participation, 76; and flourishing, xvii, 73–78, 85, 88–91; James's experience of, 73, 79–81; models of, 75; and quality of life, 77–78, 81–89, 95; secondary gain, 78

Disability Paradox, 74, 77, 82, 94

"Does Consciousness Exist?" (James), 153, 156, 159

education, higher, xvi–xvii, 31, 49; and managerialization, xvi

Eliot, Charles W., 36–37, 45–46, 48, 50n9

Emerson, Ralph Waldo, xii, xxiii, 117, 135, 197, 208; and ethics, 135; and progress, 114, 117

empiricism, 149, 153; and experience, 161; and self, 187–88

empiricism, radical. *See* radical empiricism

ethics: applied, xvii, xix, 125–44; and disability, 93–95; James's theory, xvi–xvii, xviii, 59, 90, 93, 225, 230, 246; James's theory, and gun violence, 4, 5, 11–25; and self-transformation, xv; mentioned, 102, 104, 227

ethics, animal. *See* animal ethics

ethics, business. *See* business ethics

evil, 118, 136–39, 143–44, 204, 243

existentialism, 131

experience: animal, xvii, 60–66; of disablement, xviii, 73–95; embodied, 13; and habit, xxii, 237; and James's ethics, 12, 135–39, 225–26; James on, x–xi, xix, 149–66, 218–21, 136, 201, 204–7, 213–14, 216–23; James's, of nature, 207; and meaning, 246; mystical, 86; and novelty, xxii, 12, 237; others,' 14–18; personal, xiii, xv; and relations, 24, 211; religious, James on, 82, 85, 87–88, 136, 205, 219; and self, 169–89

farming, livestock, 58–59

feminism, xv, 250

flourishing, human, 48, 226, 240

flourishing, and disability. *See* disability and flourishing

Follett, Mary Parker, 217

Franzese, Sergio, 90, 134–35, 138

free will, xi–xii, 127

Gale, Richard, 118, 120n12, 198

Gallagher, Shaun, 170, 188, 190n8

gender, 252n2

Gilman, Charlotte Perkins, 61

"Gospel of Relaxation, The" (James), 88, 89, 225

gun control, xvi, 3–25
gun ownership statistics, U.S., 5–6
gun violence, xvi

Habermas, Jürgen, 42
habit: and ageing, 238, 239, 240–41; and animals, 66; bodily, 223, 237–38; cultural, 200, 202; and ethics, 142, 227, 230; and ideas, 62; and inertia, 5, 24; James on, xi, xxii, 12, 17, 220, 223–25, 237–52; and Peirce, 61–62; and reflection, 40; risks of, 224–25
Harvard College, 32, 36, 40
Harvard University, 36, 40, 41
"Hidden Self, The" (James), 81
higher education, xvi–xvii, 31–49
Hofstadter, Richard, 42
humanism, 116
humanities, xiv, 37–38, 39, 40, 42, 45
Hume, David: and James, 181, 225; and self, 186, 187, 188, 191

idealism, ix, 154, 157, 213
ideals: James on, 13–17, 92, 136, 139, 220, 241, 245, 247–48; moral, 73; of others, 4, 10, 11, 19, 20, 22–25, 87
imperialism, xii, 246–48
individualism, 93, 136, 217, 246–47
introspection, 175, 178, 191n11, 219, 220, 230n4
"Is Life Worth Living?" (James), 63

James, Alice (sister), 73, 79, 80–81, 88–89
James, Henry (father), 79
James, Henry (brother), ix, 199, 234
James, Henry (son), 199
James, William: "Brute and Human Intellect," 63; "Does Consciousness Exist?" 153, 156, 159; "The Gospel of Relaxation," 88, 89, 225; "The Hidden Self," 81; "Is Life Worth Living?" 63; "The Moral Equivalent of War," 4, 17, 25n2, 216, 248, 253n5; "The Moral Philosopher and the Moral Life," 4, 14, 134, 135, 137, 139, 225; "On a Certain Blindness in Human Beings," 4, 16, 62, 66, 68, 89, 92, 145n4, 241–42; "The PhD Octopus," 32, 41, 44; "The Social Value of the College-Bred," 31, 32, 33, 37, 38; "Stanford's Ideal Destiny," 32; "The Thing and Its Relations," 159; "The True Harvard," 32; "What Makes a Life Significant," 89, 90, 241, 243; "The Will to Believe," 24, 34; "A World of Pure Experience," 159, 160
Jefferson, Thomas, 39–40, 42–43
Johns Hopkins University, 42, 43
Johnson, Mark, 154

Kant, Immanuel: and experience, 161; and ethics, 140, 141; method, 130; ontology, 220; practical and theoretical philosophy, 129; mentioned, 135
Keene Valley, 199, 201, 205, 207, 208
Kerr, Clark, 32, 42
Kitcher, Philip, 102–3, 105–9
Koopman, Colin, 101, 114–17, 120n9

Lachs, John, 103–4, 111–14
Lakoff, George, 10–11, 24
laws, gun safety. *See* gun safety laws
Locke, John, 181, 187, 220
lynching, xii, 244–46

management, xxi–xxii, 211–30

Marchetti, Sarin, 135, 136, 138–39
McCain, John, 10, 21
McDermott, John J., xv, 217, 219
medical materialism, 74, 81–82, 85, 86, 87, 94
meliorism: definition, by James, x, xviii; and ethics, xxii; and progress, xviii, 101–2, 104, 107–9, 113–19; mentioned, xvii, 60
meritocracy, 35–36
Metzinger, Thomas, 171, 176
Mill, John Stuart, 33, 34, 38, 49n3, 49n4
monism, 33–36, 127
moral blindness, disability and, 87–88
"Moral Equivalent of War, The" (James), 4, 17, 25n2, 216, 248, 253n5
"Moral Philosopher and the Moral Life, The" (James), 4, 14, 134, 135, 137, 139, 225
multidimensionality, 108–9, 188

National Rifle Association (NRA), 7, 8, 9, 10, 21
naturalism, 149
nature, 197–208
Nixon, Richard; 19
novelty, experiential. *See* experience, novelty

Obama, Barack, 3–4, 6, 8
ochlocracy, 35
"On a Certain Blindness in Human Beings" (James), 4, 16, 62, 66, 68, 89, 92, 145n4, 241–42
Otto, M. C., 48, 51n29
Oxford University, 41, 42

Peirce, Charles Sanders: criticism of James, 216; evolutionary theory, 61–62; method, 130, 134; origins of pragmatism, xii–xiii, 126, 149, 211; pragmatic maxim, xii; and science, 201; mentioned, x, 43, 102, 104, 107, 138, 197, 203, 213
Perry, Ralph Barton, 80, 197, 198, 200
"PhD Octopus, The" (James), 32, 41, 44
phenomenology, xv, 171, 190n6
philosophy, applied, 127–33
pluralism: and conceptualization, 224; and experience, 67, 201; and individuality, 247; and interests, 226; James on, 13, 33, 49, 62, 198, 246; and meliorism, 115–16; and monism, 127, 133; moral and ethical, 4, 34, 73, 133–38, 144; and progress, 107; and self, 180; and tolerance, 66–67
pragmatic maxim, xii, xiii
pragmatic method, 126–27, 130, 134–40
progress, and pragmatism, 101–19
Protestantism, ix
psychology, xi, xii, xiii, 44; James on, xxii, 79, 153, 155, 175, 201, 240
pure experience, 153, 155–60, 162–63, 164

race relations, xviii, 101, 108, 109–11, 119
race, James on, 243–44
Radcliffe College, 32, 38
radical empiricism, 155–56, 158, 159
relations: and experience, xix, 24, 150, 157–62, 166, 204; and mind, 204, 206; and self, 169, 175, 178, 185, 187, 198, 216; and value judgements, 93
relationships, human, with animals, 57, 59, 61–62, 65, 67, 71
religion, xi, xiii, xxii, 42, 127, 129, 132, 143, 204–06

religious experience. *See* experience, religious
Renouvier, Charles, xi, 199
Republican Party, U.S. (Republicans), 4, 7, 8, 10, 11, 22
Rorty, Richard: and experience, 149, 150; and meliorism, 102, 115–16, 117; and progress, 104; mentioned, x, xvii
Royce, Josiah, 43, 136, 213
Russell, Bertrand, 104, 158, 202

salvation, xi, xxi, 39, 117, 136, 248
Sandy Hook Elementary School, 3, 6, 20
Santayana, George, xx
science, xii, xiii, xix, 130, 135, 188, 200, 201, 251; education in, 38, 40, 42, 43, 45; philosophy of, 129, 214; and progress, 102, 104, 107, 112
self: minimal, xix, 170, 178; models of, xix; as narrative construction, xix, 170
self, James on, 169–89; and continuity, 181–83; Empirical Self, 184–86; personal, 175–81; and resemblance, 178–79, 181, 182
selfhood, 174, 177, 178
self-conception, xi, 220
self-transformation, xv
Shusterman, Richard, 154
sick-soul, 80, 138, 144
slavery, 244
social aspects of work, 216–18
"Social Value of the College-Bred, The" (James), 31, 32, 33, 37, 38
Stanford University, 32, 39, 45, 50n14
"Stanford's Ideal Destiny" (James), 32
Strawson, Galen, 169, 175, 188, 189n2, 190n9
stream of consciousness, xx, 79–80, 171, 173, 175, 180, 182, 188, 237

stream of thought, 180, 181, 184, 187
stream of experience, 179, 183, 187, 188
strenuous life, 251
strenuous mood, 34–35
subjectivity, xix, 169

teleology, and progress, 102, 105–7, 109, 213, 220
testimonial injustice, and disability, 84–87, 92
theodicy, 137, 143, 145n6
"Thing and Its Relations, The" (James), 159
Thoreau, Henry David, 114, 198, 207
"True Harvard, The," 32
Trump, Donald, xvii, 6, 7, 8, 19, 21, 24
truth: James on, xi, 4, 12, 14, 59, 71, 145n7; and progress, 102–04; mentioned, xiii, xvii, xxiii, 5, 94

Ulysses (James Joyce), 151–52
universities, 39–46
University of Berlin, 42
University of California system, 32, 42
U.S. Civil War, 43, 244
Utilitarianism, 136, 140

values: appreciation of others,' 4–5, 10, 13, 15–19, 23, 89, 94–95, 241–43, 245–47; and ideals, 5; institutional, 240; of James's time, x; moral, xviii, 141, 142; shared social, xv, 108, 213, 220; and self, xix, 170, 174, 186, 219
Veblen, Thorstein, 44
veganism, 67
vegetarianism, 67
virtues, 18, 19, 91, 130, 138, 245, 248, 250
von Humboldt, Alexander, 42

war, 17, 36, 247–52

Wells, H. G., 38
West, Cornel, 111
"What Makes a Life Significant" (James), 89, 90, 241, 243
"Will to Believe, The" (James), 24, 34
Wittgenstein, Ludwig: ethics, xix, 127, 132, 140–44; and James, 135, 138

"World of Pure Experience, A" (James), 159, 160
World War II, 44

Young, Michael, 35

Zahavi, Dan, 169–90 passim

www.ingramcontent.com/pod-product-compliance
Lightning Source LLC
Chambersburg PA
CBHW070755230426
43665CB00017B/2367